WITHDRAWN
FROM THE LIBRARY OF
UNIVERSITY OF ULSTER

[Barratt's

THE LABOUR CABINET, 1945

Front Row, left to right: Lord Addison, Lord Jowitt, Sir Stafford Cripps, Arthur Greenwood, Ernest Bevin, C. R. Attlee, Herbert Morrison, Hugh Dalton, A. V. Alexander, Chuter Ede, Ellen Wilkinson

Standing: Aneurin Bevan, George Isaacs, Lord Stansgate, G. H. Hall, Lord Pethick-Lawrence, J. J. Lawson, Joseph Westwood, E. Shinwell, E. J. Williams (Minister of Information, but not a member of the Cabinet), Tom Williams

THE BRITISH LABOUR PARTY

ITS HISTORY, GROWTH POLICY AND LEADERS

EDITED BY

HERBERT TRACEY

Chief Publicity Officer of the Trades Union Congress

VOLUME I

THE CAXTON PUBLISHING COMPANY LIMITED

CLUN HOUSE, SURREY STREET, LONDON, W.C. 2

First Published . . July 1948
Reprinted . . October 1948

Printed in the Netherlands by
Mouton & Co. of the Hague
B. L. P. 1a

LIST OF CONTRIBUTORS

TO

THE BRITISH LABOUR PARTY

(arranged alphabetically)

W. P. ALLEN, C.B.E. Formerly General Secretary of the Associated Society of Locomotive Engineers and Firemen; Member of the T.U.C. General Council, and Chairman of its Social Insurance Committee.

THE RT. HON. CLEMENT R. ATTLEE, C.H., M.P. Prime Minister since 1945. Member of Parliament for Limehouse since 1922; Secretary of Toynbee Hall, 1910; Tutor and Lecturer in Social Science at London School of Economics, 1913-23. Leader of the Labour Party since 1935.

THE RT. HON. ANEURIN BEVAN, M.P. for Ebbw Vale. Minister of Health since 1945. Was prominent in the Councils of the South Wales Miners' Federation.

W. J. BOLTON. Joined the staff of the Trades Union Congress in 1903, and during more than forty years served three general secretaries. Before he retired he had been Secretary of the International Department for a score of years.

LEONARD JAMES CALLAGHAN, M.P. Parliamentary Secretary to Ministry of Transport, 1947; Member of Parliament for Cardiff South since 1945; Assistant Secretary of the Inland Revenue Staff Federation.

SIR GEORGE CHESTER, C.B.E. General Secretary of the National Union of Boot and Shoe Operatives; Member of the T.U.C. General Council and Chairman of its Economic Committee.

THE RT. HON. JOHN R. CLYNES. Formerly Member of Parliament for the Platting Division, Manchester; Past President, National Union of General and Municipal Workers, and Chairman of its Executive Council; Parliamentary Secretary, Minister of Food, and later Food Controller, 1917-19; Chairman Parliamentary Labour Party, 1921-22; Lord Privy Seal and Deputy Leader of the House, 1924; Home Secretary, 1929-31.

PROFESSOR G. D. H. COLE, M.A. Chichele Professor of Social and Political Theory, Oxford. Director of Nuffield College Social Reconstruction Survey, 1941-44. Author of many publications on Trade Union, Labour and Social questions.

LINCOLN EVANS, C.B.E. General Secretary of the Iron and Steel Trades Confederation; Member of the T.U.C. General Council.

THE RT. HON. HUGH GAITSKELL, M.P., C.B.E. Minister of Fuel and Power, 1947; Member of Parliament for South Leeds; Principal Assistant Secretary, Board of Trade, 1942-45.

GEORGE GIBSON, C.H., LL.D. Formerly General Secretary of the Confederation of Health Service Employees; Member of the T.U.C. General Council; Director of the Bank of England; was Member of the Overseas Settlement Board, and Chairman of the Children's Overseas Committee; now Chairman of the North-west Area Board, British Electricity Authority.

ERNEST GREEN, M.A. General Secretary of the Workers' Educational Association.

E. P. HARRIES. Secretary of the Organisation Department of the T.U.C. and of the T.U.C. side of a number of Joint Consultative Committees with the Employers and the Government.

DR. SOMERVILLE HASTINGS, M.P., M.B., M.S. (Lond.), F.R.C.S. (Eng.). Member of Parliament for Barking; Consulting Surgeon and Lecturer to the Ear and Throat Dept., Middlesex Hospital; Chairman of Hospitals and Medical Services Committee, L.C.C., 1934-44.

THE RT. HON. LORD HENDERSON, 1st Baron, created 1945. Member of the Air Council; formerly Secretary of Press and Publicity Department of the Labour Party; Personal Assistant to Arthur Greenwood (Minister without Portfolio) 1940-41.

ROY JENKINS. Son of the late Arthur Jenkins, who was Parliamentary Private Secretary to Mr. Attlee for many years. Labour candidate for Solihull in 1945.

JENNIE LEE, M.P., M.A., LL.B. Member of Parliament for Cannock, Staffs. since 1945; propagandist for the social and economic betterment of the people.

DAME ANNE LOUGHLIN, D.B.E. National Organiser of the National Union of Tailors and Garment Workers; Member of the T.U.C. General Council; Member of the Welfare and Factory Board.

THE RT. HON. HECTOR McNEIL, M.P. Member of Parliament for Greenock; Minister of State since 1946; formerly Parliamentary Under-Secretary of State, Foreign Office.

THE RT. HON. HERBERT S. MORRISON, M.P. Member of Parliament for East Lewisham; Lord President of the Council, and Leader of the House of Commons.

MORGAN PHILLIPS. Secretary of the Labour Party since 1945; previously Secretary of the Labour Party Research Department and Propaganda Officer; formerly Examiner for the National Council of Labour Colleges; Secretary and Agent of the West Fulham Divisional Labour Party; Member of the Fulham Borough Council and Chairman of its Finance Committee.

J. VERNON RADCLIFFE. Formerly Labour Correspondent of *The Times* (now retired); First Chairman of the Labour and Industrial Correspondents' Group; Reporter and Special Correspondent of the *Manchester Guardian.*

WRIGHT ROBINSON. Alderman of the Manchester City Council, and Lord Mayor of the City in 1941.

T. N. SHANE. Member of the T.U.C. Publicity Department since 1926; formerly on the staff of the Labour Party and T.U.C. and on the editorial staff of national newspapers.

THE RT. HON. LORD SHEPHERD, 1st Baron created 1946. Formerly National Agent of the Labour Party and in charge of 1929, 1931, 1935 and 1945 General Elections.

THE RT. HON. LEWIS SILKIN, M.P. Minister of Town and Country Planning since 1945; formerly Chairman of the Town Planning Committee of the London County Council.

DR. EDITH SUMMERSKILL, M.P. Member of Parliament for West Fulham and Parliamentary Secretary to the Ministry of Food; Vice-President of the Socialist Medical Association; Author of "Babies without Tears."

HERBERT TRACEY. Editor of "The British Labour Party"; Chief Publicity Officer of the Trades Union Congress since 1926; formerly Director of the Labour Party's Press Department, 1917-21, and Industrial Correspondent Joint T.U.C. and Labour Party Publicity Department, 1921-26.

MAURICE WEBB, M.P. Member of Parliament for Central Bradford; Chairman of the Parliamentary Labour Party; formerly on the Head Office Staff of the Labour Party, and a special political correspondent for the *Daily Herald.*

ALLAN WINTERBOTTOM, LL.M., M.A. (Com.). Director of Studies in the T.U.C. Education Department; formerly Lecturer in Economics and Law at the City of Birmingham Commercial College. Co-Author with R. Y. Hedges, of "A Legal History of Trade Unionism."

THE RT. HON. ARTHUR WOODBURN, M.P. Secretary of State for Scotland, 1947; Member of Parliament for Clackmannan and East Stirling. Parliamentary Secretary to the Ministry of Supply, 1945-47; Lecturer in History, Economics and Finance in Labour College; Author of works on financial topics.

GEORGE WOODCOCK, M.A. Assistant General Secretary of the Trades Union Congress; formerly head of its Research and Economic Department.

EDITOR'S PREFACE

THE BRITISH LABOUR PARTY celebrates in 1950 its fiftieth anniversary. Between its foundation at the dawn of the century and the termination, half-way through the century, of its first full period of Office as a Government in possession of a clear electoral mandate, lie twelve General Elections, and two World Wars. The political alliance of the Trade Unions, the Socialist Societies and other working-class organisations, upon which the Party was founded, has sustained the shock and strain of these troubled years and these momentous events. This Book is the record of its singular achievement in the organisation of political parties. It aims at bringing within the compass of a single work a complete historical survey of the Party's achievements. It offers a review of the Party's programme, a description of its unique structure, and a portrait gallery of its founders and present leaders.

None of these factors can be left out of a full study of the British Labour Party. It owes as much to its structural peculiarities as it does to the breadth and vision of its political programme, and to the forceful personalities who built it up in the earlier days and who are its leaders at the present time. No other party in political history has exhibited quite the same consistency in organisation and policy: in structure it differs from all other parties in combining the characteristics of a federal organisation and the solidarity of individual membership, founded upon political doctrines that have almost the binding effect of a creed or articles of faith and belief. The principles that underlie the structure of the Party govern also its programme, and exercise a decisive influence upon its choice of leaders and upon the fidelity of its rank and file. The study of this remarkable phenomenon is indeed necessary for those who wish to understand the political and social history of the first half of the twentieth century.

Another work which presented a complete historical summary, review and description of the Labour Party, its makers, aims and policy, appeared twenty-three years ago, bearing the imprint of the same Publishing Company as the present Book. That earlier work owed its production to a suggestion of the head of the Caxton Publishing Company at that time, the late Sir Hedley Le Bas, whose broad sympathies and far-sighted judgment lent encouragement to the present Editor in the same way as the present Directors of the Caxton Publishing Company have encouraged the production of an entirely new work somewhat on the same lines. It has been the aim of the Editor and his collaborators, not merely to bring the earlier Book of the Labour Party up to date, but to rewrite entirely the story of the Labour Party in the light of the profound and far-reaching developments in the life of the British people between the two World Wars, with the history of the Labour Movement as the background.

Few of the contributors to the earlier Book have survived to collaborate in the production of this new Book. It is essentially, however, a co-operative undertaking, and in conformity with the plan of the Book the writers who have dealt with questions of policy and of principles, are those who now fill positions of authority and responsibility in the Labour Movement. Particular interest attaches from this standpoint to the contributions in the present volumes from the Rt. Hon. J. R. Clynes and Professor G. D. H. Cole whose continuing interest in the subjects upon which they write bridges the years between the two World Wars and gives them a vantage-point of commanding range in writing upon public affairs from the Labour standpoint today.

Not a few of Labour's most influential present-day leaders who have contributed to this Book have come into the front rank of public life in the course of the last twenty-five years. Among them must be counted the present Prime Minister, the present General Secretary of the Labour Party, and most of their colleagues and closest associates in the work of the Third Labour Government. They include Mr. Herbert Morrison, whose warm encouragement of the Editor's task is signalised by his personal contribution, in the second Volume, of the strongest and clearest defence of the principles underlying Labour's programme that—in the Editor's opinion at least—has yet appeared in print. Mr. Morgan Phillips, again, who was serving his apprenticeship to politics twenty-five years ago, contributes two chapters to the first Volume of this Book from the vantage-point of his position as successor to Mr. Arthur Henderson and Mr. James S. Middleton, as General Secretary of the Party. And so with other contributors whose names are associated with this presentation of authoritative statements of Labour policy and organisation: they hold important positions today which they were too young to occupy in politics and public life twenty-five years ago.

Special interest attaches to the third Volume of this work, devoted to biography: a volume of surpassing human interest which could have been much bigger than it is. Personality has counted for as much in the development of the Labour Movement, as the Editor wrote twenty-three years ago, as any other factor, and the representative men and women who have been included in the biographical section have been selected to show the variety of talents and the quality of service the Party has commanded in the course of the last half century. The list is not exhaustive. There are scores of other men and women whose personal history is as romantic and whose services to the Party are as significant as any dealt with in these volumes; just as there are events in the history of the Party that could perhaps have been more fully elucidated. But this Book is not a record of old, forgotten, far-off things and battles long ago: it is an account of the British Labour Party's history and experience through fifty eventful years of rapid political and social change.

HERBERT TRACEY.

HAMPTON WICK, MIDDLESEX,
January 1948.

CONTENTS

VOLUME I

PAGE

FOREWORD 1
By THE RT. HON. CLEMENT R. ATTLEE, C.H., M.P.

INTRODUCTORY: LABOUR YESTERDAY AND TODAY 3
By MORGAN PHILLIPS

SECTION 1. HISTORY

CHAPTER I

WHY A LABOUR PARTY? 13
By THE RT. HON. J. R. CLYNES

CHAPTER II

BEGINNINGS OF ORGANISED DEMOCRACY 29
By HERBERT TRACEY

CHAPTER III

THE OLD AND NEW TRADE UNIONISM 38
By HERBERT TRACEY

CHAPTER IV

THE I.L.P. AND THE T.U.C. 47
By HERBERT TRACEY

CHAPTER V

THE LABOUR REPRESENTATION COMMITTEE 55
By HERBERT TRACEY

CHAPTER VI

LABOUR'S FIRST PARLIAMENT: 1906–10 68
By HERBERT TRACEY

CHAPTER VII

DEMOCRACY WINS ANOTHER BATTLE. 77
By HERBERT TRACEY

CHAPTER VIII

PAGE

Foundations of Freedom 86
By Herbert Tracey

CHAPTER IX

Industrial Unrest and World War 94
By Herbert Tracey

CHAPTER X

Labour's First Coalition 107
By Herbert Tracey

CHAPTER XI

Social Planning and Political Reorganisation 118
By Herbert Tracey

CHAPTER XII

The First Labour Government 128
By J. Vernon Radcliffe

CHAPTER XIII

From Political to Industrial Action 138
By Herbert Tracey

CHAPTER XIV

The Way Back to Office 159
By Herbert Tracey

CHAPTER XV

The Years 1929–31 167
By The Rt. Hon. J. R. Clynes

CHAPTER XVI

From National to All-Party Government 179
By Herbert Tracey

CHAPTER XVII

Labour and the Second World War 190
By Herbert Tracey

CHAPTER XVIII

Labour's Advent to Power 206
By Morgan Phillips

CHAPTER XIX

Retrospect and Prospect 225
By Herbert Tracey

LIST OF ILLUSTRATIONS

VOLUME I

THE LABOUR CABINET, 1945 . . . . *Frontispiece*

FACING PAGE

EARLY DAYS: LABOUR LEADERS AT THE HOUSE IN 1906 70

THE LABOUR PARTY AS OFFICIAL OPPOSITION 118

THE FIRST LABOUR CABINET, 1924 130

DEMONSTRATION AGAINST THE TRADE DISPUTES AND TRADE UNIONS BILL, 1927 164

THE LABOUR CABINET, 1929 168

THE

BRITISH LABOUR PARTY

VOLUME I

FOREWORD

By the Rt. Hon. Clement R. Attlee, C.H., M.P.

The Labour Party is a characteristically British production differing widely from Continental Socialist Parties. It is the product of its environment and of the national habit of mind. It grew out of the practical necessities of society rather than from any abstract theory.

Nearly half a century has elapsed since the formation of the Labour Representation Committee, from which developed the Labour Party, but the movements from which it resulted can be traced far earlier.

Twenty-three years ago, when an earlier book about the Labour Party was published, the Labour Party had been one of the major Parties in the State for only five years. A minority Labour Government had held Office without power for a few months. This new book comes at a time when the first majority Labour Government has been in power for nearly three years and has been putting into practice the principles and policies which it has always advocated. It is facing most difficult problems, domestic and international, in a gravely disordered world. Some of these are peculiar to Britain, but most of them are occupying the minds of thoughtful men and women all over the world. It is, therefore, of high importance that there should be understanding by opponents as well as adherents, and by foreigners as well as British, not only of the current policies of the Labour Government, but of the sources from which it sprang, of the personalities who helped to build it in the past and those who maintain it today, and above all, of the moral forces and faith which give it its strength.

There are today many young men and women who have joined the Labour Movement to whom the struggles and trials of the past, which seem so recent to us older members of the Party, are ancient history. They are sometimes apt to take for granted things which their predecessors had to fight hard for years to win. I believe, therefore, that "The British Labour

Party," wherein are set out the history, ideals, and policy of the Party, and biographies of most of the notable men and women who have contributed to its success, will prove of great value to our own citizens and to many men and women outside this country who look to British Labour for a lead in the fight for freedom, democracy, and social justice.

INTRODUCTORY

LABOUR YESTERDAY AND TODAY

By Morgan Phillips

The Labour Party originated, at the beginning of the present century, as a federal alliance of Trade Unions, Trades Councils, Co-operative and Socialist Societies, and one or two other working-class bodies. The Conference in the Memorial Hall in February 1900, at which the federation was formed, set up a Labour Representation Committee composed of seven trade unionists, two members of the Independent Labour Party, two members of the Social Democratic Federation, and two Fabians. To most people the Labour Representation Committee was, as its name implies, an organisation created to get more Labour M.P.s into the House of Commons. That, indeed, was its primary aim, and its rapid evolution into a national political Party was not foreseen, and perhaps not even desired, by all who took part in the establishment of the old L.R.C. Many difficulties had to be overcome in the early days, and the most formidable difficulty of all was the attachment of many stalwart trade unionists to the Liberal Party.

The transformation of this federation into a fully organised political Party which today sustains a Labour Government with the largest majority of modern times, is an event of great political significance. Here in broad outline is a summary of the changes that have taken place in the position of the Party over a period of fifty years.

The L.R.C. had barely drawn its first breath when the Khaki Election of 1900 had to be faced. With practically no electoral machinery, the L.R.C. nevertheless put fourteen candidates in the field. Only two of them were successful—Keir Hardie and Richard Bell.

But the Movement continued to thrive steadily. It gained new strength and consolidated its position. In ten years its membership was quadrupled. Today it is the Government of the country and its membership exceeds 3½ million. The following table shows the development of the Party from the first Annual Conference:

MEMBERSHIP

	Constituency and Central Parties No.	*Total Individual Membership Men*	*Total Individual Membership Women*	*Trade Unions No.*	*Trade Unions Membership*	*Socialist and Co-operative Societies, etc. No.*	*Socialist and Co-operative Societies, etc. Membership*	**Total Membership*
1900	7	—	—	41	353,070	3	22,861	375,931
1901	21	—	—	65	455,450	2	13,861	469,311
1902	49	—	—	127	847,315	2	13,835	861,150
1903	76	—	—	165	965,025	2	13,775	969,800
1904	73	—	—	158	855,270	2	14,730	900,000

* The totals to 1917 in this column include the membership of the Co-operative and Women's Labour League affiliations, in addition to those of the Trade Unions and Socialist Societies.

	Constituency and Central Parties No.	*Total Individual Membership*				*Socialist and Co-operative Societies, etc.*		
		Men	*Women*	*No.*	*Trade Unions Membership*	*No.*	*Membership*	**Total Membership*
1905	73	—	—	158	904,496	2	16,784	921,280
1906	83	—	—	176	975,182	2	20,885	998,338
1907	92	—	—	181	1,049,673	2	22,267	1,072,413
1908	133	—	—	176	1,127,035	2	27,465	1,158,565
1909	155	—	—	172	1,450,648	2	30,982	1,486,308
1910	148	—	—	151	1,394,402	2	31,377	1,430,539
1911	149	—	—	141	1,501,783	2	31,404	1,539,092
1912	146	—	—	130	1,858,178	2	31,237	1,895,498
1913	158	—	—	†	†	2	33,304	†
1914	179	—	—	101	1,572,391	2	33,230	1,612,147
1915	177	—	—	111	2,053,735	2	32,828	2,093,365
1916	199	—	—	119	2,170,782	3	42,190	2,219,764
1917	239	—	—	123	2,415,382	3	47,140	2,465,131
1918	389	—	—	131	2,960,409	4	52,720	3,013,129
1919	418	—	—	126	3,464,020	7	47,270	3,511,290
1920	492	—	—	122	4,317,537	5	42,270	4,359,807
1921	456	—	—	116	3,973,558	5	31,760	4,010,361
1922	482	—	—	102	3,279,276	5	31,760	3,311,036
1923	503	—	—	106	3,120,149	6	35,762	3,155,911
1924	529	—	—	108	3,158,002	7	36,397	3,194,399
1925	549	—	—	106	3,337,635	8	36,235	3,373,870
1926	551	—	—	104	3,352,347	8	35,939	3,388,286
1927	532	—	—	97	3,238,939	6	54,676	3,293,615
1928	535	214,970		91	2,025,139	7	52,060‡	2,292,169
1929	578	227,897		91	2,044,279	6	58,669‡	2,330,845
1930	607	277,211		89	2,011,484	7	58,213‡	2,346,908
1931	608	297,003		80	2,024,216	7	36,847‡	2,358,066
1932	608	371,607		75	1,960,269	9	39,911‡	2,371,787
1933	612	211,223	154,790	75	1,899,007	9	40,010‡	2,305,030
1934	614	222,777	158,482	72	1,857,524	8	39,707‡	2,278,490
1935	614	246,401	172,910	72	1,912,924	9	45,280‡	2,377,515
1936	614	250,761	179,933	73	1,968,538	9	45,125‡	2,444,357
1937	614	258,060	189,090	70	2,037,071	8	43,451‡	2,527,672
1938	614	250,705	178,121	70	2,158,076	9	43,384‡	2,630,286
1939	614	239,978	168,866	72	2,214,070	6	40,153‡	2,663,067
1940	614	175,606	128,518	73	2,226,575	6	40,464‡	2,571,163
1941	585	129,909	96,713	68	2,230,728	6	28,108‡	2,485,458
1942	581	123,101	95,682	69	2,206,209	6	28,940‡	2,453,932
1943	586	134,697	100,804	69	2,237,307	6	30,432‡	2,503,240
1944	598	153,132	112,631	68	2,375,381	6	31,701‡	2,672,845
1945	649	291,435	195,612	69	2,510,369	6	41,281‡	3,038,697
1946	649	384,023	261,322	71	2,635,346	6	41,667‡	3,322,358

* The totals to 1917 in this column include the membership of the Co-operative and Women's Labour League affiliations, in addition to those of the Trade Unions and Socialist Societies.

† Owing to the operation of the Osborne Judgment it was made impossible to compile membership statistics for 1913.

‡ The Royal Arsenal Co-operative Society, through its Political Purposes Committee, continues its affiliations with the Party, and its membership is included in these totals. 1947 figures are not yet available.

In 1903 the Labour Representation Committee, the forerunner of the Labour Party, instituted a political levy of 1*d*. per member from all affiliated Societies; this was made compulsory in 1904.

In the General Election of 1906, fifty L.R.C. candidates were in the field, of whom no less than twenty-nine were elected. In addition there were fourteen miners elected, who did not join the Party until 1909.

Nevertheless, the Parliamentary Labour Party was founded with its own Chairman, Deputy Chairman, and its own Whips, and it was independent and self-governing.

Between 1906 and the outbreak of the first World War, the new Party experienced many difficulties. True, by 1909 when the miners joined the Party, the "Lib-Labs" had ceased to be, some going Liberal and others joining the Labour Party.

Then came the first World War of 1914-18. Even under the stress of war, however, this young and vigorous Party retained its faith in Democracy; its Conferences met regularly each year and full opportunity was given to minorities to express their views.

The outbreak of the Russian Revolution in 1917 marked an important turn in the history of the Party. Mr. Arthur Henderson was sent to Russia by the War Cabinet and supported the proposal for an all-inclusive Socialist Conference to be held at Stockholm. In his view this would shorten the war and save the Russian Socialist Government. His Cabinet colleagues disagreed, but the Special Conference of the Party supported him. Henderson resigned from the Government.

From this point, Party membership became more united. A statement of War Aims was prepared and issued as the considered view of the industrial and political Labour Movement. This was quickly followed by the statement of Party policy—"Labour and the New Social Order," a statement that clearly established the Labour Party as a Socialist organisation.

Perhaps the most significant development, however, was the fact that all big Trade Unions were now inside the Party. Trade Unionism has ever since been the backbone of the Party. Most members of the Party today are Trade Unionists. Everyone now recognises what has been done by the Trade Union Movement in the fight to gain better wages and conditions, to foster the spirit of independence and self-respect of the workers and to build up both the productive and constructive power of organised Labour. Workers soon recognised that no man could stand alone against combinations of employers, but they could bargain through a Trade Union, and the leaders of the Trade Union Movement gradually saw, as Keir Hardie and Arthur Henderson had seen so clearly ahead of their day and generation, that economics and politics are interwoven. It was of little use striving for better conditions in the office or workshop if there was repressive legislation to prevent fulfilment. Politics is the means to secure economic freedom—one goes with the other.

Today, close upon three million trade unionists are affiliated to the Party; they contribute much of its badly-needed income, but there are other forces powerful and vigorous in the Labour Movement. There are the virile, growing local Party organisations, there are the Socialist Societies, there is the Co-operative Movement. The Labour Movement is not a narrow, restricted thing; it goes outside trade and class; anyone can be in it; the test is simply political allegiance. So the basic national object of the Party is thus set out in its Constitution:

> "To secure for the workers, by hand or by brain, the full fruits of their industry and the most equitable distribution thereof that may be possible upon the basis of common ownership of the means of production, distribution and exchange, and the best obtainable system of popular administration and control of each industry or service."

It is a matter of historical significance that the name of the Labour Representation Committee was changed in 1906 to the Labour Party in the same hall in which the first Conference was held. As stated in the last Report of the Labour Representation Committee: "Six years have passed since our Party was constituted in the same hall where we are now to meet on the morrow of our victory. The Trade Unionists and Socialists of the United Kingdom then resolved that the time had come for Labour to assert its claim to a fair share in the control of the Government of our country. . . . Organised Labour at last has realised its power, and has learned how to use it . . . the Labour Party now sits in the House of Commons and our success at the polls has been regarded as the most significant event of the election." This success firmly laid the foundations for an independent Parliamentary Labour Party. Labour had gained a footing in Parliament. In 1923, it became the official Opposition; in 1924 a minority Labour Government took Office. It was defeated at the end of 1924, and a further minority Government was elected in 1929, which remained in Office until 1931. Though again defeated, as Arthur Henderson once said: "Labour in Office is but a stepping-stone to Labour in power." In 1945 his prediction was realised when no less than 393 Labour Members of Parliament were elected, and a Labour Government with Mr. C. R. Attlee at its head took Office with power, and a clear majority over the combined Opposition in the House of Commons.

Labour as a National Party.—The Labour Representation Committee was a Federation of Trade Unions, Socialist Societies, Trades Councils and local Labour Representation Committees, a basis of membership which continued unchanged up to 1918, when the Constitution was altered to include individual membership. The direct membership of the Socialist Societies was, and still is, comparatively small. The bulk of affiliated membership of the Party has always been Trade Unionist and the word "Labour" was generally understood to mean industrial workers.

The Labour Party was thus a co-ordination of like-minded organisations whose aim was to present the viewpoint of the working people to Parliament. Gradually this loose federation began to assume a political individuality. It is significant that at the end of the first World War the responsibilities and scope of the Party were such as to demand an amendment of the Constitution.

In 1918, when the Labour Party had shared the responsibilities of Government in the grimmest circumstances, it became clear that the country was faced with an entirely new situation. The social problems and injustices which the Party had been fighting since 1900 had been aggravated and rendered much more pressing by the three-and-a-half years of war. The Executive Committee of that date realised that if those problems were to be solved by the methods proposed by the Party, methods which went right down to the roots of society, it was essential that they should at once place their programme before the country and, at the same time, put their house in order so that the programme would have the backing of the most highly organised Socialist forces that had ever been known in Britain. Both these things were done; the programme was issued under the now famous title of "Labour and the New Social Order," and the Party was strengthened by a new Constitution which broadened the whole basis of the organisation in its previous form as a federal body. It was clear that Labour was not adequate to the great task that lay before it, because it had never previously claimed to be a National Political Party. To become an effective political force in the country it was necessary to supplement the federal membership by individual membership and the formation of local Labour Parties all over the country. The membership clause of the Constitution of the Party was therefore amended to read "The Labour Party shall consist of all its affiliated organisations, together with those men and women who are individual members of a local Labour Party and who subscribe to the Constitution and Programme of the Party."

It is impossible to exaggerate the importance of this change in the Party Constitution. It provided a definite opportunity for people from all classes in society to enter into political association. At the present time, nearing our jubilee year, it is astonishing to think there was a time, not long ago, when there were no local Labour Parties as we know them. It was upon this principle of individual membership that the new Constitution of 1918 was established and it was upon this basis that the Labour Party built itself into the great political power that governs Britain today. The Labour Party has become a truly National Organisation, and although the Trade Union members remain the backbone of the local Party, there has been a general fusion of many elements into a single organised unity.

Finance.—The Labour Party is financed through the affiliated organisations by the payment of an annual affiliation fee of 5*d.* per member. In the case of the Trade Unions this means a politically affiliated member; in the case of the Constituency Parties it means 5*d.* for individual members of the Party. This provides the Party with its chief source of income, as may be seen from the balance sheet.

The Constitution provides that "the work of the Party shall be under the direction and control of the Annual Party Conference, which shall itself be subject to the Constitution and Standing Orders of the Party." The Annual Conference is composed as follows:

(*a*) Delegates duly appointed by each affiliated Trade Union or other organisations to the number of one delegate for each 5,000 members or part thereof on whom affiliation fees were paid for the year ending December 31 preceding the Conference.

(*b*) Delegates duly appointed by Constituency Labour Parties (or Trades Councils acting as such) to the number of one delegate for each 5,000 individual members or part thereof on whom affiliation fees were paid for the year ending December 31 preceding the Conference; where the individual and affiliated women's membership exceeds 2,500 an additional woman delegate may be appointed.

(*c*) Delegates duly appointed by Central Labour Parties or Trades Councils acting as such in Divided Boroughs not exceeding one for each Central Labour Party.

(*d*) Delegates duly appointed by Federations not exceeding one for each Federation,

(*e*) Ex-officio Members of the Party Conference as follows:

(i) Members of the National Executive Committee.

(ii) Members of the Parliamentary Labour Party.

(iii) Parliamentary Labour Candidates whose candidatures have been duly endorsed by the National Executive Committee.

(iv) The Secretary of the Party.

(v) The Chairman and one delegate appointed by the Annual Conference of the Labour Party League of Youth held next preceding the Annual Party Conference.

Ex-Officio Members of the Party Conference shall have no voting power unless they are also duly-appointed delegates.

(*f*) Any special Party Conference shall be called on the same basis of representation as that upon which the last Annual Party Conference was convened.

All delegates must be members of the Party and must individually accept and conform to the Constitution, Programme, Principles and Policy of the Party. The Agenda of the Conference consists of the Report of the National Executive Committee for the preceding year, the Report of the Parliamentary Labour Party, together with Resolutions and Amendments submitted by all affiliated organisations.

A Conference Arrangements Committee is charged with the task of arranging the business of the Conference. Tellers and Scrutineers are also appointed for checking the votes. Decisions at the Conference are taken by card vote and the cards are issued on the following basis:

(*a*) National and Constituency Organisations: One voting card for each 1,000 members or part thereof on whom affiliation fees were paid for the year ending December 31 preceding the Conference.

(*b*) Federations and Central Labour Parties: One voting card each.

National Executive Committee.—The Annual Conference elects the Executive Committee for the ensuing twelve months. The Committee consists of twelve representatives of Trade Union Organisations, one representative of Socialist, Co-operative and Professional Organisations, seven representatives of Constituency Labour Parties and five women representatives. The Executive is elected by ballot vote. In addition the Treasurer is elected separately at the Conference as a member of the Committee. The Leader of the Parliamentary Labour Party is an ex-officio member of the Committee. The Secretary of the Labour Party is appointed by the Annual Conference and is the chief permanent officer.

The Executive is responsible for the maintenance and development of Party organisation throughout the country, and fulfilment of Party Policy; also to interpret the Constitution, Standing Orders and Resolutions in the event of disputes, subject always to the right of appeal to the Annual Conference.

The Executive, for convenience, appoints a number of special Sub-Committees which meet monthly. These are the Organisation, Finance and General Purposes, International, Policy, Commonwealth and Imperial Affairs, and Elections Sub-Committees.

Local Organisation of the Party.—The basis of local organisation is the Ward Committee in the Boroughs, and the local Labour Party in the County Constituencies. These Ward Committees and Parties are constituent bodies of the local organisation. Here again, as nationally, we have the characteristic federative form of the Party. We have the Trade Unions, the Socialist Societies and the individual membership.

Each Constituency Party has a General Committee as its governing body. It is composed of delegates from the local Trade Union branches, local Trades Councils, the local branches of Socialist and other societies, the Women's Sections and the Ward Committees, and local Labour Parties representing the individual members. The authority within the constituency is the General Committee. It appoints the Executive Committee to review finances, receive reports from the wards or local Parties and from Headquarters, and from the different sections within its own domain. It organises discussion groups, arranges meetings, directs efforts for increased Party membership, organises social activities and, what is even more important, the General Committee decides whether to run candidates for local or national elections. With the growth of the Party there are candidates at a national election for almost every seat. At the 1945 General Election there were 603—more than ever before.

Candidates.—Labour candidates are selected by the Constituency Parties in co-operation with the National Executive Committee. The sole test is fitness for the job and allegiance to the Socialist cause.

Any person selected to be a Parliamentary candidate must be an individual member of the Party and, if eligible, a member of a Trade Union affiliated to the Trades Union Congress or recognised by the General Council of the T.U.C. as a bona fide Trade Union. He or she must conform to the Constitution, Programme, Principles and Policy of the Party, and undertake to accept and act in harmony with the Standing Orders of the Parliamentary Labour Party. He or she must not be a member of a political Party or any organisation subsidiary thereto which has been declared by the Annual Conference of the Party, or by the National Executive Committee, to be ineligible for affiliation to the Party.

When endorsed by the National Executive, the chosen man or woman becomes a "prospective" candidate. Technically, the full status of candidate is not achieved until an election is declared. The whole process is thoroughly democratic. The Party member has a voice in his constituency, and, through delegates at the Annual Conference of the Party, in deciding the Policy of the Movement.

The membership fee to the local Party is 6*d.* per month. In fact, the funds of the Labour Party are built up by the pennies of the rank and file.

Women in the Labour Party.—From its earliest times the Labour Party has had a keener appreciation of the rights of women than any other Party, and has done more for them. In turn, the women's organisations of the Party are the finest and ablest in politics, and it is significant that in recent years the women's membership has grown faster than that of the men. Of the total individual membership of 645,345 in the last financial year, no less than 261,322 were women. These women are full members of the Labour Party, as well as being members of the specially-organised Women's Sections, of which there are now 1,650. These are grouped in Central Committees, in Boroughs and in County Constituency Parties, and in Federations and County Areas, as well as in Advisory Councils which co-ordinate the work of the women's side of the Movement over a number of constituencies.

This work is supervised by a Women's Department at Transport House, and by the skilled and experienced women Organisers in the eleven Regional Areas throughout the country.

Standing Joint Committee of Working Women's Organisations.—This Committee was first formed in 1916, when it consisted of representatives from five women's organisations: at the present time there are twenty-three organisations represented, including the General Council of the T.U.C. and Co-operative Union, and the National Executive of the Labour Party. The purpose of this Committee is to forward the interests of working women, to secure their representation on Government Committees and similar bodies dealing with matters in which women have a special interest, to set forth policy in these matters and to conduct campaigns on subjects of national interest on which combined action by working women would be beneficial. Although in its early years the Committee dealt with the problems of women in industry, the T.U.C. Women's Advisory Committee has now taken over this function, but the S.J.C. still maintains a close vigilance on the status of women as workers and citizens.

Women's Annual Conference.—A Conference of Women is convened annually, and to this Women's Sections throughout the country are entitled to send delegates. If a Labour Party has no Women's Section, then it is entitled to send delegates to represent the individual women members. Organisations (such as Trade Unions) affiliated nationally to the Labour Party are entitled to send delegates, and resolutions are taken from all organisations entitled to representation. Reports are made from Head Office, and include a report on the work of the Standing Joint Committee of Working Women's Organisations, on which the Labour Party is represented by eight members.

At the last conference 647 delegates were present, and resolutions passed by the Conference dealt with the Government's legislation, Domestic Employment, Juvenile Delinquency, Maternity Services and the National Health Service generally; Reports prepared by the Standing Joint Committee on the Care of Homeless Children, the Transition from School to Work, and the Closing Hours of Shops were adopted by the Conference.

Parliamentary Labour Party.—The Labour Party in the House of Commons is the Parliamentary Wing of the Labour Movement. It holds its own Party meetings and decides its plan for giving effect to Party policy. Provision is made for consultation between the Executive of the Labour Party and the Parliamentary Labour Party as and when required. The Parliamentary Party reports its work to the Annual Conference of the Party.

The General Election of 1945 sent to Westminster a predominantly new Party of great vigour and of varied experience, which necessitated a revision of organisation in order to enable the new Members of the House of Commons to bring new life to our Parliamentary institutions. As soon as the new Parliament assembled, a small liaison committee was set up with the primary object of maintaining close contact between the Labour Government and the back-benchers. This committee is composed of an elected Chairman and Vice-Chairman, together with the Leader of the House of Commons, the Chief Whip, one Labour Peer and the Secretary of the Parliamentary Labour Party. In addition, in order to deal adequately with business before the House as well as with problems of general administration, a series of Party Groups were formed to deal with various phases of policy covering practically the whole field of Government activity. Groups now functioning deal with:

- Agriculture and Food.
- Blitzed Areas.
- Civil Service.
- Defence and Services.
- Electoral Reform.
- Finance.
- Fuel and Power.
- Labour Questions.
- Local Government.
- Public Information.
- Tied Cottages.
- Transport.
- Arts and Amenities.
- Civil Aviation.
- Commonwealth and Empire.
- Education.
- External Affairs.
- Fisheries.
- Housing and Town Planning.
- Legal and Judicial.
- Health and Social Insurance.
- Shipping.
- Trade and Industry.

As an experiment, the Standing Orders of the Parliamentary Labour Party were reduced in number to meet the needs of the new situation, but in addition the unique experiment of suspending the operation of Standing Orders for a period of two years was agreed upon. The purpose of the experiment was to prove that free discussion combined with the spirit of good fellowship that is to be found in the Labour Movement was preferable to the rigid application of written Standing Orders.

Headquarters.—The work of the Conference and the Executive Committee of the Party is carried out at the Party Headquarters at Transport House, under the direction of the General Secretary. In addition to the Secretary, there is the National Agent, Chief Woman Officer, and the Secretaries of the International, Press, Research and Finance Departments. Throughout the country there are men and women organisers, whose activities are directed by the central office.

Fifty Years of Progress.—How the Party thus constituted and governed has grown to be a dominant political force is a question that may well be asked and answered when the Party is celebrating its fiftieth birthday. Why the Party has survived the chances and changes of fifty years can best be understood as a test and measure of the Party's response to the deepest social and political needs of the period.

CHAPTER I

WHY A LABOUR PARTY?

By The Rt. Hon. J. R. Clynes

Yes, why a Labour Party? Certainly not in order merely to have three Parties instead of two. A political Party is not easily formed in this country. If it grows and tends to become a dominant body you may be certain that there were very sound causes and many good reasons for starting it. A few new Parties, backed by great effort and large sums of money have in our time been worked into existence of a sort only to be broken, buried and forgotten. If a new Party like ours, born in poverty and viewed with indifference or contempt, not only survives but becomes both the challenger and the conqueror it has been transformed from a harmless nuisance or novelty to an absolute and longed-for necessity.

So far as it was treated seriously in its early years the Party was assailed in terms of unconcealed prejudice as guilty of unwarranted intrusion into a privileged area where there was not room for one more. It was not we who first asked "Why?" It was our opponents, and by the question they meant that two Parties were quite enough and that anyhow little more remained to be done, as it was now the duty of individuals to take care of themselves. On the contrary, when we asked "Why a Labour Party?" we showed how little had even been attempted and how numerous and far-reaching were the weighty subjects never yet touched either by Parties or Parliament.

That was the stage where our opponents were puzzled and also became very angry. Their feelings deepened into disgust when we revealed conditions concerning the houses of the people, their work, low wages, long hours, a travesty of education, workshop accidents and no compensation for the victims. These and a score of kindred matters must, we said, be forced into the House of Commons and we would get on the floor there to start the job. These pressing human problems must have a priority in Parliament!

Thereupon they were much amused and believed that we did not understand that our "prior problems" were, as they said, outside the scope of House of Commons service, being matters for individual will and activity and, of course, for private enterprise. When we derided that view our opponents were not much disturbed because they told us we had nothing wherewith to move ahead. Nothing? They were thinking of influence, organisation, Party power, a Press and money. They soon saw, however, that we were not without substantial assets. We had abiding faith in a cause, a missionary zeal to preach it in face of every sign of derision, and best of all *we had the facts on our side* and when we uttered the facts the people knew that we merely spoke their own everyday experience. People then did more than listen, they were moved; they had lived enslaved and impoverished but did not know it, so accustomed were they to injustice and hardship. They were not poor because they did not work, but because they did, and they began to see that in the main the richer folk were the idlers. Many of that class did not think themselves favoured and, indeed, were well intentioned sympathetic patrons of the poor. It was the way of life, but we said that it was the wrong way. We declared that while we were not the foe of any group we were the resolute enemies of an evil and unjust system. In that mood we went from place to place and our gatherings grew from a few to thousands. The pioneers were encouraged but the Tory and Liberal Party managers were as yet unafraid.

A Leader For Pioneers.—Fear later began to show itself, and alarm came next with the advent of a powerful Labour Advocate with rare leadership qualities—Keir Hardie. It was still the tireless, small groups of individual pioneers who spread political principles destined to change the character of legislation in Britain. Out of their ceaseless efforts the Labour Party was formed. That was in 1900, but the groups from which it sprang had been active for years. At the start, we were not taken seriously, and as the Trade Unions formed the greater part of the membership it was thought better then not to proclaim ourselves a Party. The title assumed was "Labour Representation Committee."

As I have held, at some date, principal positions in the organisation in the country, and in the Parliamentary Party also, I gathered first-hand knowledge of our growth to full strength and victory. Others will deal with personalities, pioneers and founders, but having acted with Keir Hardie over fifty years ago, I must write a little about the undaunted spirit who led us when all our political apparatus had to be created out of nothing and definite shape given to the troublesome but imperative course we were doomed but glad to follow.

Hardie is the sufficient answer to all who made light of Leadership and who even now urge that people ought to be left more to lead themselves. The advent of such a figure at such a time marked him as the natural head of a new movement whose march must be slow because of the enormous influence wielded by the leaders of the other great Parties. That influence was against us and in those days, more than now, the masses more readily followed an eloquent or commanding personality than a doctrine or programme. Indeed, there was little in any old Party programme which touched the lives and interests of the poor.

To the pioneers the most magnetic and revered name was that of Keir Hardie. He symbolised the determined warrior, and though gentle and courteous in manner, he was inflexible and resolute in the pursuance of objects which were unpopular but which gathered strength as he toiled for them.

I was a member of one of the groups and attended a meeting called by Keir Hardie in those early days to establish our work on a national footing. That began a record of valiant propaganda effort for the making of Socialists all over Britain. Branches of the Independent Labour Party were then active, and as a national body it acquired greater power.

It was a hard line of life for Hardie, with many privations. Cars, taxis, buses or trams were unknown, and it often meant walking miles from one meeting to another. There were no railway passes or expenses, for even Members of Parliament, and travelling often required us to look out for midnight excursions.

Remember that before Hardie could make a Party we had to make a Movement. It was of little use asking people to come to listen to him—we had to go to them and make them listen. Those who stopped at street corners or in the market place did listen. And they wondered at the words of this rugged, yet picturesque, pitman who imparted to them some share of the missionary spirit. He did not upbraid his fellow men. He sought to persuade and inform them so that they would readily seek freedom from their old but fruitless Party attachments. He did not preach hate of the fortunate or rich folks, but exposed the injustice and defects of a system which gave most to the least deserving and kept those who toiled hard and long even below the poverty line.

His fine instinct was bettered by his experience and surroundings. The grim facts of life were described so vividly that the victims of injustice became aware of the facts for the first time. His Socialism was explained, not as something which he had lifted from the tomes of industrious authors: it went deeper than textbooks, and was exalted to a doctrine of human justice and wisdom. As men listened, they gave him not only warm regard, but affection, and they heard him preach on the homely topic of their lives like one inspired.

After reaching the House of Commons, he fought a lonely battle with little aid and without fear. He lived down some instances of rudeness by educated men who laughed at his purpose and method, while thinking that they were well-bred, but were not. Later on he won the goodwill of these men and other critics who paid him the high tribute of being "The Member for the Unemployed."

Missionary Methods.—The early conclusion of other Party Leaders was that we would always remain a small and harmless number; the accepted doctrine in our country being that only two Parties had existed in the past and that they would continue. A charming and innocent view, which left out of account the probability that we would take the place of one of the old Parties! This is what happened, not at a jump, but by steady and approved stages.

In these stages the work was not limited to lectures and public meetings. Wherever we could, we fought in local and Parliamentary elections, and though we scarcely ever won, each result was taken as a moral victory and any number of votes was an advance on nothing. That was the point where we started and only the other side had anything to lose!

It is comparatively easy to instruct when the teacher can appeal to reason which is not chained to an old prejudice and can leave the facts to do their work. But forty or more years ago people had a fixed label in politics, and to that period belonged the sentiment in one of the highly popular songs of Gilbert:

> "I often think it's comical
> How nature always does contrive,
> That every boy and every gal
> That's born into this world alive,
> Is either a little Liberal
> Or else a little Conservative!"

Few people had thought of the term *Labour* as the title of a political Party and many deemed it unattractive for common use. Gradually, however, the term acquired a dignity of its own and people began to feel a pride in the name *Labour* which we said ought to be the *most honoured word in our language*.

Party attachments were usually steadfast, though political knowledge was very slight. It was seldom that either of the two Parties *made any impression on the other*, and the arguments of each fell on barren ground. But a third Party, equipped with new arguments and a refreshing line of human appeal, won over austere electors who had previously been faithful to their side. These men not merely changed their politics. They had, so to speak, adopted a religion, for their politics were now held as a faith, and the zeal of the missionary stimulated the activities by which, with unremitting toil, the propagandist work of the Labour Party was carried on.

We had more than new arguments which dealt with the affairs of humble people. Our men made politics not only interesting but entertaining. Small orchestras and choirs were organised. Hymns and music made our crowds feel how delightful and sociable Socialists could be. People were now not only ready to listen, but pay to be admitted and ask for a collection—if we did not.

The chief value of this more cheerful side of our efforts lay not in sharing the temporary pleasure of a brightened life, but in the growing conviction that soon we would be able to realise a few of the aspirations expressed in our programme and Party doctrine. Progress was no doubt slow but it now seemed sure, and to those who felt they were too old to see great changes there was a glow which displayed their content as they left our meetings.

In its first year the Party strength was 350,000. At the time of the First Labour Government the number had risen to more than three million. This membership was altogether Trade Union, apart from about 35,000 drawn from small Socialist and Co-operative Societies. The rapid growth in the total strength of the Party was due in part to the more lively opposition directed against us as our challenge to the other Parties became more threatening.

Yes, opposition grew, but so did a tendency to buy it off by concessions to our claims and by some approach to imitation in the speech and pledges of our enemies. We were a long way from the strength of a Labour Government in power, but we had passed from the stage of feeble appeal, to a point where our opponents were compelled to grant instalments of our claim. "Why a Labour Party?" had become a different question from the time when it was intended to mean that there was no need whatever for it. The Party could now point to results of substance which in the absence of the Party would never have been conceded. We were too weak to make a law ourselves but just strong enough to make others do it.

In Office and—Out.—Our progress landed us in Office in 1924, as the First Labour Government. We had not measured how near we were to that great event, and, frankly, we were not fully prepared for it. While we had men ready and fit for Office, a few Ministers had to be lifted from outside our ranks. They were sympathetic and willing to co-operate in our work, and they filled certain technical posts and Law Offices with complete loyalty and satisfaction. Our state, however, was rather one of training for the future than present achievement. The results, both in growth and in proof of ability to govern, were, later on, clearly in our favour.

Results from any legislative action were in keeping with what a Minority Government could not do, and very likely there were many who wished us well but who did not quite understand the limitations of a Government without a majority to support its policy. Administrative effort was not lacking as a means to redress some of the balance against us, and most welcome results were attained in that way. There were a few who thought that, not being able to go our own way, we should resign. We, however, knew that we would be defeated by superior numbers just as soon as our opponents felt that it was a suitable time for them to join together and turn us out. That we knew would do less injury to our cause than a refusal to face the task as long as we were allowed. We could face the difficulties of being a minority but not the suspicion of being political cowards or the immense handicap we should be under by giving our job to others. They would shout that we had run away as indeed they did at the end of the next Labour Government, when in fact the two Parties had combined to defeat us.

The life of our first Minority Government was shorter than was expected, but as the two other Parties easily outnumbered us, they took occasion by the hand, and acting together they turned us out in short of a year. The trumpery reason for this action was that we had tampered with the law by not prosecuting a Communist for using seditious language! The Labour

Government saw no reason for staging a political trial in our Law Courts, but in the General Election which soon followed, we found that forgery was among the devices employed to connect us with the Communists, whose repeated approaches to join us we have firmly rejected.

Some days before voting was due to begin, a letter alleged to have been sent from Russia to British Communists was given a great display in the Press of this country. It suggested mutiny in the British forces, or worse, and the Labour Party was linked with its sentiment and objects. M. Rakovski, acting then in London for the Soviet Government, sent a statement to our Foreign Office, denouncing the letter as "a clumsy forgery." The letter did its evil work, and our Party suffered at the time. Anyone could get a copy of this precious document, but when I asked Sir Austen Chamberlain whether even he as Foreign Secretary had seen the original letter, his answer in the House of Commons was "No." That reply has remained unaltered.

At that time Russia was much misunderstood and the Russian Revolution had aroused many doubts and suspicions. The Labour Party, however, believed that the Soviet Republics ought to have a fair chance of survival, and we had not only shown our sympathy, but pleaded for friendship and the restoration of the trade and economic relations of previous years. Goodwill was gradually established as time went on and admiration followed upon the astonishing successes of Russian arms and leadership in the course of the second World War. The line we took in those years was worth the political reverses we thereby had to endure.

In the circumstances our reverse was not felt as a crushing blow and the weapon of a forged letter did not daunt our spirit as would a defeat on straight issues concerning our principles and programme. The victory of our foes did not quite rid them of the taint of foul fighting and the two Parties who had united to turn us out did not long maintain a unity which could win them any lasting public confidence or Parliamentary strength.

A short term in Office had served a valuable purpose and given to Labour men for the first time a personal training in the responsibilities of government which was turned to good account during the succeeding years of active opposition. This condition gave a new aspect to our state of growth with the feeling that our quite unexpected advent to office, as a Government unprepared, must not be repeated. Formerly our work had been done with due regard to its educational value, and its propagandist results. Now and onward the work in Opposition must also be done to extract the maximum concessions from a hostile Government and to prepare ourselves and our supporters for assuming the liabilities of a Labour Government, however short the notice. Our leading men had therefore to be not only valuable members of the House of Commons, but must train to become accomplished and qualified members of a Ministry fit and ready to govern.

Lock-out: Then a Strike Exploited.—The chief occurrence in Labour affairs from now on to the General Election of 1929 was the National Strike in 1926. The Labour Party did not organise, prompt or desire the strike. It happened, and though it was an industrial encounter, the Tories turned it into a great political event. They saw votes in it.

How did the trouble start, anyhow? It began with the prior lock-out of 1,000,000 mine workers for resisting a further wage reduction. The strike may not have been prudent, and *such a course was never a part of Trade Union plans or policy*. Mr. Baldwin at the time declared the strike to be "a show of sympathy with the distressed miners," and for proof of compassion for others and a display of solidarity to aid men so often wronged, that stoppage stands alone in Labour history.

The Tories hurried to reap a Party harvest from a distracting industrial conflict. They did not consider the matter, or any mandate to limit their Act of Parliament to industrial subjects. Frequently we tried in the following years to modify a revengeful and odious Law, but they always said the time was unsuitable.

Before the war was the wrong time; during the war was not the right time, and after the war was the worst time to attempt an alteration. When the Act was passed the Tories chose the time best suited to their Party. They aimed the blow while feeling was high.

I am not going to discuss technical and legal points. The great issues covered democratic practice, majority government, and the division of Union membership into a group paying for legislative benefits and men who got them for nothing.

The law made a mockery of democratic practice, which is the observance of majority rule in the internal affairs of all manner of associations to advance their avowed objects. If a group resolves to act together in even the running of a Tory club or a tennis court, majorities determine the payments, management, and the rest. A man who tried to escape his fee or levy because he was in a minority, and still enjoy any benefit he could get, would be treated as a cad with complete Tory approval.

The 1927 Act ensured the enthronement of minority dictatorship. It provided that a Union may take a ballot of its members on whether they would establish a fund and pay a contribution for political purposes. The result usually was in favour. But that meant nothing, for the minority could walk away without obligation of payment, and the majority do nothing unless men individually signed a form empowering them alone to pay. That was called contracting-in, and it permitted men to do just what they could have done without any ballot whatever.

The Tory excuse for it all was that it was against the conscience of some men to pay for politics. We know that the conscience of a few sincere men revolted against taking life in war. They were ridiculed by the Tories and branded as cowards in what was a matter of life and death. In a matter of about one half-penny a week for Parliamentary service we were asked to shield the creatures who disliked paying it! We, however, never met a man who refused the benefits. The Party lost large sums of money, as did the Unions; but with the Act now swept away the Tories have lost any credit they ever had for fair treatment of political opponents.

Offshoots? Or to Shoot at Us?—Our Party in its period of growth, and especially in its middle years, could not help having to march some distance alongside other formations which had not much in common with it, but even less with other political bodies. Some of them were little more than half alive during a short existence and have long been dead. Even their names cover no stirring records, but we have memories of the Anarchists, the Syndicalists, and of course, the Communists.

The Anarchists were always a few, usually furious with others, often violent and ever ready for heated controversy with everyone. They did not propose to do things so much as organise to leave things undone. Their notion was that we had too much government and all of it always wrong. Their doctrine was that men could only be free if left fully alone to do as they pleased. With an aim so negative their ideas could scarcely be expressed in a programme, and ordinary people let them talk about their perfect world in the midst of imperfect peoples who grasped their objects only to disapprove them.

The Syndicalists, though never a large body were, for their number, turbulent, and often troublesome. In the Journal of the Post Office Workers' Union there was an article some time ago which would introduce the Syndicalists to some who had never heard of them. Indeed, outside parts of France and Spain, their life was a short one, and success, had they enjoyed any, would no doubt have hastened their end as fast as failure. Apart from evidence of breakages they left little trace of results for as the *Post* article said:

> "Syndicalism was effective as a criticism of the collectivist conception and in its distrust of the value of unsupported political action; it was effective also in providing a philosophy of action. . . .
>
> "The Syndicalists aimed at the workers in each industry securing control of their own undertakings and directing them on the basis of industrial democracy. Such centralised power as they envisaged would flow from the federal connection of the various industries thus directed by the workers."

There might have been a philosophy of action, but it was action of the sort which required no philosophy to direct it and its advocates were as a rule exhausted by their efforts. "Industrial democracy" may have attracted support from workers in industries whose output could take the form of enjoyable personal possession and fill our homes and cupboards with pleasing and usable articles to serve the individual needs of the day. The sense of control and direction would be different, however, in the case of millions of men whose labour was linked with, say, sewers, drains, tanneries, roads, waterworks, gas plants, sanitary services, cemeteries, and scores of other undertakings. Indeed, there are numerous necessary occupations over whose control and possession the workers would find little to rejoice. Such political diversions as these organisations provided had a value only to our opponents by causing much misunderstanding, and driving some people to believe that they must be a part of our Socialist effort.

The Communists were the group which made recurring trouble, and seemed most contented when it could do most mischief. It maintained a misleading pretence of friendship for the Labour Party, but spent its energies less in advocating a Communist faith than in vilifying our Party and traducing its leaders. Doctrine or principles they rarely advocated, and gave their time and a wide range of reckless abuse to attacks on people in positions of responsibility. An attempt at unity with the best of such men would be farcical; with the worst of them it would be fatal.

The Labour Party should admit to its ranks only those who believe in it; not those who sought for years by every means to discredit and defeat the Party.

They are not akin to us in spirit, aim, methods, or final object, and the class dictatorship they seek finds no place in our conception of popular government.

Take them in for the sake of unity? Self-deception could no further go. Inside, they would divide and disrupt. Divisions and conflicts would be common in the outside districts, and an artificial unity would drive out of the Party far larger numbers than the Communists could bring in.

Their hostility was the most bitter when our Party was most in need of help; that was when we were fighting the cause of Labour in elections. They would treat Tory candidates far better than the candidates of the Party they so often tried to join. Their manner of trying to join aroused suspicion. At one time they would cringe in their terms of supplication, but soon returned to their line of common abuse without ever enlisting trust in their good faith.

The most paraded part of the stock-in-trade of the Communist Party was an incessant demand for working-class unity. Appeals were showered upon thousands of Branches and Executives of Trade Unions and local Parties.

Rebuffs did not deter them, and they were resolved to mind anything except their own business. When they did, the results were often disastrous, and next to their appeals for unity there stands very high in the lists the number of their internal quarrels, expulsions, resignations, and denunciations of their former comrades. To such people unity consists in breaking away from the main Labour forces, running a rival affair till they see proof of failure, and then shriek for others to unite with them!

In the early days of the Communists in this country many were sympathetic and disposed to admit them to the Labour Party. Very soon, however, they revealed their allegiance to foreign authority and developed the alien methods which they have since continued.

They became the anti-Labour Party, and their coarse hostility to us has often been shown with greater virulence than to Capitalist organisations. We have become hardened to their gross misrepresentation, and to the falsehoods with which they have tried to damage the reputation of Trade Union and Labour officers. So bad has their conduct been that libel actions have been undertaken to stay their hand. I do not suppose they will be silenced by the last emphatic refusal to admit them to the Party. For anything may be expected from a body which claimed that the "activities of the Communist Party were vital factors in bringing about the defeat of the Tories" at the 1945 General Election! There we may leave it.

The Party and Defence.—Those who knew the Labour Party well would entertain no doubt whatever about its attitude towards the rise of Hitler in Germany and the trend of events which sustained the demogogic Dictator in Italy. The Party well understood the causes which in both cases hurried the advent of these disturbing and menacing forces in Europe. The objective of the Hitler Dictatorship was not only obvious, but proclaimed in its early stages. It was based upon the hatred of surrounding countries deemed to be inferior races, and especially directed against us, mainly because we had defeated Germany in the first Great War which she persisted in starting. A second war, with a German victory, would therefore be sweet revenge followed by complete and immediate domination of her foes. The stages of a detestable Dictatorship were not skilfully used to conceal the foul purpose in view, and apart from unashamed lying, the massive military machine of Germany would, it was believed, speedily register absolute success. The horrifying consequences of the encounter, and the bestial devices of the Dictator did not trouble Hitler—at the time.

And what did the Labour Party do about the greatest event in the modern world? It had no power as a Government, and it was no easy matter to arouse those who had. Onward from 1935 we continued the cry of alarm and warning in the face of the vast warlike preparations in Germany. The Government at that time did not seem to expect serious trouble, and certainly was not preparing to meet it. Hitler continued to build for every phase of modern warfare with the confidence that this country would not interfere unless threatened, and of course Hitler was too crafty for that. His subtle line was to pretend the utmost friendship with the frequent avowal that he wished us well.

At the Conference of the Labour Party in 1937 I submitted on behalf of the Executive a Report on International Policy and Defence which was adopted by a great majority. The Report described the kind of Government required in our country to deal with the international position, said that it must be strongly equipped to defend this country and play its full part in collective security, resist any intimidation by the Fascist Powers designed to frustrate the mighty readiness for resistance which the occasion demanded. At such a moment, faced with an enemy so ruthless and prepared, Britain was fortunate in having a Party so well organised to speak and so resolved to resist an attack upon Freedom, which this country could not enjoy unless it were retained by others. Unity of action and profound belief in a cause were the joint assets which gave the Party its supreme value. That is why, when a leader of the Party was speaking in the House of Commons during a time of high tension, many members who were not of our Party called to him in terms of warm invitation "speak for all of us, speak for England!" He spoke amid approving cheers and the unanimous goodwill of the House. In like manner it may be said, that though my Report to our Conference was framed by a Party it carried conviction to a Nation and those who dissented would have gone further. I take from the official report a few lines of what I said in expressing the thoughts of Labour as we faced our problems about ten years ago:

> "The Report dwells justly upon the universal fear of war. Our feelings are harrowed by the daily repetition of evil signs and threats of disaster. It may be that we are becoming hardened by this repetition, but that does not lessen the risk. Indeed, it may tend to increase it by creating an indifference or a feeling that war will not occur. A powerful voice has been added within the last day or two to these utterances of alarm. President Roosevelt has now drawn the attention of the world to the increasing conflict between dictatorships and democracy, particularly in certain countries of Europe.
>
> "We cannot imagine that the Fascist States are accummulating arms upon a vast scale in order never to use them. Those States are becoming more and more offensive, aggressive and assertive in glorifying war and in calling their men and their boys to arm and prepare for conflict.
>
> "Two or three countries at least are not arming for defence. They have pursued their warlike action without even proclaiming war. Japan is not invading China in defence of the Japanese, but in its own interests. Abyssinia has been invaded and crushed, not to defend Italian soil, but to acquire for Italy the country of a weaker Power."

Like others who spoke in fulfilment of our obligations, I expressed the view that the League of Nations could be made strong again by a Government which would base its policy on the declarations of the British Labour Movement. The Conference decision was the prompter of hundreds of meetings, and of activities which increased until the crash of the second World War fell upon Europe. What followed until the war began and happened before it ended does not belong to this chapter, and others will deal with the formation of the Coalition Government and the great Labour victory at the General Election.

Of all places, however, it is here most fitting to note how the unshakable facts, as events are unfolded, offer an eloquent answer to the question "Why a Labour Party?" Assume the absence of such a Party and imagine the degree of danger to the nation at such a moment of unparalleled crisis.

Suppose that just when every aspect of national safety was dependent upon the labour and courage of the masses, the masses could speak and act only through impotent groups or separated sects. What an immense difference that would have meant in making the most effective preparations to surmount the dangers then coming so near. In peace-time or war, and in the periods between there has been no combination of persons or interests ahead of Labour in readiness and competence to defend not a sectional interest, but the nation. It does not parade its patriotism, or provoke the hostility of others by bragging about its own might and greatness. But its patriotism is there not as a show-piece, but as an asset in reserve for full use when required in the defence of a people and the country of all of us.

Colonies and Empire.—In the years of its propaganda service the Labour Party had frequently to spend its efforts and time in disproving the most absurd mis-statements circulated against it. The title of Empire denoted greatness among nations and implied the possession of vast territories far away and ruled by Authority in London. The free and inappropriate use of the term Imperialism did much to discredit the name of Britain and mislead unthinking people as to the motives of different political Parties in retaining attachment to Colonies and Dependencies of mixed peoples having little in common with the English population. We were often unfairly denounced as being in favour of a "Little England" only.

The origin of attachments varied and could be traced to purchase, gifts, favour, conquest, adventure or merely to getting there first. I need not dwell upon the causes of growth or upon usefulness according to position or opportunity. The outlook of the Labour mind to these remote outposts of Empire was human and considerate with a firm resolve for fair dealing. It dwelt upon the economic conditions, employment, liberty and life of the people. They were not viewed as our private property; they had their own rights of possession and birth, whatever their colour or beliefs. We knew they would be employed at some sort of tasks under orders and that their treatment should attest our good behaviour towards them. Some of these groups of people have increased and progressed to the stage of now being nations themselves and though living with us under the title of Dominions they enjoy the forms, status and substance of government equal with our own. Their prosperity was always welcomed by us, not because of greater chances of profitable investment or for territorial or private business reasons. We were delighted to know of any advance in their education, social and economic affairs, and greater knowledge in the art of how to govern themselves wisely.

Indeed, in respect to all matters of high importance which covered life conditions in these lands so remote, Labour men possessed a far higher understanding and deeper sympathy with the problems of the people than a number of Tory leaders displayed.

It is going far back to quote the words written about ninety years ago by Disraeli: "These wretched Colonies will all be independent too in a few years, and are a millstone round our necks." That was no doubt provoked by the success of America in winning her Independence. And why not win it? Nothing is more natural than that people who feel they are being unjustly treated should strive to free themselves and seek justice through Independence. Many years later the same Tory feeling was expressed in like sweeping terms of contempt by Balfour when resisting the restoration of self-government in South Africa. He denounced the concession in the House of Commons as "the most reckless experiment ever tried in the development of a great colonial policy." How fortunate for us that it was tried. We had every means of seeing what uses for mischief a powerful Germany could have made with a disappointed and bitterly discontented South Africa. The loose talk of Party leaders was all the worse when it reflected, as it did, the view of their followers: the Tory mind was seldom at ease when looking upon the progress of others.

The position is now, of course, totally different and the growth of the Labour Party has very largely caused the change. The view of former years which dominated colonial relations was narrow, superior and exhibited the characteristics of ascendant chief and appealing subordinate. Government was carried on as though there had to be some degree of fear of the governing power and while the party of second place could crave a concession, he ought to have the patience to wait for it. The melancholy experiences relating to India and Ireland are prompters which may still have for us both future and fruitful values. The Labour Party did not frown upon tendencies towards independence when others claimed it, and it preferred to let peoples have some practice in the art of self-government to fit themselves for it.

Foreign Policy.—Any force which ever lived in the cry that "Labour was not fit to govern" was scattered long before the last General Election, but free use was made of an up-to-date variant. The Tory Press, literature and platforms bid the electors "not to put the conduct of foreign affairs into untried hands." How could working men know anything about these grave, immense, and delicate matters! Yet who now dare compare the work of any Tory Foreign Secretary with the achievements of Ernest Bevin? Indeed, no Tory Minister ever had to face such uncommon and often baffling problems, and not only satisfy his side, but win the approval of a nation. It is not an isolated success, so I recall another.

The late Mr. Arthur Henderson left his task in 1931 with an unexcelled record as Foreign Minister and left a more composed Europe than had been known for many years. I could fill pages with rousing censures on Tory Governments uttered by Mr. Churchill when foreign affairs were in Tory hands. We were the first to educate the masses on the high importance of fine international understanding. We sent Trade Union and Socialist delegations overseas and by conferences, literature and meetings sought to rid the world of the curse of war. We are proud of our pioneer work in making good neighbours and in giving proof that we could be one ourselves. The results of leaving foreign policy in the hands of others for nearly a quarter of a century have been expressed in friction, conflict, jealousies and horrifying wars. The straight Labour line of action and open, honest dealing have evoked praises from an Empire.

On Ill-Starred Times and Some Errors.—It has been the singular fate of the Labour Party to undertake the tasks of national government at periods of unusual distraction and abnormality. Long before the great Labour victory in 1945 we foretold the appalling state in which Europe would be found after the end of the war. It would not, we said, be a condition of merely devastated countries turned from their true function of yielding food and riches for mankind. It would be lands with hating, jealous and distracted populations who would feel the pangs of famine, but who could not at once be lifted to the level of a civilised life. It is for history to say how surviving statesmen deal with the harrowing legacy of the second World War. As the Labour Party will govern, not for a sect or an interest, but for a nation, and will do it with a comprehending and international mind, I have no fear of the final verdict.

It was a few years after the first World War that Labour was called upon to govern, though not to rule with the power of a majority elected to support us. Our advent followed close upon the heels of a disturbing aftermath of a war which had settled little, but unsettled very much. It was to a great extent a war of exhaustion for both the people in the Services and the civilians. Their experiences had produced a crop of new and perplexing problems while the Ministers who formed the Government were themselves quite new to the job. Now was the time when it was doubly likely that Labour would justify the sneer that they were not fit to rule. That is what our opponents thought and what a few of them said. The contrary happened and though our minority position permitted only secondary efforts at legislation, there were excellent and welcome results reached by administrative action and by a competence which again upset the fiction that "Labour was not fit to govern." Many of our men had served some apprenticeship in great organisations, societies and public authorities. They stepped with assurance and ease into kindred State service and were doing so well as a team that it was planned to clear them out without delay.

I have already covered that and other lines of experience as part of an answer to the question "Why a Labour Party?" I may conclude now with a brief commentary on a few of the common errors about the Party, for although these errors have often been corrected, denied and disproved, they do not die.

There is the belief that without us changes would have taken place. That is no doubt true, for no political Party can long live upon its past, and "something would have to be done." But the changes due to our existence and activities have been deep, abiding, far-reaching, and fundamental. Capitalism is no longer praised as ideal, and none now will offer an unqualified defence of it. It has been subject to ceaseless correction and restraints by barriers, regulations and statutes for which public opinion and safety have called, and which Tory Governments often applied. As an idol worshipped in former years competition scarcely exists. It was deemed to be indispensable to our trade and commerce. Now our industries, though different, are not thought to be opposite, and great amalgamations have grouped a variety of interests together. Even these formidable properties are dwarfed by the colossal Co-operative Movement—an ally of the Labour Party.

The most singular of the errors about the Party is that it is dominated by the Trade Unions and that somehow an unconstitutional influence or authority is exerted to determine the actions and policy of the Party and Government. This error is the more strange because there is not a single fact or figure to support it. If such domination existed I do not think the outcome would be calamitous because there is not on any point of substance a material difference between the Unions and the other units who mingle together on equal terms and make the membership in the country and the Parliamentary Party in the Commons.

It is a fact that in the early years of the small Parliamentary Party the entire body was largely composed of Trade Union officials. The men who were then fit and free for the work were few and organisation with mobile resources scarcely existed outside the Unions. Now only about 20 per cent. of the large Parliamentary Party are drawn from the Unions, but long before this change there was no clique or sectional spirit seeking to secure a group advantage. The Party Officers in the Commons are chosen on merit, and not because of their job. Only about a quarter of the Cabinet can be classed as Trade Union officials. The Labour Party in the country appoints its Chairman yearly by the rotation process, while the Unions long ago agreed to concede to other sections a total number on the National Executive which gives them a balance of power should a difference arise on a matter of importance. I have never known such a case. If the Unions desired to dominate they would begin at the source and prefer one of their own when candidates are being chosen. That statement is not disturbed because in a few coal areas mine workers' agents are often selected as the result of conditions created years ago by mine owners themselves. To be wrong on a point of fact is bad enough, but to have no facts whatever to support a complaint is conclusive.

A close relation of the error with which I have just dealt is the one that Labour is "a class Party." Founders and followers throughout the years have repudiated this view. In 1903 Keir Hardie wrote:

> "To claim for the Socialist Movement that it is a class war is to do Socialism an injustice and indefinitely postpone its triumph. It is lowering it to the level of a faction fight. Socialism offers a platform broad enough for all to stand upon who accept its principles. It makes war upon a system, not upon a class."

The opening words in the declaration of the objects of the Party are:

> "To secure for the *workers by hand or by brain* the full fruits of their industry and the most equitable distribution thereof that may be possible."

That is an invitation to all except the utterly useless, and no one is asked any question about his occupation or rank. The test for the Party is not a man's job or class, but his convictions and beliefs, with respect to our objects and the way to attain them. That way is the orderly democratic method of majority rule to which we submitted during the long years when power was wielded by others and which we shall not abuse now that the power is ours. To help the working people was less a class act than a human service giving aid first to those in need of first aid.

Those who remain unconvinced by words might look at the Party personnel in the House of Commons and see there the great variety of members drawn from almost every group and grade of the men and women who compose the trades, professions, services, pursuits and occupations in the country. Nor do we say: "Alone we did it!" No, we have drawn upon the perseverance, sacrifice and valour of men and women who had a tougher fight than we in times much worse than ours. We can now offer to the memory of our brave predecessors a monument of great achievement in the industrial, social and economic life of millions of people as some reply to the question: "Why a Labour Party?"

CHAPTER II

BEGINNINGS OF ORGANISED DEMOCRACY

By Herbert Tracey

Political history offers no parallel to the rapid rise and sweeping success of the Labour Party in the first half of the twentieth century. When the century dawned there were no more than three members in the House of Commons who claimed to be associated with the distinct "Labour Group" which had been called into existence by the famous resolution of the Trades Union Congress in 1899, under which a Labour Representation Committee was set up to secure independent Labour representation in Parliament. Within five years the number of Labour Members in the House had grown from three to twenty-nine, and they had formed themselves into a separate political Party with its own constitution, rules and policy, with its own leader and whips. Twenty years later the Labour Party was the largest single Party in the House of Commons, and held office for a hundred days as the first Labour administration in 1924. This was a minority Government, at the mercy of the two older Parties which eventually combined to eject it from office in the autumn of the latter year.

For the succeeding five years the Labour Party was the official Opposition. It reached Office again in 1929, but still without a Parliamentary majority. The Second Labour Government fell, in political circumstances and in a convulsion of Party loyalties that might have caused its disappearance from history. But its roots were by this time so deeply embedded that it survived the severest shock that a political Party can suffer. Within the next decade it recovered and more than redeemed its place in the political leadership of the British people. Its representatives held many of the highest and most responsible offices in the Coalition Government formed in the spring of 1940, at the instance of the Labour Party, to wage resolute war against the Nazi-Fascist powers, until victory was assured and a just and durable peace could be made.

When victory was won, in mid-1945, the Labour Party, resuming freedom of action, entered the General Election with a determination to win; and win it did. By the unmistakable vote of the electors it was placed in Office for the third time, but this time with a majority of nearly 200 seats over all the other Parties and groups combined.

How were these astonishing results achieved? The answer to this question carries us back to the beginnings of organised democracy in Britain. To unfold the story of the Labour Party's rise to power, it is not necessary, however, to trace the historical developments which have made it possible to change Governments by peaceable means without resort to civil war. These developments are bound up with the evolution of representative Government and Parliamentary institutions. It has been held as a fundamental theory that historically the Party system is a substitute for revolution. For long ages the only practical way of changing unsatisfactory Governments was by armed revolution on the part of the governed. In the seventeenth and eighteenth centuries there grew up in Britain, and was carried from Britain to almost every civilised country on earth, the procedure by which Party Government became the substitute for revolution.

Historians like Macaulay and Guizot attribute the origins of the political Parties in Britain to the Parliamentary struggles that arose in the second session of the Long Parliament in 1641. Henry Hallam traces the record of the Tory and Whig Parties to 1679. Other historians identify the first Parties as early as the Ministry of Clarendon, between 1660 and 1675, and as late as the reign of William III. An American historian who specialised in the history and development of political Parties saw them fashioned, slowly and clumsily, as he put it, during the quarrels between Cavalier and Roundhead. But it is perhaps enough to say that Parties began to function as an instrument of Government under the later Stuarts and William III. They were so well established and strongly entrenched as to be able to withstand the reaction to personal Government by the Monarch which was engineered by George III.

But the modern system of representative Government came after the first measure of Parliamentary Reform, in 1832. The first clear instance of a whole Ministry resigning after failure to win a General Election was the fall of the Peel Ministry in 1835. Thenceforth the principle of responsibility to the electorate was generally acknowledged.

In the evolution of representative Government and Parliamentary Institutions, the year 1832 is a significant date. Before there can be Parties, in any effective sense, there must be an electorate: for more than 150 years between 1677 and 1832 no alteration was made in the system of Parliamentary representation, although in the course of these years the population increased from less than 5,000,000 to more than 14,000,000, and great concentrations of urban population were formed, under the impact of the Industrial Revolution. None of these new industrial centres possessed the Parliamentary franchise. So far as the franchise extended, up to 1832, it was exercised by a very limited number of people. In the towns it was generally only members of the municipal council who possessed the right to vote; and these municipal bodies were not themselves elected. The number of electors throughout the country was ludicrously small before 1832. Seats in the House of Commons were treated as the personal property of a small class of wealthy landowners and the lesser gentry. It is on record that seats were openly bought and sold, for prices ranging from a few shillings to hundreds of pounds. In some cases the sole elector was the proprietor of the Borough. Ruined villages, without a single inhabitant, had representation in the unreformed Parliament, and great cities like

Liverpool, Manchester, Leeds, had no representation at all. There was no secret ballot, and only one polling station in each constituency. There were only two political Parties, and both represented the same aristocracy of privilege and wealth. Often the proprietors of seats in Parliament, belonging to these Parties, made a bargain one with another to divide representation of constituencies. Sometimes a wealthy proprietor would warn off candidates of another Party by publicly announcing how much money he was prepared to spend to win or hold the seat: as much as £20,000, £30,000 or £40,000 being not infrequently spent on a single contest.

Not only were the wage earners outside the franchise, but the middle class as well. It was from the rising middle class, created by the Industrial Revolution, the owner-capitalist, proprietor and controller of factories and workshops, that the agitation for Parliamentary Reform derived its leadership; and it was this class that benefited by the first Reform Act of 1832. It left the property-less working class, likewise the product of the Industrial Revolution, still without the franchise.

In the perspective of history it was perhaps not altogether a misfortune that the wage earners, the proletariat herded together in the gloomy factory towns, were shut out by the Act of 1832 from any direct participation in political affairs. It gave them time and supplied them with compelling reasons to concentrate upon the building up of their Trade Unions. The roots of the Labour Party are in the Trade Unions. In the development of the institutions of democracy, the year 1824 is as significant a date as 1832. In 1824 the right of the wage earners to establish and maintain their Trade Union organisation was formally recognised by Parliament.

Repeal of the Combination Laws in 1824 was, it is true, accomplished by stealth and without Parliament and the governing classes realising the forces that were then liberated. It made a much bigger breach in the age-old citadel of privilege than was made by the enfranchisement of the middle class in 1832. The working class achieved their political emancipation by the organisation of their economic strength, in the Trade Unions and the Co-operative Movement. Even when the Chartist Movement arose, as the second wave of Parliamentary Reform, after the disappointment of the 1832 Act, it did not divert the workers' energies from the building up of their Unions. It is not wholly a chronological accident that the collapse of Chartism, after 1848, synchronised with a new and tremendously important development in Trade Union organisation, which from the middle of the century onwards took the form of amalgamating small localised bodies of craftsmen into powerful National Unions. The Trade Unions, which were to become at the end of the nineteenth century the strong pillars of the Labour Party, were guided by a sure instinct in giving their support to the Chartist Movement, but not losing themselves in it.

The Chartist Movement, nevertheless, derived much of its inspiration and its force from the unenfranchised masses that were being formed into strong Trade Unions and Co-operative Societies. These voluntary associations of working people were not only schools of democracy, but its instrument. Trade unionists like William Lovett and other leaders of the metropolitan Unions were deeply interested in educational, moral, and political reform. Indeed, the chief political organisation of the working class which gave driving force to the movement for Parliamentary Reform, originated amongst the carpenters who formed, in 1831, an association of Metropolitan Trade Unions. William Lovett, who was president of his Union, a Society of Cabinet Makers, was a leading spirit amongst them, and he later formed the London Working Men's Association, which was definitely political in its outlook and purposes; in fact, Lovett wrote the first draft of the Charter. Through such agencies as Lovett's Association, the London Trades Council and similar kindred bodies in other parts of the country, trade unionists and the working class generally were educated in politics and imbued with the idea of direct Labour representation in Parliament. The creation of the Trades Union Congress in 1868 provided the forum in which this question could be discussed, by the only organised body capable of attaining the end in view. The issue was first raised in the second Annual Congress, when the question of "the best means to secure the direct representation of Labour in the Commons House of Parliament" was opened for discussion by delegates from the Amalgamated Coopers (H. A. Gaunt) and the National Association of Miners (J. Norman Sell), and Congress advised working-class constituencies to adopt as their candidates for Parliament either the officials of trade societies or men actually working at their trade.

The credit of being the first Labour candidate belongs, indeed, to a trade unionist who was a full-time officer of his Union. Credit is often accorded to George Odger as being the first Labour candidate, and he fought the three-cornered contest at Southwark in 1870. But the distinction really belongs to William Newton, one of the founders of the Amalgamated Society of Engineers (now the Amalgamated Engineering Union) who fought Tower Hamlets in 1852—a thing unheard of in the days of the unreformed Parliament—on the restricted franchise of the 1832 Act. Yet William Newton, without a Party organisation, and contesting the second largest constituency in the Kingdom, under the conditions then prevailing, with no popular franchise, no secret ballot, and no safeguards against corrupt electoral practices, received on the hustings the largest show of hands: he won the seat by popular acclaim, but a poll was demanded and his total of votes, although it exceeded a thousand, was the lowest of the three totals cast, in this three-cornered fight by a trade unionist against influential and wealthy representatives of the two great Parties. The journal of the A.S.E. was an ardent supporter of the principle of independent Labour representation for nearly two decades before the second Reform Act of 1867 enfranchised the general body of the urban working class. It strenuously urged trade unionists throughout the country to form operatives' committees in every town and county to put forward their own candidates.

Another Labour candidature was promoted ten years before the 1867 Act, with the encouragement of John Stuart Mill: it was at his instance that George Jacob Holyoake stood in 1857, and by a coincidence in the same constituency, Tower Hamlets, in which William Newton made the first bid for working-class representation by a British working man. But it was not until the franchise was widened by the Act of 1867 that practical steps were taken to organise the working people to secure representation in Parliament for themselves. In the summer of 1869 several meetings of trade unionists and others were called in London for the purpose of establishing a central association embodying all sections of London working men. These meetings led to the formation of the Labour Representation League. There were in existence at the time a few working-class bodies, outside the metropolitan area, which were local Labour Parties in all but name. The most notable instance was that of the workers in the arsenal and dockyards at Greenwich, which, in the 1857 General Election, put forward its own candidate against the Government candidate; and at the hustings he received, like William Newton before him, a show of hands in his favour, but in the poll he received only 1,577 votes against 2,913 recorded for his opponent.

The Labour Representation League itself had a forerunner, in the Political Reform Union, which Ernest Jones, the Chartist, Holyoake, William Newton, William Allen, and other Trade Union and Co-operative leaders combined with a number of middle class Radicals and reformers, including Charles Bradlaugh, to form in 1858. Delegates from such Unions as the Westend Boot and Shoe Makers, the Operative Masons, the Painters and Glaziers' Society, and other Unions in the London building trades, were represented in the conference at which the Political Reform Union was established. But it was the Labour Representation League, established a decade later, which gave the clearest definition to the political aspirations of the workers. It proclaimed as its purpose the promotion throughout the Kingdom of an organisation which would register the votes of working men "without reference to their opinions or Party bias":

> "Its aim being to organise fully the strength of the operative classes as an electoral power, so that, when necessary, it may be brought to bear, with effect, on any important political, social, or industrial question, in the issue of which their interests are involved. Its principal duty will be to secure the return to Parliament of qualified working men: persons who, by character and ability, command the confidence of their class, and who are competent to deal satisfactorily with questions of general interest as well as those in which they are specially interested." [1]

[1] The Prospectus of the Labour Representation League from which this extract is quoted is given in full in an appendix to A. W. Humphrey's "History of Labour Representation."

The aims set forth by the Labour Representation League received the endorsement of the Trades Union Congress. But the Trade Unions at that stage were more disposed to build their immediate political hopes upon their own Parliamentary Committee which the second Congress decided to set up with the obligation to watch legislation in the interests of Labour generally and to promote Labour legislation by drafting Bills that were to be entrusted to members of Parliament well disposed to Labour; and this Parliamentary Committee was vested with the authority of voicing the views of the organised trades in deputations to Ministers, and in the lobbies of the House of Commons. For a good many years the Parliamentary Committee of the T.U.C., (now transformed into its General Council) exercised these political functions on behalf of the Trade Union Movement. But this does not mean that the idea of independent Labour representation disappeared from discussion in the Annual Congresses. It is by no means true to say that the Trade Unions lost interest in the project, or that they neglected the opportunities afforded by the appearance on the scene of the Labour Representation League.

Within a year of the League's formation, it ran its first candidate at a by-election in Southwark, and its choice of a candidate fell upon George Odger, who was then secretary of the London Trades Council. He came within measurable distance of winning the seat. The League came into existence too late to take part in the General Election which followed closely upon the enactment of the Reform Act of 1867. Even so, Radical or Liberal working men's associations existed which promoted working-class candidatures—among them the candidature of George Howell at Aylesbury, W. R. Cremer at Warwick, and E. O. Greening at Halifax. Cremer, who later devoted himself to the peace movement and was knighted, was by trade a carpenter, and one of the founders of the Amalgamated Society of Carpenters and Joiners (now the Amalgamated Society of Woodworkers). George Howell was by trade a bricklayer, who became the first secretary of the London Trades Council, and later secretary of the Parliamentary Committee of the T.U.C. Greening, too, was a trade unionist.

The real opportunity of the Labour Representation League came at the General Election of 1874. Under its auspices, directly or indirectly, about a dozen working-class candidatures were promoted and the first two trade unionists to take their seats in the House of Commons were returned at this election. Thomas Burt won Morpeth, and Alexander Macdonald carried Stafford. They were both of them leaders of the mine workers, but they belonged to the Liberal Party, and neither of them can be said to have been identified with the movement towards independent Labour representation in Parliament. They both held their seats in the General Election of 1880, and they were joined in the House by Henry Broadhurst, who won a seat at Stoke-on-Trent; Joseph Arch, who fought the Wilton division, was another Trade Union candidate.

Broadhurst was a stonemason who held the general secretaryship of the T.U.C. for about a dozen years, assuming that office in 1875; and Arch was the founder of the Agricultural Labourers' Union. In this decade the working-class group in Parliament, all of them identified with the Liberal Party, rose to eleven, and one of them—Broadhurst—was made Under-Secretary at the Home Office; later, in 1892, Thomas Burt also reached ministerial status as Parliamentary Secretary of the Board of Trade in the Rosebery Government.

At this point we enter upon the period of "Liberal-Labour" relationships which influenced the development of the principle of independent Labour representation for a considerable time. Although numerous discussions arose in the Trades Union Congress on the question of direct representation of Labour in Parliament—Henry Broadhurst read a paper on the subject in the 1874 Congress, and resolutions in support of the principle were adopted by Congress in 1875 and in many Congresses thereafter—only tentative efforts were made to set up an effective political organisation. In 1876 a Direct Labour Representation Association was started—by W. J. Davis, a member of the T.U.C. Parliamentary Committee—in Birmingham and it secured representation on the Town Council and the School Board. In the General Election of 1879 the T.U.C. Parliamentary Committee for the first time issued a General Election manifesto setting forth nine points: these included workmen's compensation, reform in the administration of justice, increased factory and workshop inspectorate, abolition of imprisonment for debt and a number of reforms in electoral law, among them the extension of hours of polling in provincial boroughs, and payment out of rates of returning officers' charges. In the 1881 Congress the T.U.C. Parliamentary Committee was instructed by resolution to give every encouragement to bona fide Labour candidates; but in the 1883 Congress a motion to create national and local funds for the support of members in Parliament was rejected. In the General Election of 1885, for which the T.U.C. Parliamentary Committee again issued a manifesto, which this time, by direct instruction of Congress, included a demand for votes for women, ten trade unionists belonging to the T.U.C. were elected to Parliament: namely, Thomas Burt, Henry Broadhurst, Joseph Arch, William Abraham ("Mabon"), W. Crawford, W. R. Cremer, Charles Fenwick, George Howell, J. Leicester, and J. Wilson. Arch, Leicester and Wilson, however, lost their seats in the July election of the same year, after the rejection of the Home Rule Bill.

Encouraged, no doubt, by the growth of Trade Union representation in Parliament, the T.U.C. in 1886 decided to set up a Labour Electoral Association, with a Committee appointed by and from the Congress, to represent nine territorial divisions or areas. The rules of the Association prevented any but bona fide societies affiliating. This was a beginning, but a very tentative one, and it was tainted by "Lib-Lab" sentiment. It must be remembered that at this time the influence of Gladstonian Liberalism was all-pervading and tremendously powerful. It is difficult now to comprehend the ascendancy which Gladstone established over the working-class leaders in the last two decades of the nineteenth century. Their veneration for him was real and profound, and there is no doubt that his hold over them retarded for nearly twenty years the creation of a genuinely independent Labour Party. It is a notable fact that as soon as his great and over-shadowing figure passed finally from the political scene, the movement amongst the workers towards political independence became more pronounced.

A powerful impetus was imparted to the movement, towards the end of the 'eighties, when the Trades Union Congress was halting between two opinions; when the Labour Electoral Association was being drawn on the one hand in the direction of a separate and distinct Labour Party, and on the other hand was being assailed, even in Congress, as being too closely allied with the propaganda for an independent Labour Party. The balance of opinion among the delegates to the Congresses of this time was clearly against "Lib-Lab" politics: a resolution at the 1888 Congress in favour of the Labour Electoral Association giving its support to candidates other than Labour who, "judged by their past and present conduct can be relied on always to place the rights of labour before the interests of any political Party" was lost by 82 votes to 18. In connection with the same Congress, too, a meeting was held in the Congress city (Bradford) with the avowed purpose of inaugurating an independent Labour Party: present at this meeting were men whose names will always be associated with the creation of the Labour Party—among them Keir Hardie, Tom Mann, John Hodge, and others who had a good deal to do with the propaganda of Socialism which was then taking an organised form.

We are here at the point, in time and place, where two convergent streams of thought and action meet. In two decades of intensive organisation the wage-earning class had built up the Trade Union Movement, whose unity of purpose and growing power were represented in and through the Trades Union Congress. Developments were impending in Trade Unionism which were immensely to widen its scope, and to fortify it by the unionisation of hitherto unorganisable masses of workers. Amongst these workers a new ferment was working, in the propaganda of the Socialist Societies. What is called the "New Unionism" made its influence felt inside the Trades Union Congress simultaneously with the entry onto the floor of Congress of ardent socialists who were also the apostles of an independent Labour Party. In the Congress of 1887 Keir Hardie made his first appearance as a delegate, and participated in the discussion of a resolution the object of which was to commit the Trade Unions to support of the Labour Electoral Association. "Lib-Lab" arguments were used in this debate against Hardie's insistence that Labour's representatives should be independent of the older political Parties; but leaders of the Congress, including John Wilson (who was then president of the Labour Electoral Association), Ben Pickard, who held a miner's seat in Parliament, and James Holmes, the railwayman who was, a dozen years later, to move the Congress resolution that brought the Labour Representation Committee into existence and cemented the alliance of socialists and trade unionists, all declared themselves emphatically in favour of a Labour Party separate from the two great political Parties. Two years later, in 1889, came the great Dock Strike which heralded the advent of the New Unionism and demonstrated the creative idealism of the Socialist Movement.

CHAPTER III

THE OLD AND NEW TRADE UNIONISM

By Herbert Tracey

The Labour Party as we know it today is the product of an alliance between the Trade Unions and the Socialist Societies, which found their point of contact in the idea of an independent Labour Party. The 1880's saw the birth of Socialism as an organised force in the formation of the Social-Democratic Federation and the Fabian Society. In the same decade the spread of Trade Unionism from the craftsmen and skilled operatives to unskilled and semi-skilled workers and wage earners of every description over the whole field of industry profoundly affected both the rank and file and the leaders of the working-class movement. The Trade Unions which weathered the storms in the middle decades of the nineteenth century were the great organisations of the craftsmen and skilled operatives; and they had done their work well. From Parliament they had secured a series of Statutes which legalised their beneficent activities, afforded protection for their funds, and gave (as they believed) immunity to their organisation in the furtherance of trade disputes, by giving effect to the principle that it was not wrong for men to do in combination what it was not unlawful for them to do individually and alone. True, the Unions had still to win general recognition and many bitter fights had yet to be waged before employers, who were themselves strongly organised in many industries, conceded the right of the Trade Unions to bargain collectively on their members' behalf. Collective bargaining had nevertheless become an established procedure in industry. Membership of the Unions was rising steadily year by year: the aggregate membership of the Unions affiliated to the T.U.C., which was less than half a million in 1880, was nearly a million-and-a-half in 1889. The powerful amalgamated societies of craftsmen, which were the mainstay of the Trades Union Congress, had built up an imposing system of insurance for their members providing substantial cash benefits of a trade and Friendly Society character. These factors made for stability, but they also perhaps tended to restrict the range of Trade Union organisation to the relatively well-paid skilled workers and artisans. Beneath them in the social scale was a vast mass of unorganised workers, ill-paid, housed in slums, and working long hours in heavy manual employment, at the docks, in the transport services, in the gas works, in foundries and shipyards where general labour was required to do jobs which the craftsmen disdained to do.

Inevitably this horizontal division of the wage-earning class produced a conflict of views on the policy of the Labour Movement, as between those who were turning their attention to the organisation of the great body of general labour, and the older school of trade unionists, who believed that the best results for their members could be achieved by the practice of collective bargaining with their employers. There was a divergence of view, too, on the merits of political action as compared with the value of the traditional methods of Trade Union action. For several years, inside the Trade Unions and on the floor of the Trades Union Congress, a dispute raged on the question of the eight-hour day, in which leading trade unionists found themselves opposing one another on the proposal that the standard of working hours should be a legally enacted eight-hour day. The more conservative-minded leaders held that the State should not interfere with conditions regulating the hours of work of adults. The only law regulating hours of labour at the time was the Act put through by the efforts of Alexander Macdonald, which limited the hours of boys to ten per day. The younger school of "new unionists" fought steadily to get the support of the whole Trade Union Movement for the enactment of a legal eight-hour day. Disagreements on this subject, which was obviously fundamental and with a direct bearing upon the question of creating a Labour Party as the instrument of the workers' political aims, threatened more than once to disrupt the whole Labour Movement. In the end the younger school won support for the commonsense view that there are many Trade Union aims and objectives which cannot be attained and fully safeguarded by industrial action alone, but require legislation.

Discussions of this nature drew much of their illustrative material from existing industrial conditions, as these were brought under the searchlight of Socialist criticism. A number of inquirics and investigations into social conditions instigated by reformers and philanthropists of the middle class, brought to light appalling facts about the prevalence of poverty, destitution, and exploitation of labour: the work of the Salvation Army in the slums of London and other great cities which provided the material for such books as "The Bitter Cry of Outcast London"; and the systematic statistical investigation set on foot by Charles Booth, a philanthropic ship owner who, at his own expense, engaged the services of such social experts as Beatrice Potter (later Mrs. Sidney Webb), to produce the monumental survey of "Labour and Life of the People."[1] Similar investigations carried on in provincial towns and rural districts underlined the conclusions reached by these metropolitan investigators. Seebohm Rowntree's "Poverty: A Study of Town Life" applied the standards and methods of Booth's investigations to a typical English town like York, and afforded proof that the miserable conditions prevailing in London, the wealthiest city in the world, were not peculiar to London, but were widespread and arose out of the prevailing economic system. These investigations, so far from disproving the Socialist indictment of society under capitalist rule, sustained it. They shattered the comfortable assumption dear to middle-class defenders of the existing order

[1] The first two volumes of Charles Booth's Survey were published under this title in 1889-91, but the whole work ran in the end to eighteen volumes, published under the title of "Life and Labour in London."

that all poverty was due to vice or drink: it was proved beyond dispute that "the destruction of the poor is their poverty." In Booth's inquiry a "poverty line" was fixed which made no allowance for anything but the bare necessities of life, and he and his team of research workers were forced to the conclusion that over a million and a quarter of the people of London were living below this poverty line: for the population as a whole 32 per cent. were living, in the world's wealthiest city, in a state of chronic poverty; and in London's East End the proportion rose to 60 per cent. Rowntree's investigation in York showed the same proportions of dire poverty, comfort and riches as holding for the masses and classes of York as for those of London.

Against these grim and squalid conditions of life the masses of unskilled and unorganised labour made their protest in great strikes, like the strike of the London dockers in 1889, which brought them within the orbit of Trade Union organisation. The dockers' strike, like the strike of the London match girls, which occurred about the same time, signalled the rise of the New Unionism. Its success derived from the energetic impulse of these exploited masses, but their organisation into powerful general labour Unions was the work of trade unionists who belonged to the older Unions—to men like Tom Mann and John Burns, both of them members of the Amalgamated Society of Engineers (as it was then called), who joined with Ben Tillett, Will Thorne, and other strong and able men drawn from the ranks of London's East End workers, to build up the new Unions.

The attitude of these men towards the older form of Trade Unionism was clearly indicated by John Burns, who wrote in 1887: "Constituted as it is, Unionism carries within itself the source of its own dissolution. Their reckless assumption of the duties and responsibilities that only the State or the whole community can discharge in the nature of sick and superannuation benefits, at the instance of the middle class, is crushing out the larger Unions by taxing their members to an unbearable extent. This so cripples them that the fear of being unable to discharge their Friendly Society liabilities, often makes them submit to encroachments by the master without protest. The result is that they have degenerated into mere middle- and upper-class rate-reducing institutions."

Implicit in such a statement is the social philosophy which the Labour Party—with which, incidentally, John Burns himself was never identified—has translated into a political programme, and which the Third Labour Government, since 1945, has used its ample majority to implement in a great series of social security Acts of Parliament. Burns, Tillett and Tom Mann were saying at that time what the street corner propagandists of the Socialist Societies were saying, and what the Fabian pamphleteers and essayists were proving—and what the unemployed workers were experiencing in their own persons. Unemployment in the middle 'eighties was the most urgent of social problems. John Burns called the unemployed the real Fourth Estate. Mass meetings of the unemployed were a regular feature of life in London, and their effect was not unlike that produced upon the ruling class at the beginning of that century, when repressive legislation was passed by Parliament directed against the combinations of working men. A demonstration of the unemployed in Trafalgar Square in February 1886 threw the authorities into such a panic when it became a march through the West End of London, that four prominent Socialists, leaders of the Social-Democratic Federation—Hyndman, Burns, Champion and Williams—were indicted on a charge of sedition. All four were acquitted. But in November of the following year, what is known in the annals of the Socialist Movement as Bloody Sunday occurred, when the unemployed workers, under the leadership of John Burns and R. B. Cunninghame Graham, then a Radical Member of Parliament and an aristocrat to his finger-tips but with strong Socialist convictions, sought to hold a demonstration in Trafalgar Square which was closed to them by the police under instructions from the Home Office. Repulsed from the Square the demonstrators made their way past the police barrier; but Burns and Cunninghame Graham, trying to force their way through, were roughly handled by the police and arrested. A number of people were wounded, too. (In another demonstration three months later, in similar conditions, a workman named Sinnel was so seriously injured that he died.) Burns and Cunninghame Graham were tried at the Old Bailey and sentenced to six weeks' imprisonment.

Such events as these were the birth throes of the New Unionism and the other Socialist Societies. It was in 1886 that Ben Tillett made the first attempt to organise the London dockers, beginning with the tea operatives and general labourers in the warehouses and wharves in the Tilbury area. Almost simultaneously Will Thorne, with Tom Mann, John Burns and Tillett, were striving vigorously to organise the gas stokers in the London district. The Union they formed put forward two years later a demand for a three-shift system in the industry which would enable the hours of work to be reduced from twelve to eight per day, and also to secure an increase in the daily wage. The Union obtained these concessions without an actual stoppage of work. This success encouraged Tillett to resume the task of organising the London dockers. In August 1889, the Union, still struggling to establish itself, took part in a minor dispute concerning the handling of a cargo at the South West India Dock. Out of the original claim of the men concerned for a bonus over and above 5*d.* an hour, there arose the demand for the famous "dockers' tanner"—the claim for 6*d.* an hour, with 8*d.* an hour for overtime, the abolition of sub-contract and piece-work and the stipulation that no man should be "called on" for a period of less than four hours' work at a stretch. Within three days 10,000 men at the docks joined in the fight for these terms, and with the assistance of Tom Mann and John Burns, as the struggle went on, the Union extended its organisation. The dockers' strike roused a great deal of public sympathy. Tillett's eloquence and the dramatic leadership of Burns, who daily organised huge processions of dockers, culminating in great meetings on

Tower Hill, attested the vitality of the new Movement. Under the pressure of public opinion a conciliation committee, of which Cardinal Manning, and the then Lord Mayor of London were leading members, negotiated a settlement which gave the dockers most of the Union's claims, and their organisation which took the name of the Dock, Wharf and Riverside Labourers' Union, when the strike came to an end, had a membership of 30,000, and was presently extended to all the other ports. In the same year Havelock Wilson's Union of seamen and firemen, founded in 1887 reached a membership of 65,000. "The full round orb of the Dockers' Tanner"—a phrase coined by Ben Tillett—illumined the whole labour world. The New Unionism added more than three quarters of a million members to the Trades Union Congress between 1886 and 1890, and the advent of the delegates of these new Unions to Congress greatly strengthened the trade unionists who were working for the establishment of an independent Labour Party.

Outside the Trades Union Congress, but in close touch with its active and militant elements, were the organisers of the Socialist Movement. As this is the story of the Labour Party and not a general history of the Labour and Socialist Movement, full justice cannot be done in these pages to the part played by all the men and women who carried on Socialist propaganda, and created the Socialist Societies which did so much to unite the Movement in support of the Labour Party. Not all the leaders of the Socialist Movement were trade unionists by any means: the most influential and tenacious of them belonged to the middle class and the intelligentsia: they were literary artists, thinkers, artist-craftsmen, with brilliant gifts, and not a few of them with much learning, and possessed of remarkable talents for the platform. They did not see eye to eye with one another, either on Socialist theory or on matters of Socialist organisation and method. Hence appeared almost at the same time several Socialist Societies, to one or another of which these brilliant people belonged.

A leading spirit among them was Henry Mayers Hyndman, son of wealthy parents, endowed with a strong personality, and possessing a wide knowledge of politics and economics, and an intense dislike of modern commercialism. His upbringing and temperament gave his mind a distinctly conservative, not to say imperialist, bias; but this characteristic was combined with a strong and almost romantic sympathy with social revolutionary ideas. He was the first English Marxist, after Marx, and he was mainly instrumental in infusing into the first Socialist Society formed in this country the Marxist view and ideology. In Hyndman's circle were such people as Professor Edward Spencer Beesley, the positivist; Helen Taylor (the step-daughter of John Stuart Mill); Joseph Cowen, the Radical M.P.; and others who were, like Hyndman, critical of the existing state of society. In June, 1881, a conference was held at which a society calling itself the Democratic Federation was formed, which recruited amongst it members William Morris, Ernest Belfort Bax, Eleanor Marx, Harry Quelch, Jack

Williams, James Macdonald (not to be confused with James Ramsay MacDonald), and others who all rendered notable service later to the avowed Socialist Movement. Under Hyndman's leadership the Democratic Federation made unsuccessful attempts to bring in the London Radical working men's clubs, amongst whose members were to be found old grey-haired men, survivors of the army of Chartism, who lingered on into the 'nineties, discoursing when occasion offered, of the teachings of Bronterre O'Brien, Feargus O'Connor, Ernest Jones, Oastler and Stephens, Spence, and Robert Owen. In 1883 the Democratic Federation proclaimed its Socialist faith and assumed the name of the Social-Democratic Federation. The writings of Hyndman and William Morris, Belfort Bax, and other Socialist scholars, were the greatest asset of the S.D.F. But its weekly journal *Justice*, was also a considerable asset. It made its appearance at the end of 1883, Edward Carpenter, poet, philosopher and Socialist Communist, whose writings likewise exercised great influence upon that generation, and later ones too, providing the funds to start the journal. For some years the S.D.F. had practically a monopoly of the talents of the middle-class and upper-class intellectuals, artists and writers, who embraced the Socialist cause; amongst them, William Morris, Walter Crane, H. H. Champion, Herbert Burroughs, and many others, who did the spade work of Socialist propaganda at street corner meetings, in the parks, and in workmen's clubs, and who sold *Justice* and Socialist literature at open-air gatherings everywhere. Hyndman, in silk hat and frock coat, did not disdain to sell *Justice* every week in the Strand, nor did William Morris consider it beneath his dignity to hawk the journal and Socialist pamphlets at the propaganda meetings. Unfortunately, the S.D.F. could not harbour in its bosom all the able and outstanding personalities who have just been named, and a split occurred in 1884 which led Morris, Walter Crane, Belfort Bax, Eleanor Marx and many others to leave it and to found the Socialist League. Hyndman, Champion, Harry Quelch, Jack Williams, Herbert Burroughs, Hunter Watts, John Burns (for a time), Will Thorne, and many others who were leaders of the New Unionism remained to carry on the S.D.F.

The Socialist League, with William Morris as its greatest figure, lived only a few years. As poet, craftsman, artist, and writer, Morris was one of the great figures of the age. He remained a Socialist to the end of his life, and he made his residence, Kelmscott House at Hammersmith, the centre of the Hammersmith Socialist Society, and gathered there the brains and genius of the Socialist Movement as long as he lived.

But all the brains and genius of the Socialist Movement were assuredly not inside either the Socialist League of William Morris, or Hyndman's Social-Democratic Federation. The brightest galaxy surrounded with dazzling light the Fabian Society, formed in November 1883, with George Bernard Shaw, Sidney and Beatrice Webb, H. G. Wells (for a time), Sidney (later Lord) Olivier, Hubert Bland, Cecil Chesterton (for a time), Annie Besant, and many other distinguished people to carry on its literary propaganda and its lectures, discussions, and social investigations. The work of the Fabian Society deserves a chapter to itself, as does, indeed, the S.D.F. and the Socialist League. Its contribution to the education of the working-class movement in Socialist principles, and in social science, politics, and political philosophy, is of immeasurable value. Most of the present-day leaders of the Labour Party, and many leading trade unionists, learned Socialism and politics as members of the Fabian Society.

Yet it was left to still another Socialist Society, the Independent Labour Party, to energise Socialist propaganda amongst trade unionists; and to another unattached group of Socialists, Robert Blatchford, Alex Thompson, R. B. Suthers, and the other able journalists who carried on the weekly *Clarion*, to popularise Socialism amongst the people. Robert Blatchford's "Merrie England" and "Britain for the British" made Socialists literally by the hundred thousand. It might be said that the Fabian Society spread Socialism on the upper levels of our national life; whereas the I.L.P. and the Clarion Group spread Socialism among the masses—the I.L.P. in particular impregnating the organised working-class movement. The Fabian Society, as such, was not interested in the formation of a Labour Party. The best short summing up of its aims and policy is perhaps contained in the following extract from Tract No. 70, Report on Fabian Policy (1896):

> "The object of the Fabian Society is to persuade the English people to make their political constitution thoroughly democratic, and so to socialise their industries as to make the livelihood of the people entirely independent of private capitalism.
>
> "The Fabian Society endeavours to pursue its Socialist and democratic objects with complete singleness of aim, for example:
>
> "It has no distinctive opinions on the Marriage Question, Religion, Art, Abstract Economics, Historic Evolution, Currency, or any other subject than its own special business of practical democracy and Socialism.
>
> "It brings all the pressure and persuasion in its power to bear on existing forms, caring nothing by what name any Party calls itself or what principles, Socialist or other, it professes, but, having regard solely to the tendency of its action, supporting those which make for Socialism and democracy and opposing those which are reactionary.
>
> "It does not propose that the practical steps towards social democracy should be carried out by itself, or by any other specially organised society or Party."

This declaration is, and was intended to be, a defiant challenge to dogmatic Marxism. It is also clearly a repudiation of the idea of an independent Labour Party. It is true that individual Fabians embraced the purpose of an independent Labour Party, and the influence of the Fabian Society, in the field of political organisation, was rather directed against the project of organising a Socialist Party on similar lines to those pursued on the continent, notably in Germany. In 1892, in fact, just before the General Election, a Fabian election manifesto, written by Bernard Shaw, severely and acutely criticised both the existing Parties, and told the working classes that they could form their own Party if they cared as much for politics as they did for horse racing. Again, in 1893, when the Liberal Government had failed lamentably to carry out the promise made by its leader, Sir Henry (then Mr.) Campbell-Bannerman, "to show themselves to be the best employers of labour in the country," Bernard Shaw and Sidney Webb wrote an article in the *Fortnightly Review* entitled "To Your Tents, O Israel!" which pointed out that with rare exceptions none of the Government Departments had done anything to redeem Campbell-Bannerman's pledge; and the workers were called upon to abandon Liberalism and form a Trade Union Party of their own and to run fifty candidates for Parliament. This article was afterwards reprinted, with much additional matter drafted by Bernard Shaw, as Tract No. 49, "A Plan of Campaign for Labour." It had a wide circulation. As it showed in considerable detail how a Workers' Party ought to be established, it no doubt had no small share in the development of the Movement which, seven years later, brought the Workers' Party into being under the title of the Labour Representation Committee.

Nevertheless, it was the I.L.P. and Blatchford's Clarion Group which finally hammered home the idea of the Workers' Party. The I.L.P. can be said to have originated in the disappointment of strong supporters of the principle of independent Labour representation when they tried to transform the Labour Electoral Association into a body that would give no support to Parliamentary candidates belonging to other Parties, but who could be relied upon always to place the rights of Labour before any Party interest. Controversy on the question inside the Congress was confused with other issues involving the official Trade Union policy on the question of the eight-hour day, and also the position of the general secretary of the T.U.C. who was a strong and conscientious supporter of the Liberal Party and had, in fact, become a member of the Government. Heated debates took place which retarded the slow change of opinion that was taking place amongst the older and more conservative-minded leaders of the Trade Union Movement. The convinced Socialists who were delegates in the Congresses of this period, with Keir Hardie as their principal spokesman, were unable to secure the support of a majority of the delegates for the idea of a new Party, when its advocacy was complicated by considerations of personal loyalty towards the older Trade Union leaders. But whilst the argument proceeded from one Congress to another and was carried on with great vigour by the leaders of the New Unionism, an important development took place in Scotland.

In 1888 definite steps were taken to bring into existence in Scotland a separate and independent organisation for the working people. Keir Hardie in that year stood as a Labour candidate in a mid-Lanark by-election in definite opposition to the two older Parties. It was only the year before that Hardie had made his first appearance at the Trades Union Congress as the delegate of a small Union of Ayrshire miners. In the mid-Lanark by-election he gave effect to the doctrine he had preached in the Congress by proclaiming the necessity of severing the Trade Unions from the existing political Parties and forming an entirely independent Labour Party. He failed to win this by-election, obtaining no more than 712 votes. Two months later the Scottish Labour Party was formed in Glasgow, with Hardie as its secretary. The new Party found a chairman in Mr. R. B. Cunninghame Graham, who was then M.P. for North Lanarkshire, a seat which he had won as a Liberal in 1886. The advent of a militant Labour Party in the North had a great deal to do with the sporadic efforts that were made to form an organisation on similar lines in some of the industrial towns south of the border, particularly in Yorkshire: the most successful attempt in this direction being made at Bradford, where a political body, calling itself the Labour Union, was founded as the result of an extensive local strike in 1890. The propaganda in the provinces was carried on chiefly by Ben Tillett, Robert Blatchford, Joseph Burgess, editor of a once influential weekly journal *The Workman's Times*. And in 1892 a new impulse was imparted to the Movement in the General Election of that year, by the return to Parliament of John Burns for Battersea, Keir Hardie for West Ham, and J. Havelock Wilson for Middlesbrough, all of whom stood either as Socialists or independent Labour candidates. Ben Tillett fought in this election as candidate at Bradford, and was supported financially by the Fabian Society: he polled 2,749 votes but failed to win the seat.

CHAPTER IV

THE I.L.P. AND THE T.U.C.

By Herbert Tracey

The success of independent Labour candidatures gave much encouragement to the leaders of the campaign to detach the workers from the older political Parties, and to unite them in one of their own creation. In the autumn of 1893 a Conference was held at Bradford for the purpose of uniting the various scattered local independent Labour organisations into a national Party. About 120 delegates were present at this Conference, including five from the Social-Democratic Federation and twelve from the Fabian Society. The Conference decided to form a new organisation with a Socialist programme but without a Socialist title, and this took form as the Independent Labour Party. Neither the Fabian Society nor the S.D.F. joined the new body. Robert Blatchford and the Clarion Group, though they had been instrumental in making Socialists by the thousand, did not identify themselves very closely with the I.L.P. in its youthful days. Its most active spirits, with Keir Hardie as their leader, were not actively identified with the Trade Unions either; but among them were John R. Clynes, Pete Curran, Ben Tillett, Ben Turner, Tom Mann, George N. Barnes, and others who were beginning to exercise great influence in their Trade Unions. Associated with them were men and women who achieved on the I.L.P. platform recognition as political leaders of high competence: Ramsay MacDonald, Philip Snowden, W. C. Anderson, Bruce Glasier; and notable women like Mary Macarthur, Margaret Bondfield, Enid Stacey, Katherine St. John Conway (later Mrs. Bruce Glasier), Margaret Macmillan, Caroline Martin, Mrs. Emmeline Pankhurst, and many others who gave themselves whole-heartedly to the propagation of the Socialist gospel. The I.L.P. was, of course, avowedly a Socialist Party, and unlike the Labour Party, which was formed later, it was built upon a foundation of individual members rather than upon the affiliation of organised bodies. It lacked the essential element of political support which the later Labour Party secured from the Trade Unions. In spite of three years' widespread and steady propaganda by talented speakers who could draw popular audiences far larger than those willing to listen to the spokesmen of the two older Parties, the I.L.P. failed in the General Election of 1895 to secure the return to Parliament of any one of its 28 candidates. Keir Hardie himself lost his seat at West Ham. Throughout the country the I.L.P. candidates received rather less than a combined vote of 45,000. It was encouraging, but it did not mean that organised Labour had found yet the right path to tread.

Trade unionists could win seats in Parliament, but trade unionists who fought as Socialists, whether under the auspices of the I.L.P. or the S.D.F., seemed foredoomed to failure. The confused state of mind among trade unionists was well illustrated by the attitude of the Trades Union Congress, when the project of an independent Labour Party was discussed in connection with the propagation of Socialist propaganda. In the 1893 Congress, the year in which the I.L.P. was founded, a resolution dealing with Labour representation in Parliament came under consideration. It embodied a concrete scheme for the establishment of a fund to assist independent Labour candidates in local and Parliamentary elections. It was proposed that contributions to the fund should be optional on the part of societies that wished to affiliate with the Movement; but those who did affiliate would be required to subscribe annually to the election fund 5*s.* for each 100 members. Administration of the fund it was proposed to entrust to a committee of thirteen persons, elected annually at the Congress, by and from the delegates representing the contributing societies. Selection of Parliamentary candidates whom the fund would assist, was to rest in the first instance with the constituencies; but the scheme provided that a list of suitable candidates should be approved by the committee of the fund and made available to constituencies that could not find a satisfactory local candidate. It was stipulated that all candidates receiving financial assistance from the fund must pledge themselves to support the Labour programme as agreed upon from time to time by the Congress.

This resolution stood on the Agenda of the Congress in the name of John Wilson, M.P., who had been the chairman of the Labour Electoral Association; but he delegated the duty of moving the resolution to Ben Tillett who said that it was not intended to reflect upon the activities of any existing Association: the object rather was to found one central organisation for the promotion of direct and independent Labour representation. In the previous three years they had seen growing among trade unionists a wish to move in this direction, and he hoped that the various bodies already in existence, that were connected with and favourable to the Movement for independent Parliamentary representation, would fall into line with the Congress scheme.

In this debate there was criticism of the Labour Electoral Association, which one delegate declared to have degenerated into a wing of the Liberal Party. An amendment was proposed by James Macdonald, who had influence among the delegates as secretary of the London Trades Council, and this amendment required candidates receiving financial assistance to pledge themselves "to support the principle of collective ownership and control of all the means of production and distribution," as well as the Labour programme agreed upon from time to time by the Congress. Macdonald declared that the future political welfare of the workers required this new independent political Party to have a solid basis on which to act. Pete Curran seconded this amendment, and amongst others who spoke in support of it were Havelock Wilson and John Burns. The latter declared that the amendment affirmed a principle "which cut right to the kernel of the social and labour problems—it stripped all the husks off party politics, whether Liberal or Tory, and five or six of the bogus independent Labour Parties that had come into existence." Burns' speech was clearly directed against the I.L.P. He did not distinguish between the collectivist principles proposed in the amendment, and the Socialist doctrine which was being preached, he said, all over the country, in the name of independent Labour and Socialism. Till the Independent Labour Party was put out of existence (Burns said) there was nothing between Trade Unionism on the one hand, and Trade Unionism plus a Socialist Labour Party on the other. "These parties were at present separate, but if they were blended together they would be invincible." J. R. Clynes also gave his support to the amendment, remarking drily that he would watch with interest to see how the textile delegates in the Congress would vote. For the amendment moved by James Macdonald, 137 votes were registered, with 97 against—a majority of 40. And the announcement of the figures, as the official T.U.C. report records, was "received with loud cheers by the Socialist delegates."

But the official T.U.C. report goes on to summarise a debate which then followed on another resolution, moved by Keir Hardie. This expressed the view that the claims of Labour in Parliament should be asserted irrespective of the convenience of any political Party; "and to secure this it is necessary that the Labour Members in the House of Commons should be unconnected with either the Liberal or Tory Party and should sit in opposition to any Government until such time as they are strong enough to form a Labour Cabinet." Hardie made it clear that his intention was to give his motion exclusive reference to M.P.s who might be elected under the scheme of Parliamentary representation to which the Congress had just agreed. He said they might be told there were two sides in the House of Commons and that a member must either sit on the Liberal or the Tory side. But there was no such thing as a Liberal or Tory side, he pointed out. There was the Government side and the Opposition side, and he thought that an independent Labour Party should follow the example of the Irish Members and sit always on the Opposition side of the House. It might be true that the Party which had brought in most of the reforms that had worked for the advancement of the working class was the Liberal Party; but he was of opinion that if there were a party of ten independent Labour men acting together, they would be able to approach any Government and obtain from it concessions which they could not otherwise obtain. Hardie's motion was seconded but there was no discussion—and when it was put to the vote it was lost by 119 against 96, a majority of 23; the delegates seemingly were unaware of the contradictions and inconsistencies which were thus left for a later Congress to reconcile.

Nothing came immediately from the decision of this Congress to establish a political fund to finance independent Labour candidates. The

Parliamentary Committee of the Congress drew the attention of delegates, in the next year's assembly, to the fact that the previous Congress had taken no steps to set up the Committee which was to take charge of the organisation and administer the funds in accordance with the Macdonald resolution. The Parliamentary Committee had called the attention of affiliated societies to this omission, and had invited those who were prepared to give effect to the Macdonald resolution to send representatives to a Conference which the secretary of the Parliamentary Committee was authorised to call for the purpose of establishing the fund and setting up the necessary committee of management. Only two replies came from affiliated societies in response to this invitation, and it was therefore impossible for the Parliamentary Committee to proceed further. No delegate at the 1894 Congress apparently challenged the Parliamentary Committee's conclusion; although it rejected by a large majority an amendment moved by a delegate suggesting that a clause should be added to the Parliamentary Committee's report regretting that the time of Congress should be taken up by discussing and agreeing upon a subject that evidently had not the support or approval of the societies represented.

It is clear from the discussion that took place in the annual Trades Union Congress, in these years, that many trade unionists who were not without influence, were hostile to the I.L.P., and this hostility affected their view of the growing movement towards the setting up of an independent Labour Party. In the General Election of 1895, none of the twenty-eight I.L.P. candidates secured a seat, and leading members of the Congress, including George Howell, Sam Woods (only recently elected the secretary of Congress), W. C. Steadman, and W. R. Cremer, who held seats in the outgoing Parliament, were among the defeated candidates. The president of the Congress in that year made a strong attack upon the I.L.P. as being responsible for (as he said) converting the term Labour candidate into a by-word of reproach and mistrust. Its name, he said, was misleading, and from its public performances he had reluctantly to conclude that the I.L.P. was anti-Labour and anti-trade-unionist. It was at this Congress, moreover, that alterations were made in the system of representation by which delegates from local Trades Councils became no longer qualified to sit in the Congress: the rule was then laid down that delegates to Congress must be either full-time officials of the affiliated Trade Unions, or members of these Unions actually working at their trade. The amendment to the Standing Orders of Congress had the unfortunate effect of excluding from it John Burns and Henry Broadhurst, as well as Keir Hardie.

The deadlock on the question of independent Labour representation received further illustration in the 1896 Congress. A motion was put forward instructing the T.U.C. Parliamentary Committee to submit the following question to the affiliated societies:

> "Are your members willing to subscribe *1d.* per quarter to a fund for the purpose of contesting seats and supporting bona-fide trade unionist candidates for

Parliamentary honours pledged to neither of the old political Parties—Tory or Liberal?"

This proposal was defeated by 136 votes to 62. Implicit in such decisions was the division of opinion among trade unionists on the question whether the proposed Labour Party should be a Trade Union Party, or an independent Party embracing all, whether trade unionist or Socialist, who were prepared to make it the instrument of working-class opposition to the older political Parties.

The resolution proposing that an inquiry should be made among the Unions to ascertain the attitude of their members towards the principle of free and independent Labour representation actually had the support of the president of the previous Congress (John Jenkins) who had assailed the I.L.P. in his presidential address. John Jenkins declared that he believed it was necessary to have a national organisation of Labour, but that it must be under the auspices of the Trades Union Congress. But the project of establishing a political fund which the Congress of 1893 had sanctioned, evidently misfired. It disappeared as a topic of discussion from the Congress, and it was not until the 1899 Congress assembled at Plymouth that the final decisive step was taken which resolved the ideological conflict inside the Trade Unions and produced the real solution of the problem. The historic decision was then taken which separated the political organisation of the working-class movement from the general functions of the Trades Union Congress.

In the previous year, indeed, the president of the Congress, James O'Grady, had suggested that "a committee should be appointed to draft a scheme of political organisation for the Trade Union world on the ground that, just as trades federation is a matter of vital necessity for industrial organisation, so will also a scheme of political action be of vital necessity, if we wish Parliament to faithfully register the effects of the Industrial Revolution on our social life." O'Grady pointed out that the Trade Unions were agreed upon their objective, and the trend of modern industry was clearly in the direction of collectivism: with the certainty that it implied the only solution of the social problems facing them today, as practical men they must (he said) use every agency at hand, industrial and political, to work consciously towards that goal; and he included political agencies because he thought they were generally agreed that Trade Union action alone would never bring about industrial emancipation. He was convinced, he made it clear, that the Trade Unions could only obtain their objective by the creation of an independent Labour Party. He quoted calculations that had been made in the *Westminster Review* in 1897, that a subscription of 1*d.* a week from trade unionists would amount to about £224,000 in one year, and in four years, when the existing Parliament would be nearing its close the fund would amount to £898,000. "With this sum we could, if need be, threaten every seat in the Kingdom," O'Grady said. The first step was taken at the 1899 Congress in the following year, to accomplish this result.

James O'Grady's suggestion bore fruit in the following way. Although Keir Hardie and the leaders of the I.L.P. and the Socialist Movement generally, were excluded from Congress under the revised Standing Order which limited representation to full-time Trade Union officials or members actually working at their trade, they still took an active part behind the scenes at Congress. The resolution on Labour representation which came before the 1899 Congress was, in fact, actually drafted in the office of the *Labour Leader*, the official organ of the I.L.P. It was entrusted to James Holmes, one of the railwaymen's delegates, and was seconded by James Sexton. It was in the following terms:

> "That this Congress, having regard to its decisions in former years, and with a view to securing a better representation of the interests of Labour in the House of Commons, hereby instructs the Parliamentary Committee to invite the co-operation of all the Co-operative, socialistic, Trade Union, and other working-class organisations to jointly co-operate on lines mutually agreed upon, in convening a special congress of representatives from such of the above-named organisations as may be willing to take part to devise ways and means for securing the return of an increased number of Labour members to the next Parliament."

James Sexton, who seconded the resolution, declared that its object was to avoid the existing disgraceful confusion, in which prominent Labour men opposed each other on separate political platforms, and this state of affairs in some of its aspects constituted a reflection upon the intelligence and common sense of the Congress. Ben Tillett and Pete Curran, too, who supported the resolution, insisted upon the necessity of putting an end to the confusion that prevailed inside the working-class movement. Margaret Bondfield said that the Shop Assistants' Union, which she represented in Congress, had instructed her to support "any means that were considered practicable for securing some concerted action on the part of trade unionists, socialists, and Co-operative Societies," for they had already experienced the impossibility of obtaining anything like satisfactory legislative action from the older Parties. Opposition to the proposal came from some of the older Trade Union leaders whose spokesman was Thomas Ashton, secretary of the Amalgamated Spinners. He declared that the proposal, if passed, would have no notice taken of it by one trade unionist out of ten thousand. Trade Unionism would come to grief, he contended, if it interfered in politics. After other speeches were made, the divided opinion of the Congress found expression in a vote which recorded 546,000 in favour of the motion, and 434,000 against it.

No vote was taken on another resolution which might have committed the Congress, if it had been discussed, to the organisation of a distinct Trade Union Party. It was proposed in this resolution that every Union affiliated to the T.U.C. should contribute the equivalent of ½*d.* per member each year towards a Parliamentary election fund, and that this fund should be used to pay the expenses of candidates who ran directly under the auspices of the T.U.C. Parliamentary Committee; that these candidates if they secured election to the House of Commons should act in accordance with the policy laid down by the T.U.C., as interpreted by its Parliamentary Committee; and that when the fund came into operation, any Union which did not contribute was to lose its representation at the Congress. This resolution was withdrawn, in view of the later discussion impending upon the resolution put forward by James Holmes.

Steps were taken immediately to give practical application to the resolution of Congress. A special committee was appointed for the purpose of carrying out the Congress decision. Four members represented the Parliamentary Committee, namely Sam Woods, W. C. Steadman, Will Thorne and Richard Bell; Keir Hardie and J. Ramsay MacDonald were selected to represent the I.L.P.; George Bernard Shaw and Edward R. Pease, were chosen for the Fabian Society; and Harry Quelch and H. R. Taylor for the Social-Democratic Federation. On a committee thus constituted the Socialists were in a majority, and being more energetic, and with very clear views of the aim they wished to attain, they had very much their own way in the preliminary arrangements by which a date for the Conference was fixed, and a basis for discussion drawn up in the form of proposals. These have their proper place here, as it was upon them that the Conference laid the foundations of the Labour Party. The principles embodied in these resolutions governed the Party for nearly a score of years after it was founded. These proposals, the first of which bear obvious marks of the compromise as between the Socialists on the one hand, and the older trade unionists on the other, were in the following terms:

(1) *Object of Conference:* A resolution in favour of working class being represented in the House of Commons by men sympathetic with the aims and demands of the Labour Movement.

(2) *Labour Members in the House of Commons:* A resolution in favour of establishing a distinct Labour Group in Parliament, who should have their own whips and agree upon their policy, which must embrace a willingness to co-operate with any Party which, for the time being, may be engaged in promoting legislation in the direct interest of Labour, and be equally ready to associate themselves with any Party in opposing measures having an opposite tendency.

(3) *Constitution of Committee:* The Committee shall consist of twelve representatives from Trade Unions, ten from Co-operative Societies, provided they are represented as a body at the conference, two from the Fabian Society, two from the I.L.P., and two from the S.D.F.

(4) *Duty of Committee:* This Committee should keep in touch with Trade Unions and other organisations which are running Labour candidates.

(5) *Financial Responsibility:* The Committee shall administer the funds which may be received on behalf of the organisation, and each body shall be required to pay 10*s.* per annum for every 1,000 members or fraction thereof, also that it shall be responsible for the expenses of its own candidates.

(6) *Reporting to Congress:* It should also report annually to the Trades Union Congress and the annual meetings of the national societies represented on the committee, and take any steps deemed advisable to elicit opinion from the members of organisations to which the Committee is ultimately responsible.

(7) *Basis of Representation:* Societies, by whatever name they may be known, shall be entitled to one delegate for every 2,000 members or fraction thereof and they must pay 10*s.* for each delegate attending the conference.

(8) *Voting:* The method of voting shall be by card to be issued to the delegates of trade societies according to their membership and paid for on the principle of one card for every 1,000 members.

The implementation of the 1899 Congress decision, on the basis of the foregoing proposals took place at the Special Conference held in obedience to the Congress mandate on February 27-28, 1900. It was with this Conference that the history of the Labour Party really began. The calling of the Conference at the behest of the T.U.C. marks the end of the pioneer period of the Labour and Socialist Movement in Britain. The foundations of the Labour Party were laid, and during the following years a massive structure was built upon these foundations rapidly and securely. How the industrially organised workers were able to make common cause with the Socialists in organising a political Party at the beginning of the present century the next chapter will explain.

CHAPTER V

THE LABOUR REPRESENTATION COMMITTEE

By Herbert Tracey

When the Conference which was called in obedience to the resolution of the Trades Union Congress in 1899 met in the Memorial Hall, London, on February 27, 1900, the conflict of tendencies within the Trade Union and Socialist Movement prevented a clear-cut decision being taken to establish the new political organisation as an independent Labour Party. The Trade Union Group of Members of Parliament considered themselves to be a separate group in the House of Commons. They had, in fact, constituted themselves as a separate group under the auspices of the Parliamentary Committee of the T.U.C. with their own chairman and whips. There were nine of them, including John Burns and Thomas Burt, with several others who remained attached to the Liberal Party, and who never identified themselves with the Labour Party. John Burns, at the Memorial Hall Conference said the Group had been definitely organised for four or five years past with Sam Woods and himself as whips: they had not called themselves independent, but they had done the work; and he proceeded to warn the Conference against too much dictation. On the other hand, there were trade unionists at the Memorial Hall who certainly did not regard the Trade Union M.P.s, or some of them at least, as Labour Members of Parliament, as they had been found ready to work with capitalist interests against the interests of the workers in Parliament. When Ramsay MacDonald, ten years later, said of the Memorial Hall Conference that some of the delegates met "to bury the attempt in good-humoured tolerance, a few to make sure that burial would be its fate, but the majority determined to give it a chance." he summed up the situation fairly accurately.

Seventy working-class organisations were represented in the Conference by 129 delegates who were entitled to cast altogether 591 votes on the basis of one vote for every 1,000 members (or fraction thereof) whom they represented. All told, more than half a million organised workers were represented in the Conference, the largest Trade Union being the Amalgamated Society of Engineers with 85,000 members, and the smallest the Amalgamated Society of Waiters, with 200 members. The delegates of the Independent Labour Party, seven of them, including Keir Hardie, Philip Snowden, Ramsay MacDonald, F. W. Jowett, and Joseph Burgess, claimed to represent 13,000 members. The Fabian Society which was represented by its secretary, Edward R. Pease, had a membership of 861. The Social-Democratic Federation had four delegates, including Harry Quelch and James Macdonald, representing 9,000 members. The largest individual delegation was that of the Gas Workers and General Labourers' Union, numbering thirteen, with Will Thorne at its head, and with J. R. Clynes, Pete Curran, Arthur Hayday, and others later to be known as stalwarts of the Labour Party, in the delegation. Arthur Henderson's Union, the Friendly Society of Ironfounders, was represented in the Conference, but he was not its delegate. Co-operative Societies, and also the Co-operative Union, had been invited, along with other working-class bodies, to send representatives, but the Co-operative Union, in the absence of any mandate from their last Annual Conference, were unable to pledge their organisation. As a matter of history, the only Co-operative Society which has remained in affiliation with the Labour Party for any length of time is the Royal Arsenal Co-operative Society, which maintains to this day, through its Political Purposes Committee, an affiliated membership of about 25,000, and is represented on the National Executive of the Labour Party by one elected member.

The lines of division in the Conference separated three well-defined groups: there was the point of view represented broadly by the Socialist delegates from the I.L.P. and the Fabian Society, and (with reservations) the S.D.F.; along with them stood the group of trade unionists representing the New Unionism; and opposed to them were the older Trade Union leaders who remained faithful to the Liberal (or Radical) principles instilled into them in their earlier days. This latter group wanted representation of the workers in Parliament to include "men sympathetic with the aims and demands of the Labour Movement," but not necessarily in opposition to the two older Parties. The Socialist Group wished to have Labour represented in Parliament only by avowed Socialists who were prepared to form a separate Party "based upon a recognition of the class war, and having for its ultimate object the socialisation of the means of production, distribution and exchange." The third group were content to insist that representatives of the workers in Parliament must belong to the working class.

These conflicting points of view were reflected in the resolutions which came before the Conference. It opened with a brief and fairly non-committal speech from the chairman of the Parliamentary Committee of that year (J. T. Chandler) who explained how the Conference had originated, and expressed the hope that the outcome of its deliberations would be the evolution of a scheme which "would command the support of the trade unionists and of the non-unionists of the country, and as a result they would have a much larger number of friends in the House of Commons in the future than they unfortunately had at the present time." As the Parliamentary Committee's chairman was not a delegate to the Conference, it proceeded thereupon to elect W. C. Steadman, an M.P. who was the delegate of the Barge Builders' Union, a small but sturdy organisation of 400 members, and a member of the T.U.C. Parliamentary Committee, who became secretary of the T.U.C. a few years later (1905-10). Steadman admitted to the Conference that he was one of the trade unionists who believed, until events taught him otherwise, that the workers could attain their objective of better conditions by voluntary efforts through their trade organisation. But experience had convinced him that the leaders of the advanced movement who believed in political action were right, and he was wrong. "The great industrial army of the country, the men who were endeavouring to raise mankind, not by the shedding of human blood but by the peaceful conquest of the ballot box, were the only class who were insufficiently represented in the House of Commons." For the first time in the history of the Labour Movement all sections of it (with the exception of the co-operators) had drawn together, and whether they formed a Labour Party or allied themselves to other political parties in the House of Commons, let them (he said) be represented by men of character. And after this exhortation the Conference proceeded to deal with resolutions which expressed the varying trends of opinion among the delegates.

The first resolution, proposing that the working classes should be represented in the House of Commons by members of the working classes, would have excluded members of the Socialist Societies who were not manual workers. It was rejected in favour of an amendment moved by George Barnes, of the A.S.E. This was in the following terms:

> "That this Conference is in favour of working-class opinion being represented in the House of Commons by men sympathetic with the aims and demands of the Labour Movements, and whose candidatures are promoted by one or other of the organised movements."

John Burns seconded this resolution, because he was convinced the time had come in the history of the Labour and Socialist Movement when they should not be prisoners to class prejudices but should consider parties and policies apart from all class organisation. He said that if the Conference declared itself in favour of working-class candidates only it would be bad enough, but to give a definition of those working-class candidates would be infinitely worse. The motion put forward by Barnes was then accepted by 102 to 3 votes. The Conference thus decided that the new political movement was not to have an exclusively working-class character. But was it to be a Socialist party? This issue was presented in a challenging form by James Macdonald, on behalf of the S.D.F. He moved the following resolution:

> "That the representatives of the working-class movement in the House of Commons should form there a distinct party, with a party organisation separate from the capitalist parties, based upon a recognition of the class war, and having for its ultimate object the socialisation of the means of production, distribution and exchange. The party shall formulate its own policy for promoting practical legislative measures in the interests of Labour, and shall be prepared to co-operate with any party that will support such measures, or will assist in opposing measures of an opposite character."

To this uncompromising declaration Alex Wilkie (of the shipwrights) moved an amendment proposing that a Labour programme of five or six points should be framed on questions with which the vast majority of the workers were in agreement, and that Labour candidates should be pledged to act together in support of these points, and also to co-operate with any Party which, for the time being, might promote legislation in the direct interests of Labour, or to associate themselves with any Party in opposing measures which would be detrimental to Labour: but on all purely political questions Wilkie's amendment proposed to leave Labour representatives entirely free.

This was the "Lib-Lab" point of view. James Sexton, who represented the dockers, said it was magnificent, but it was not war. It was rejected by 59 votes to 35. Then came a motion, presented by Keir Hardie in the name of the I.L.P. which defined the issue with sufficient clarity, and was accepted by the Conference unanimously. It was in these terms:

> "That this Conference is in favour of establishing a distinct Labour group in Parliament who shall have their own whips, and agree upon their policy, which must embrace a readiness to co-operate with any party, which for the time being may be engaged in promoting legislation in the direct interests of Labour, and be equally ready to associate themselves with any party in opposing measures having an opposite tendency; and further, members of the Labour group shall not oppose any candidate whose candidature is being promoted in terms of resolution One."

Hardie emphasised the meaning of his motion by saying that it aimed at the formation in the House of Commons of a Labour Party having its own policy, its own whips, and acting in all that concerns the welfare of the workers in a manner free and unhampered by entanglements with other parties. It left each of the affiliated organisations free to select its own candidates, the one condition being that when returned to Parliament the candidate should agree to form one of the Labour group there, and act in harmony with its decisions.

Acceptance of this motion did not put an end to the controversy as between the "Lib-Lab" elements on the one hand and the uncompromising Socialists on the other. But it did lay down the conditions upon which the new Party was enabled to come into existence. The Conference was in a position then to proceed to the election of an Executive Committee. It was decided that this should consist of twelve members. Seven members were chosen to represent the Trade Unions; namely, Frederick Rogers (Vellum Bookbinders), Thomas Greenall (Lancashire Miners), Richard Bell (Amalgamated Society of Railway Servants), Pete Curran (Gas Workers and General Labourers), Allan Gee (Yorkshire Textile Workers), Alex Wilkie (Shipwrights), and John Hodge (British Steel Smelters). The two members chosen to represent the I.L.P. were Keir Hardie and James Parker. The members representing the S.D.F. were James Macdonald and Harry Quelch. The Fabian Society's member was its secretary, Edward R. Pease. James Ramsay MacDonald (I.L.P.) was unanimously elected secretary—and the office of the Committee was part of a room in his flat at 3 Lincoln's Inn Fields. Frederick Rogers was chosen as the first chairman, and the newly-elected body was designated the Labour Representation Committee.

After passing a number of resolutions on details of organisation, including one which instructed the Executive Committee to invite Trades Councils to send representatives to the next Conference on the basis of one delegate for every 25,000 members affiliated, the L.R.C. was left to get on with its task. It made an encouraging start. In its first year its Committee was able to report the affiliation of just over forty Trade Unions, with an aggregate membership of about 353,000. The three Socialist Societies had nearly 23,000 members divided among them, and half a dozen Trades Councils had a combined membership of about 100,000; the latter aggregation, of course, overlapping to some extent the affiliated Trade Union membership. Some of the largest Unions, like the Amalgamated Society of Engineers, the Boot and Shoe Operatives, and others in the printing and textile trades and in the mining industry, were not in the first year's list of affiliations; but in reporting on the position to the T.U.C. Parliamentary Committee, Ramsay MacDonald, as hon. secretary of the L.R.C., explained that several of the large Unions were balloting their members upon affiliation, and the probabilities were that the membership of the L.R.C. would very soon be doubled—it was, in fact, nearly trebled in the course of the two following years.

These were important formative years. In 1900 the Khaki Election which followed the South African war found the Labour Movement deeply divided, and the L.R.C. were able to run no more than fifteen candidates. Only two, Richard Bell and Keir Hardie, were returned; but they were joined in the course of the next couple of years, at by-elections, by David Shackleton, Will Crookes, and Arthur Henderson. But the controversy which had arisen inside the Trade Union and Socialist Movement did not die down when the L.R.C. fought its first General Election. It came up again, both in the Congress and in the L.R.C. Conference, sometimes as an abstract principle, and at others in connection with personalities. An attempt was made at the T.U.C. in 1903 to restrict membership of the Labour Representation Committee to the same basis as for the Trades Union Congress. This proposal was made by way of an amendment to a resolution presented by Pete Curran and seconded by Robert Smillie, which asked the Congress to endorse the policy of direct Labour representation, and to urge all Trade Unions not yet affiliated to the L.R.C. to join forthwith "so that the entire Labour Movement may be consolidated for definite political purposes." The amendment to this resolution proposed to add that the qualification for membership of the Labour Representation Committee should be the same as for the Trades Union Congress—a proposal which was supported by, amongst others, Richard Bell, who had just ceased to be the Chairman of the L.R.C. He interpreted the principle of independence differently, he said. His own idea was independence and co-operation, as opposed to independence and isolation. Bell was in trouble at that time because he had given his support to Liberal candidates in a matter involving the interests of his own Union and of the Trade Union Movement generally. He was subjected to considerable criticism both in the Congress and in the L.R.C. Conference, but the main issue was clarified in the latter assembly by the amendment of the L.R.C. constitution which defined its objects in the following terms:

> "To secure, by united action, the election to Parliament of candidates promoted, in the first instance, by an affiliated society, or societies in the constituency, who undertake to form or join a distinct Group in Parliament, with its own whips and its own policy on Labour questions, to abstain strictly from identifying themselves with or promoting the interests of any section of the Liberal or Conservative Parties, and not to oppose any other candidate recognised by this Committee. All such candidates shall pledge themselves to accept this constitution, to abide by the decisions of the Group in carrying out the aims of this constitution, or resign, and to appear before their constituency under the title of Labour candidates only."

This settled the question, and in good time. It was henceforth recognised that the new political Movement was to be independent, and history has more than ever justified the prescience of the men who fought for it. But the unity of the Movement was cemented not by amendments to the constitution so much as by the course of political events. And an event had just taken place which riveted the attachment of the Trade Unions to the new Party. The Taff Vale Judgment, which was given by the House of Lords in 1902, supplied a final and convincing argument for an independent Labour Party.

A telegram read to the delegates at the Trades Union Congress in 1900 was the first intimation that an issue had been raised by the Taff Vale Judgment which was destined to cement the relations of the Trade Unions with the Labour Party. Richard Bell, on behalf of his Union, read the telegraph message, which announced the decision of the Judge involving not only his own Union, but the whole Trade Union Movement: an injunction had been granted against the Union in a judgment which implied that the Union (the Amalgamated Society of Railway Servants) and its funds, were liable for wrongs committed by its agents in the course of the dispute that had arisen with the Taff Vale Railway Company. The Trade Unions were quick to make up their minds about the significance of the Taff Vale Judgment. Their view of it was sharply defined in the recommendations which the T.U.C. Parliamentary Committee placed before the next Congress in 1901, in the following terms:

> "In view of the decision of the House of Lords in the Taff Vale case, rendering the funds of societies liable in damages for the illegal acts of their agents, this Congress empowers the Parliamentary Committee to take a test case to the House of Lords, to ascertain how far picketing may be carried on without infringing the law, and rendering the funds of societies liable in damages. Further, that a Fund should be established for the purpose, in the first place, of carrying this out, and as it appears in recent cases in Court, that employers and the various insurance societies acting on their behalf, are endeavouring to establish principles of law against Trade Unionism generally by attacking societies numerically and financially weak, this

Fund should be available for resisting such principles where it is endeavoured to establish them against trade unionists of the country and of protecting the interests of Trade Unions generally. Further, that each society should so amend its rules that so far as possible protection may be obtained against some of the consequences of the decision in the Taff Vale case. Acting in conjunction with our Standing Counsel we shall thoroughly consider this latter matter after Congress is over and communicate with the organised trades of the country without delay."

There was no reference in this statement, which became a motion before Congress, to political action by the Unions; but an amendment was proposed to add that each Society should use its best endeavour "to bring about such an alteration in the law as will meet with the approval of this Congress." Richard Bell supported this amendment. His society, he said, was about to be sued for £20,000 by the railway company—actually the Union had to pay the railway company £23,000 in satisfaction of all damages and costs, and altogether the Union spent nearly £42,000 in defending a principle that was vital to the existence of Trade Unionism. Into the details of the Taff Vale dispute it is not necessary to enter. In the course of it the railway company secured an injunction against the Union, its general secretary and its organising secretary for picketing and molestation; and another injunction was secured from the Court to restrain the Union trustees from spending Union money in defence of its officers. Proceedings against the workers involved who were summoned for breach of contract were dropped: but the railway company pursued its case against the Union, and it was carried finally to the House of Lords which handed down a decision in 1902 that was universally regarded as a mortal blow at the Unions generally. This was not only the view of trade unionists. Distinguished jurists like Frederic Harrison took the view that the legal decision meant the end of Trade Unionism. He argued that the Taff Vale case, with others, had so crippled the Trade Unions, that to enter into strikes at all was dangerous, and that the new weapons used against them in the industrial war would smash up all the Unions in time.

The newly-formed L.R.C. interpreted the Taff Vale Decision as evidence of deepening hostility to the whole Labour Movement. In its report to the 1902 Conference of the L.R.C. its Executive Committee described the decision as an attempt "to crush out Trade Unionism by claims upon its funds: the attack upon Trade Unionism on its legal side is an attempt to restrain its action, so that its power to protect the workmen will be but a shadow"; and referred to articles in the Press as part of a well-organised movement to prejudice public opinion against the Unions. "Menaced on every hand, in workshop, court of law, and Press, Trade Unionism has no refuge except the ballot box and Labour Representation," said the L.R.C.

As the full significance of the Taff Vale Judgment spread amongst trade unionists, they turned almost with one accord to their Labour representatives in Parliament. In a single year the number of Unions affiliated to the L.R.C. doubled, and their combined affiliated membership rose from 455,450 to 847,315. The number of Unions affiliated at the first

Conference of the L.R.C. was forty-one; it had grown in 1904 to 165, with a combined membership of very nearly a million. The growth of the L.R.C. testified to the conviction implanted in the minds of trade unionists by the Taff Vale Judgment that such "Judge-made law" could only be rectified by legislation. It is true to say that no single factor contributed so much as this legal decision to the early up-building of the political Labour Movement.

It had, for example, the effect of bringing into the L.R.C. practically the whole of the cotton workers of Lancashire, represented by the United Textile Factory Workers, which affiliated almost immediately. A by-election in the Clitheroe Division, a textile constituency, gave the leaders of the new political Labour organisation the opportunity to support the candidature of David Shackleton, of the Darwen Weavers, who was returned unopposed: the older political parties showed no anxiety to contest the seat against the new and almost unknown Movement. Shackleton became immediately a force in the House of Commons and a leader in the later fights that took place there for the reversal of the Taff Vale Judgment and amendment of the law relating to industrial disputes. This was not the only indication of the growing influence of the L.R.C. in its earliest years. A by-election in Woolwich in 1903 enabled the local Labour forces to concentrate upon the candidature of Will Crookes, then an active figure in East End politics, and he won the contest handsomely with 8,687 votes to 5,458. A few weeks later, when the political world was thrown into a ferment by Joseph Chamberlain's sudden opposition to the Free Trade policy and his advocacy of a system of Colonial preference, Arthur Henderson was elected in another by-election, at Barnard Castle in a three-cornered contest, in which both Tariff Reform and the Taff Vale Judgment were hotly-debated issues.

Thus, the political questions which were to decide the outcome of the then approaching General Election took shape as the organisation of the workers' political Movement was strengthened. In the conferences of the L.R.C. in those years, as well as at the Trades Union Congress, from year to year, the controversy between those who wanted the new Party to be simply a Trade Union party, and those who sought to make it a genuinely representative party of the people founded upon Socialist principles had to be fought out. The Committee of the new Party told the Conference of 1902 that there was some danger in the action of constituent bodies which made the Labour member the representative of one trade rather than of the general interests of wage earners. "It is the wage earner, and not only the miner, the engineer, or the railway servant, who needs representation," (said the Committee) "and any methods of carrying our ideas into effect which debars from Parliament capable men belonging to the smaller Unions is a mistake." It was indicated that the Committee intended before the next General Election to establish a Parliamentary fund, subscribed to by societies and individuals interested in Labour representation for the purpose of aiding bona-fide Labour representatives, irrespective of the

Union to which they belonged: "only in this way can they be won for *Labour* Representation, and not merely for *trade* representation."

This latter project was carried into effect at the 1903 Conference of the L.R.C. Contributions were fixed at the rate of 1*d.* per member per year for affiliated societies, and the scheme provided that all members elected under L.R.C. auspices should be paid from the fund an equal sum "not to exceed, for the present, £200 per annum"; and the Committee was authorised to pay 25 per cent. of the Returning Officer's expenses in respect of its approved candidate, so long as the total sum so expended did not exceed a quarter of the Parliamentary Fund. Later on it was decided by a vote of the Conference that 5 per cent. of the annual income of the Fund should be transferred to the Committee general funds to pay for working expenses and carrying on propaganda. Provision had to be made for the maintenance of members in Parliament, as there was at that time no Parliamentary salary paid from public funds.

Another by-election which occurred about that time, at West Monmouth in 1904, marked the entry of the mine workers' organisation into the new political Party. At its annual meeting in that year the Miners' Federation of Great Britain decided that its candidates in future should run as Labour candidates and co-operate with the L.R.C. group in the House of Commons. The secretary of the South Wales Miners' Federation, Thomas Richards, stood as a Labour candidate with the support of the L.R.C. in the West Monmouth by-election, occasioned by the death of Sir William Harcourt, and in the result secured the seat by 7,995 votes against 3,360 by the opposing candidate, who stood as a Tariff Reformer. There was a remarkable growth, too, in the constituencies of local L.R.C.s modelled upon the constitution of the national body, and it was recognised that these local committees would, sooner or later, have to be regarded as an integral part of the political Labour Movement; as, in fact, they did, under the title of local Labour Parties.

Developments of this kind helped to clarify the relations between the Parliamentary Committee of the Trades Union Congress and the Labour Representation Committee. Difficulties arose often, in the early years of the political Movement, from the overlapping of functions between the Executive Committee of the L.R.C. and the Parliamentary Committee of the T.U.C.: the latter's objects were still largely of a political character, despite the creation of the newer body charged specifically with political work; and there were difficulties, too, in the relations of the L.R.C. with the Management Committee of the General Federation of Trade Unions, a body which at that time occupied a somewhat anomalous position, claiming almost co-equal authority with the T.U.C. Frequent pronouncements on current affairs, both national and international, and the endorsement of Parliamentary candidates by the Executive bodies of both the T.U.C. and the General Federation of Trade Unions, made it necessary to establish something like a common point of view. Consultations between them and the Committee of the L.R.C. resulted finally in the framing of a concordat on the following lines:

(1) All candidates adopted by the Labour Representation Committee under its constitution shall receive the loyal and hearty support of all sections of the Labour Party.

(2) All Labour and Trade Union candidates approved by the Parliamentary Committee, in accordance with the Standing Orders of the Trades Union Congress, shall receive the support of the L.R.C. insofar as its constitution allows, and in the same manner as Mr. T. Richards in West Monmouth.[1]

(3) Members of the Labour Representation Committee shall not be considered disloyal in refusing to support any Labour candidates adopted on any Party platform except that of Labour, and, further, that the candidates approved by the Committee represented here today shall offer no opposition to each other.

(4) That the Labour Representation Committee make it clear that their national constitution does not require abstention on the part of electors in constituencies where no Labour candidate is running.

These declarations served to promote the further solidarity of the Trade Union and Labour Movement, without entirely removing the grounds of difference. Such differences were rooted in the political sympathies of so many of the older generation of trade unionists. They were intensified by the growing bitterness of the political struggle against the ascendancy of the Tory Party, which, under the leadership of Arthur Balfour, the then Prime Minister, was profoundly out of touch with the sentiment of the country, as the General Election was shortly to prove. The Tariff Reform controversy antagonised the Labour Movement of those days almost as much as it revitalised the Liberal Party: but the real driving force of the political working-class movement at that time was unquestionably the resentment of Trade Unionists over the continuing effects of the Taff Vale Judgment. Legal decisions of a like nature had hit the South Wales Miners' Federation, the Yorkshire Miners' Federation and other Unions. The President of the Trades Union Congress in 1904, who happened to be Richard Bell, declared that the position of Trade Unions was then serious: "for it is held that Unions can be held for civil damages, though they are not 'legal' entities; the Judges will issue injunctions to restrain their collective action, though they are not corporations; the courts will interpret and enforce their rules, and peaceful persuasion is held to be illegal and criminal. If an officer of a local branch, however subordinate he may be, has acquiesced in such persuasion, the Union can be made answerable in heavy damages."

Trade Union protests had not brought any remedy from the Balfour Government. It had appointed a Royal Commission, but because of its inequitable and non-representative character, the T.U.C. had decided that no evidence nor information should be supplied to the Commission by the Unions. More than one Bill was drafted to legalise the peaceful conduct of trade disputes and to alter the law affecting the liability of

[1] In the successful by-election fought by Thomas Richards at West Monmouth as a nominee of the South Wales Miners, the L.R.C. could not give him its formal endorsement as the Miners' organisation had not at that time actually affiliated, but he received its friendly and active support.

Trade Union funds, as these were jeopardised by the Taff Vale Judgment. Labour members in the House were unsuccessful in the ballot which would have enabled one of them to bring forward the Bill that had been drafted in consultations between the T.U.C. Parliamentary Committee, Sir Charles Dilke, Sir Robert Reid and other distinguished M.P.s who were sympathetic with the Trade Unions. But the Bill was brought to a second reading by a majority of 39. The Prime Minister's refusal thereupon to make it a Government measure, or to provide facilities for its further passage through Parliament, did not endear him to the Trade Unions.

So the L.R.C. entered upon the election of 1906 in a much better state of preparedness, with a much more strongly based organisation in the Trade Unions, than it had in the Khaki Election six years earlier. Political circumstances favoured it, despite its rigorous repudiation of any electoral understanding with the Liberal Party. Its leaders paid no heed to the clamour against Labour candidates, in three-cornered contests, "splitting the progressive vote." There were fifty L.R.C. candidates put forward in the General Election, and the following twenty-nine were returned, to form a compact Parliamentary Party wielding considerably greater influence in the House of Commons than its mere numerical strength implied:

Members	*Societies*	*Constituencies*
G. N. Barnes	A. S. Engineers	Blackfriars
C. W. Bowerman	London Soc. Compositors	Deptford
J. R. Clynes	Gasworkers	Manchester, N.E.
Will Crookes	Coopers	Woolwich
Chas. Duncan	A. S. Engineers	Barrow-in-Furness
A. H. Gill	Textile Workers	Bolton
T. Glover	Miners (Lancs.)	St. Helens
J. Keir Hardie	I.L.P.	Merthyr Tydfil
A. Henderson	Ironfounders	Barnard Castle
John Hodge	Steelsmelters	Gorton
W. Hudson	A. S. Railway Servants	Newcastle-on-Tyne
J. Jenkins	Shipwrights	Chatham
F. W. Jowett	I.L.P.	Bradford, W.
Geo. D. Kelly	Lithographers	Manchester, S.W.
J. Ramsay MacDonald	I.L.P.	Leicester
J. T. Macpherson	Steelsmelters	Preston
Jas. O'Grady	Furnishing Trades	Leeds, E.
J. Parker	I.L.P.	Halifax
T. F. Richards	Boot & Shoe Operatives	Wolverhampton, W.
G. H. Roberts	Typographical Association	Norwich
J. A. Seddon	Shop Assistants	Newton
Philip Snowden	I.L.P.	Blackburn
T. Summerbell	I.L.P.	Sunderland
J. W. Taylor[1]	Colliery Enginemen	Chester-le-Street
Will Thorne	Gasworkers	West Ham, S.
Stephen Walsh	Miners (Lancs.)	Ince
Geo. J. Wardle	A. S. Railway Servants	Stockport
Alex Wilkie	Shipwrights	Dundee
W. Tyson Wilson	Carpenters & Joiners	Westhoughton

[1] J. W. Taylor joined the Party subsequent to the Election.

Certainly, more was involved than the rise of the number of independent Labour Members in the House of Commons from four (in the outgoing Parliament) to twenty-nine in the new one. The L.R.C. Executive Committee was justified in claiming that the six years of organisation, propaganda and preparation had not been wasted. "Suddenly politicians of all parties realised that a new factor in politics had appeared," (said the Committee); "that organised labour as a political force is already a menace to the easy-going gentlemen of the old school who have slumbered for so long on the green benches of St. Stephens. Everybody is asking: 'What does it all mean? What does the Labour Party want? What will it do?'" The L.R.C. Executive promised that these questions would be answered in due time, but one thing, it declared, was already clear. A new Party which could place its candidate at the head of the poll in the historic constituency of Newcastle-on-Tyne, with one of the highest votes in the whole country, which could win seats in Bradford and Glasgow, in Dundee, and in London, against the nominees of both Liberals and Tories, had a future before it and would have a hand in the making of history. Nobody perhaps then foresaw that history would move so rapidly to the point where the Liberal Party would virtually disappear as an effective political force, and that in due time even the Tory Party, headed by the most powerful and influential Prime Minister of modern times would suffer a decisive defeat at the polls, and a Labour Government with an adequate majority would take its place. Not all the portents of the 1906 election could be read in that way. The gains of L.R.C. candidates in the 1906 election were mainly at the expense of the Conservative Party. In twenty-two single-member constituencies where Labour was opposed by Conservatives only, the L.R.C. won sixteen seats; in double-member constituencies where they were opposed by thirteen Liberal and Tory candidates they won ten seats. Out of a total vote polled by all Parties of 859,518 (these being the days of the limited franchise), the L.R.C. candidates polled a total of 323,195, or 37 per cent. of the aggregate vote. In no single constituency even where the L.R.C. candidates were unsuccessful, did any of them poll less than in previous contests, and in most cases the successful candidates materially increased their poll—Snowden at Blackburn, with more than 10,000 votes, as against a previous Labour vote in that constituency of just over 7,000, Ramsay MacDonald in Leicester with 14,685 votes against a previous Labour vote of 4,164, Will Thorne at West Ham with more than 10,000 against a previous vote of 4,439, Keir Hardie with more than 10,000 at Merthyr Tydfil against a previous vote of 5,745, and so on.

But the 1906 General Election did not wholly solve the problem of the relations between the old and the new Labour Parties. In addition to the twenty-nine L.R.C. members, there were twenty-two Trade Union M.P.s who continued to maintain a separate Trade Union Group. It consisted in the main of Lib-Labs. Most of them owed allegiance to local Liberal

Associations. But in many instances, for example, in the case of the Miner M.P.s, they were dependent upon their Trade Unions for their election expenses and maintenance. Following are the names of this Trade Union Group:

Members	*Societies*	*Constituencies*
W. Abraham	Miners	Rhondda
Richard Bell	A. S. Railway Servants	Derby
W. Brace	Miners	Glamorgan, S.
H. Broadhurst	Stonemasons	Leicester
T. Burt	Miners	Morpeth
W. R. Cremer	Carpenters and Joiners	Haggerston
Enoch Edwards	Miners	Hanley
Charles Fenwick	Miners	Wansbeck
Fred Hall	Miners	Normanton
J. Haslam	Miners	Chesterfield
John Johnson	Miners	Gateshead
W. Johnson	Miners	Nuneaton
Fred Maddison	Typographical Association	Burnley
George Nicholls	Agricultural Labourers	Northants, N.
Tom Richards	Miners	Monmouth, W.
W. C. Steadman	Barge Builders	Stepney
H. Vivian	Carpenters and Joiners	Birkenhead
John Ward	Navvies	Stoke
John Wadsworth	Miners	Hallamshire
John Williams	Miners	Gower
John Wilson	Miners	Durham
J. Havelock Wilson	Sailors and Firemen	Middlesbrough

As more than a dozen of the group represented mining constituencies, the decision of the Miner's Federation in 1910 to affiliate to the Labour Party, necessarily led to the dissolution of the group as a whole, and only two or three of it continued to remain in isolation as "independent" members, though they continued to accept the whips of the Liberal Party. Among these independents were Thomas Burt, Charles Fenwick, John Ward, Havelock Wilson, and one or two others.

CHAPTER VI

LABOUR'S FIRST PARLIAMENT: 1906-10

By Herbert Tracey

From the historical standpoint, the results of the 1906 General Election marked the turning point in the relation of the political Parties one with another. They were in the long run fatal to the Liberal Party, though at the outset they seemed to portend a revival of Liberalism. The Liberal triumph was, in the political circumstances of the time, overwhelming: the Party gained 377 seats in the new House against 167 Conservatives; there were 83 Irish Members, and the two Labour Groups combined to strengthen the position of the Liberal Government—which would, however, have had a majority of 84 if all the other Parties and Groups had combined against them.

Not only their numerical strength, but the quality of the Liberal M.P.s, especially on the Front Bench, gave that Party an ascendancy in debate, particularly upon the political issues which had decided the election against the Balfour Government. Mr. Balfour (as he then was) had resigned at the end of 1905 in the belief that there were divisions inside the Liberal Party on the question of leadership that would disable them in their election campaign and give him an advantage: but Sir Henry Campbell-Bannerman was skilful enough to form a strong Government without alienating the group of Liberal imperialists headed by Asquith, Edward Grey, and Haldane. The Government Front Bench in the 1906 Parliament presented a dazzling array of political talents; whilst behind them they numbered amongst their supporters men of outstanding ability and distinction in public life.

At the outset of the 1906 Parliament the Liberal Government had things pretty much their way, on matters like the introduction of Chinese labour in South Africa, and the Tariff Reform controversy. More importance attached then to the latter question than attaches to it today. The Liberal Government gloried in its defence of free trade, and in its promise of far-reaching measures of social reform. Mr. Asquith claimed that the defeat of the Tory Party's tariff policy was of even more significance than the appearance of the Labour Party on the political stage. In a speech made at the beginning of 1906, after the General Election, Mr. Asquith said:

> "When the nation was told that the advent of a Labour Party in the House of Commons, with a programme such as its leading members had put forward, brought this country within measurable or perilous distance of revolutionary change, he thought the question might be asked: 'Who were the people from whose lips proceeded this charge?' They were the lips of men who, if the country had given

them their way, would have made by far the most revolutionary change in our system that had ever been propounded in our time. There was not an item put forward by these Labour colleagues in their programme which involved so fundamental, and certainly not so disastrous, a change in the conditions of life in this country as the return from free trade to protection."

Phrases occur in this passage which betray the Liberal Leader's conviction at the time that the new Labour Party [1] was no more than an appendage to their own Party. Mr. Asquith referred to "these Labour colleagues," and to their programme in a manner which suggested that he did not anticipate any strong demonstration of independence from them. There was nothing to suggest that he had any premonition of the "revolutionary change" which the Liberal Government's social policy and its commitments on the question of Irish Home Rule were to bring about before the Parliament had run its term. On the Home Rule question, the Liberal Party, before the General Election, had lost Lord Rosebery as its Leader. On the policy of social reform, the Party had yet to discover the dynamic force of Lloyd George's leadership. The combination of both was to produce an explosive situation, with civil war as a possibility by no means remote, and a constitutional revolution arising out of a conflict with the House of Lords, which left that venerable institution shorn of many of its powers.

For the Labour Party in Parliament the question of liveliest concern at the beginning of the session was the righting of the wrongs arising from the Taff Vale Judgment. The T.U.C. during the lifetime of the Balfour Government had taken vigorous steps to secure the passage of a Bill to amend the law relating to trade disputes. Its Parliamentary Committee drafted a Bill which did not get beyond its second reading in 1904, but was introduced again after the Parliamentary Committee had circularised every Member of Parliament asking them to ballot for the Bill to have a place in the legislative programme. More than a hundred replies came from M.P.s of all Parties, and twenty promised to give the Bill first place; but the majority, while expressing sympathy with the object, stated that they were already committed to other measures in the ballot. The trade unionist M.P.s of course, undertook to give first place to the Bill if they were successful in the ballot. The T.U.C. Bill was ultimately introduced by a Liberal Member, T. P. Whittaker (M.P. for Spen Valley).

Meanwhile the T.U.C. conducted a campaign throughout the country calling upon the Government to afford facilities for the passage of the Bill, and pledging trade unionists everywhere not to support any Parliamentary candidate who failed to declare his intention to vote for the Bill. The measure was wrecked in Committee, when amendments were moved which the Trade Union M.P.s regarded as fatal to its purpose, and the Trade Union M.P.s considered it necessary to take the exceptional step of leaving

[1] One of the first decisions of the Labour M.P.s under the auspices of the L.R.C. was to adopt the title "Labour Party"—the name by which it was officially known thenceforth.

the Committee and resolving to withdraw the Bill altogether. The Balfour Government was plainly opposed to amendment of the law in the sense desired by the Trade Unions. It appointed a Royal Commission in 1903 to which it submitted the question whether and how the law relating to conspiracy should be relaxed in regard to peaceful picketing—and the degree of exemption to be accorded to Trade Union funds from liability in action for damages for wrongful acts.

Such was the Liberal Government's inheritance from its predecessor, and in the early stages of discussion upon the revision of Trade Union law there were divisions inside the Cabinet which, but for the bold decision of the Prime Minister (Sir Henry Campbell-Bannerman), would have seriously disturbed its relations with the Labour Party. The new Labour M.P.s had taken their position seriously when the session began, and had organised themselves at once as a Party on proper lines. A room was secured at the House for the Party's exclusive use. Whips and other officers were elected; Keir Hardie was chosen as Chairman; daily meetings of the Party officers were arranged; the Party itself met weekly to consider the business before the House, to allocate speakers for the debates, and to receive reports from the various Party Committees set up to deal with different phases of Parliamentary affairs. Members of the Party were fortunate in the ballot, and the Party took the earliest opportunity to introduce its own draft measure for the reversal of the Taff Vale Judgment. It was not, of course, strong enough to secure the passage of its own Bill, which gave place to consideration of the measure which the Government, under its commitments, undertook to introduce. The Government Bill, as originally introduced, however, followed so closely the recommendations of the Royal Commission appointed by the Balfour Government, as to deserve the description of it as a "Lawyer's Bill," and the Trade Unions found it entirely unacceptable.

The Liberal Government possessed an unusual number of distinguished lawyers—among them Asquith, who was strongly opposed to writing into any Statute a form of words that would give (he said) workmen as such, a privilege not enjoyed by other citizens. The lawyers' handiwork was apparent in the first draft of the Government Bill. It merely provided that an action fastening liability upon the funds of a Union for damages in respect of any wrongful act committed in contemplation or furtherance of a trade dispute, should not lie, "unless the act was committed by the 'Trade Union' Committee, or by some person acting under their authority: provided that a person shall not be deemed to have acted under the authority of the Committee if the act was an act or one of a class of acts expressly prohibited by a resolution of the Committee, or the Committee by resolution expressly repudiate the act as soon as it is brought to their knowledge."

Labour Members of Parliament were not alone in thinking that this way of dealing with the freedom of the Unions to carrying on a trade

EARLY DAYS: LABOUR LEADERS AT THE HOUSE IN 1906
Front Row, left to right: Arthur Henderson, J. Ramsay MacDonald, Keir Hardie, D. J. Shackleton
Back Row: G. H. Barnes, Philip Snowden, John Hodge, Will Crookes, J. O'Grady

dispute was full of loopholes and loose ends, with which the Courts could make endless mischief. Why, if it were the intention to exempt Trade Union funds from liability, they asked, could not the Bill say so in plain words? Having their own Bill in hand, the Labour Members were prompt to use it as a weapon against the Government, and it was put down for second reading as a Private Member's Bill a couple of days after the Government's Bill received its second reading. Labour spokesmen in the debate that then arose proved their capacity, and the Government found itself in a serious difficulty which the Prime Minister, to the dismay of Asquith and other of his colleagues, solved by telling the House that the Labour Party's Bill was the better of the two and had his support. The solution finally reached was embodied in the clause of the 1906 Trade Disputes Act which ran:

> "Any action against the Trade Unions, whether of workmen or masters or against any members or officials thereof, on behalf of themselves and all other members of Trade Unions, in respect of any tortious act alleged to have been committed by or on behalf of the Trade Union, shall not be entertained by any Court."

Over other measures introduced by the Liberal Government in the first session of the 1906 Parliament there were fewer grounds for dissension. As a direct outcome of pressure by the Labour Party an Act was passed to provide school meals for necessitous children. The Labour Party made its position clear on old age pensions, votes for women, unemployment, and the position of labour in the sweated trades, by moving resolutions on them in the House. In due course legislation was carried on most of these questions, including the Old Age Pensions Act, the Trade Boards Act, and the Labour Exchanges Act. But there were ominous indications, before the first session came to an end, that the Government would have to deal with the obstruction of the House of Lords.

Two of the three principal measures of the session were destroyed in the Second Chamber, namely the Education Bill and the Plural Voting Bill. The Trade Disputes Bill did not suffer the same fate because the Lords were unwilling to risk a conflict with the Unions. The attitude of the House of Lords towards Liberal Reform measures was so plainly obstructive that the Liberal Cabinet, even before the end of 1906, seriously considered whether they should not risk their strong position in Parliament by dissolving and having another General Election. Sir Henry Campbell-Bannerman resigned the office of Prime Minister in 1908 and Mr. Asquith succeeded him, without making many changes in the personnel of the Government: the principal change affecting its fortunes were that Mr. Lloyd George became Chancellor of the Exchequer in Asquith's place, and Mr. Churchill succeeded Lloyd George at the Board of Trade. There were many contentious questions raised by the legislation proposed by the Asquith Government, and some of them received no mercy in the House of Lords. Although the Peers were not prepared to challenge organised Labour on the Trade Disputes Bill, they did not hesitate to mutilate the miners' Eight Hours Bill; for example, by an amendment to exclude permanently from the computation of hours, both winding times.

Before his Government was a year old, Asquith as Prime Minister saw clearly that the Liberal Party was nearly at the end of its resources, and could not hope to succeed unless something could be done to remove the obstruction placed in its way by the House of Lords. He put the thing plainly in a speech he made at the end of the year by saying that the existing system enabled the Leader of the Party which had been defeated and repudiated by the electors at the polls, to determine through the House of Lords what should, and should not be, the legislation of the country. "The question I want to put to you, and to my fellow Liberals is this: Is this state of things to continue? We say that it must be brought to an end, and I invite the Liberal Party tonight to treat the veto of the House of Lords as the dominating issue in politics—the dominating issue, because in the long run it overshadows and absorbs every other."

It was an issue upon which the Labour Groups, still to achieve complete unity, were certainly at one. Trade Union M.P.s of the "Lib-Lab" trend found no difficulty in working with the L.R.C. Group on most Parliamentary questions. An agreement was reached that the two groups should co-operate in the House, and that they should not fight each other in the country: that is to say, the Trade Union Group undertook to support the L.R.C. candidates in Parliamentary by-elections, and the L.R.C. in its turn agreed to support T.U.C. candidates as far as its constitution permitted this to be done. But the L.R.C. would not on any terms agree to support the T.U.C. group on other than Labour platforms.

Not for the first, or for the last time, the Liberal Party managers tried to make Party capital out of the existence of two Labour Groups. In the spring of 1906 a letter was sent to all "Lib-Lab" M.P.s suggesting that they should form themselves into a separate organisation, as a Labour Party within the Liberal Party. This proposal was put forward in a letter signed by the Liberal agent for Westminster, who intimated that it was not being circulated to the twenty-nine L.R.C. Members in the House. It was in the following terms:

> "The opinion has been freely expressed to me by Liberal leaders (who have promised considerable financial support) that a separate organisation should be formed to represent the views of the Liberal-Labour Members of Parliament and to secure a substantial increase in their numbers at the next General Election.
>
> "It is thought that a Labour Party within the Liberal Party will be a source of great strength to both, and I am requested to ask your views thereon as a Labour M.P.
>
> "Will you please be good enough to send me a reply with suggestions, during the week, so that steps may be taken to call an early meeting."

Nothing came of this proposal, and the suggested National Liberal-Labour League was never formed. The experience of Trade Union M.P.s in trying to get measures through the House upon which they had set their heart had something to do with their unwillingness to swallow this bait. Among the Bills for which they made themselves responsible on behalf of the T.U.C. were measures for the regulation of hours of labour in bakehouses, street traffic regulation, housing of the working classes, Saturday and Sunday hours for textile workers, a Bill defining the rights of employees to a "character" note from their employers on leaving their jobs, and Bills dealing with elementary education, nationalisation of the mines, education of the blind, and similar reforms. But wider vistas of social reform were opened up by the new Chancellor of the Exchequer, and these vistas were darkened by the coming storm with the House of Lords.

Before Lloyd George introduced his first Budget in 1909, schemes for sickness and unemployment insurance were in preparation. Like old age pensions, these subjects had engaged the active interest of the Labour Movement. Much of the influence the Labour Party acquired in the early years was due to its keen advocacy of such social reforms. Although the Liberal Party could claim credit for legislation on them, it is beyond question that the pace of Parliamentary action and the nature of the measures themselves must be attributed to the advent of the Labour Party and the pressure of its presence in the House. If the tendency of legislation from 1906 has been socialistic, the credit is due almost exclusively to the Labour Party. And it was not only in the matter of Social Reform that the Labour Party's influence made itself felt: it was equally apparent in the direction taken in matters of financial policy in the Budgets introduced by Lloyd George.

Before we come to deal with the Lloyd George Budgets, and the social reforms connected with them, leading up to the conflict with the House of Lords, it is relevant to summarise at this stage the results of the Labour Party's activities in relation to other measures of social amelioration to which Parliament devoted its attention in these early years. With the Trade Disputes Act of 1906 we have already dealt. Another measure which was in its way a landmark for which the Labour Party was responsible, was the Act providing for meals for children in public elementary schools. The agitation in favour of such provisions had been going on for some time before the advent of the Liberal Government. Evidence submitted to a Commission set up in 1904 to inquire into the causes of national physical deterioration, showed that under-feeding was prevalent both in rural and urban districts throughout the country. Labour used the report of this Commission to press for legislation. It called a Conference in January 1905, to ventilate the subject and organised support for a measure to deal with the problem. Propaganda carried on resulted in the passage of an Act in 1906. Discussion began upon the Labour Party's Bill, which was introduced in February of that year, and passed its second reading; whereupon a Select Committee was appointed, of which Arthur Henderson became a member, to consider the matter: the Bill as it passed through Parliament was a much less satisfactory measure than the Labour Bill would have been: instead of being made obligatory on local Education Authorities, it was amended in its passage so as to make the obligation of providing school meals merely permissive, and by an amendment in the House of Lords its application was limited to England and Wales. Labour was forced to accept this limitation in order to save the Bill. As was feared, the permissive powers of the Act rendered it in many places non-effective. An attempt made by the Party in 1908 to rectify matters by an amending Bill, providing for medical inspection of school children, making the power to provide meals compulsory, abolishing the limit of a halfpenny rate imposed in the earlier Act, and requiring medical inspectors to present annual reports on the physical condition of school children in their areas, did not reach the Statute Book.

The Labour Party, in the same way, made the unemployment problem their special concern. Unemployment was increasing (reaching 6 per cent. in 1904) and the Labour Movement took steps to define its policy on broad lines. It declared that the problem was national and not local, and must be treated on a national basis. It advocated therefore, the setting up of a new Ministry to be called the Ministry of Labour. It proposed that through this new Government Department, schemes of national utility such as afforestation, reclamation of foreshores and wasteland, new roads, the erection of public buildings, and similar enterprises, should be prepared to provide employment in times of trade depression. It was laid down as a principle that everyone had a right to work at standard Trade Union rates of pay, and that it was the duty of the State to provide work when ordinary channels failed. The first attempt to cope with the unemployment problem was made by the Balfour Government, which introduced the Unemployed Workmen's Act of 1905; but this hardly did more than acknowledge that the problem existed, and that Parliamentary action was essential to solve it. The "Right to Work" remained an essential part of Labour's programme, and in 1907 the Party's Unemployed Workmen's Bill proposed the setting up of local and central employment authorities, empowered to set going schemes of reasonable work with provision for public maintenance of genuine and willing workers in periods of unemployment, and this Bill also proposed machinery for the registration of all unemployed persons. Notwithstanding the huge Liberal majority in the House, this Bill never reached its second reading. It was introduced again in 1908, and in later sessions, but it never reached the Statute Book in that form. It was not until 1910 that Labour proposals for the registration of unemployed workers took shape in the Labour Exchange Act.

For many years before the creation of the Labour Party the Trade Unions had urged the establishment of a system of old age pensions. The agitation grew out of conferences between Trade Union leaders and Charles Booth, the author of the monumental work on the life and labour of the people of London, which did so much to awaken the social conscience of that generation. The outcome of these conferences, in which Margaret Bondfield, Will Crookes, George N. Barnes, and others now well known or remembered as prominent members of the Labour Party, took part, as the creation of the National Committee of Organised Labour for the promoting of old age pensions. This Committee had for its secretary Frederick Rogers, who was the Labour Party's first Chairman. The Movement went forward under his guidance and a prepared public opinion awaited the Liberal Government's action after the triumph of the 1906 General Election. As Chancellor of the Exchequer in the Campbell-Bannerman Government, Mr. Asquith made some modest financial provision for a scheme of old age pensions. In his second Budget, which is notable too, for having introduced the differentiation, for the first time, between earned and unearned income, he provided the means to start old age pensions, on an estimated cost of about £2¼ million in the first year, to reach £6 million or so in the next two years. In May 1908, he introduced the Bill which gave, in its final form, 5*s.* a week to persons at the age of 70, whose income from other sources was not more than £21 a year, or 8*s.* a week, with smaller pensions on a sliding scale down to 1*s.* a week for those with an income of not more than £31 10*s.* a year. The Bill went through both Houses within two months. Amendments were made in the House of Lords, including one which limited the duration of the Bill to seven years; but the Speaker ruled out most of the Lords' amendments as breaches of the privilege of the House of Commons in respect of Bills disposing of public money. The Peers themselves were not then ready to open the inevitable conflict by challenging the financial prerogatives of the House of Commons, and the Bill reached the Statute Book under criticism from the Labour Party, who considered its provisions niggardly and inadequate. What the Labour Party wanted was a non-contributory universal scheme at the age of 60. It objected strongly to a proposal from the Government that the pension for couples living together should be reduced to 3*s.* 9*d.* each.

Apart from legislation on the problem of the drink traffic, the most important measures which received Labour's support in the field of social and economic reform were the Coal Mines (Eight Hours) Act, and the Act relating to the sweated trades. The latter question had been much agitated in the country in previous years, and Anti-Sweating Conferences and exhibitions which the Labour Party helped to organise, had revealed terrible conditions in the dressmaking, tailoring, cardboard box, chain making and other trades. In 1909 a Bill based upon one drafted and introduced by Arthur Henderson was enacted under the title of the Trade Boards Act.

Timid and inadequate as most of these social reform measures were, they kept the Labour Party more or less in step with the Liberal Government, and made it an ally of the Liberal Party in the struggle that began with the House of Lords over Lloyd George's Budget in 1909. There was a strong current of criticism directed against the Labour Party in these years, because it was alleged to be too closely identified with the Liberal Party. It was charged against the L.R.C. Members in the House of Commons that they had, in the main, supported the Liberal Government, and that their independence was more assumed than real. Keir Hardie put it in this way in his first report to the Annual Conference of the Party in 1907, as chairman of the Parliamentary Group: "This objection" (wrote Hardie) "proceeds on the assumption that it is the business of the members of an independent Party to be always running amok at the Treasury Bench. Such critics forget that these would be the tactics of despair, and that we are not in despairing mood. Thirty men cannot hope to monopolise the time of Parliament, and the most that can be expected from them is to see that value is received for the support which is given to the Government of the day. We have supported the Government, and opposed the Government, just as we deemed the interests of the workers required." Hardie claimed that the Party's record in Parliament justified this claim to its essential independence, had demonstrated its vitality, and its possession of Parliamentary aptitudes.

Two by-elections in 1907 in which Labour candidates (one of them Robert Smillie) were unsuccessful; four in 1908, one of which, Jarrow, was won by the Labour candidate (Pete Curran); and two in 1909, in which neither of the Labour candidates succeeded, showed that the Liberal Party still held the ascendancy in the country. But there were indications in the municipal elections of these years that the Labour Party organisation in the constituencies was becoming more efficient and good spade work was being carried on from year to year. But before the Party's second trial of strength came in the first General Election of 1910, the democratic forces involved in the struggle with the House of Lords, which reached its final reckoning in that year, had still to keep in step.

CHAPTER VII

DEMOCRACY WINS ANOTHER BATTLE

By Herbert Tracey

When the battle was joined with the House of Lords at the end of the first decade of this century, the Labour Party had reached adult stature. Its relations with the Trade Union Movement had been placed upon a better footing by the establishment of a Joint Board representing the Parliamentary Committee of the Trades Union Congress and the General Federation of Trade Unions on an equal footing with the Labour Party. Each of the three national bodies appointed three representatives with their respective secretaries to constitute the Board as the body "to determine, on the application of one of its constituent bodies, the bona fides of any Trade Union affiliated, or applying for affiliation, to any of the constituent organisations"; and with authority to consider and decide references made to it by any one of its constituent bodies "regarding questions affecting them jointly, or about which some doubt or difference may have arisen as to which body they properly belong." The Board, moreover, was required to consider and agree upon joint political or other action deemed to be advantageous or necessary, which was agreed to by all the constituent bodies. This constitution was framed and adopted as a basis for the action of the Joint Board, at a time when a new peril menaced the existence of the Labour Party.

John R. Clynes was the President of the Party's Annual Conference in 1909. In his address from the Chair he referred to the Party's growing strength. From a membership of less than 400,000 at its first Conference, the Party had grown to more than a million and a half, including the miners, who had just decided to join. Mr. Clynes went on: "As the industrial activities of the Labour Movement were threatened a few years ago by law court decisions, which later legislation had to remedy, so now our political activities are menaced by Judgments which, if upheld, will take from Trade Unions the right which every other body possesses, namely, that of deciding its internal business, and by a majority of its members resolving whatever the whole of its members should do." The reference was to a decision of the law courts known as the Osborne Judgment, a case in which a member of the Amalgamated Society of Railway Servants, W. V. Osborne, had challenged its expenditure upon political objects and its support of the Labour Party. It was not the first challenge of the kind. Two years before a member of the South Wales Miners' Federation brought an action against it because he objected to pay any contribution towards the expense of returning and maintaining representatives to Parliament. The attack failed, but in view of matters which developed later, it is interesting to note that Mr. Justice Darling took the view that the definition of a Trade Union contained in the Trade Union Acts 1871-76 was not intended to be exhaustive, or to have the effect of preventing the association from lawfully doing other acts beyond those stated; and in this view Mr. Justice Phillimore concurred.

Then in July 1908, the proceedings started which resulted in the Osborne Judgment. W. V. Osborne was the secretary of the Walthamstow Branch of the Amalgamated Society of Railway Servants, and a foreman porter at Clapham Junction. The A.S.R.S. had been established and registered as a Trade Union since the year 1872. In 1903 words were added to its objects "to secure Parliamentary representation"; and in 1905 and 1906 further amendments to its rules were made so as to include a clause to the effect that all candidates should sign and accept the constitution of the Labour Party and be subject to its whip. W. V. Osborne objected to these alterations. He began legal proceedings against the Society and its trustees to restrain them from spending Union money on any objects other than those specified in Section 16 of the Trade Union Act of 1876. This section runs as follows:

> "The term 'Trade Union' means any combination, whether temporary or permanent, for regulating the relations between workmen and master, or between workmen and workmen, or between masters and masters, or for imposing restrictive conditions on the conduct of any trade or business, whether such combination would or would not, if the principal Act had not been passed, have been deemed to have been an unlawful combination by reason of some one or more of its purposes being in restraint of trade."

The reference to the principal Act, of course, is to the Trade Union Act of 1871. The point involved in the citation of this clause is whether it provided an exhaustive definition of the objects that a Trade Union could lawfully pursue.

The historical importance of the Osborne Judgment lies in the remedy that had ultimately to be sought and found, for the restrictive interpretation placed upon the existing Trade Union law in its application to the political activities of Unions. The principal legislative result of the Osborne Judgment was the Trade Union Act of 1913, as much a landmark in the history of the Labour Movement as the Trade Disputes Act of 1906, and the much later Trade Disputes and Trade Unions Act of 1927. When the Osborne case was heard, in the first instance, by Mr. Justice Neville, he considered himself bound by the decision by Mr. Justice Darling and Mr. Justice Phillimore, to which reference has just been made. But in the Osborne case the Judge expressed the view that given the right to spend their money in promoting their interests in the House of Commons, the question of how they could do so was purely a question of policy with which the courts would not concern themselves. In effect, the Judge found that Parliamentary representation in the interests of its members was not *ultra vires* under the existing law, and Osborne's action against the society was dismissed with costs against him.

Osborne was dissatisfied with this result and was able to find means to carry the case to the Court of Appeal. Its Judgment was unanimously against the Society, substantially on the ground that to secure Trade Union representation in Parliament was not one of the objects contemplated or authorised by the Act of 1871 or the amending Act of 1876. The Court of Appeal took the view, expressed very clearly by the Master of the Rolls, (Lord Justice Cozens-Hardy) that the definition of a Trade Union, and of its purposes in the 1871-76 legislation, was a limited and restricted definition. It was not competent for a Union, the Judge said, to add to its objects "something so wholly distinct from the objects contemplated by the Trade Union Acts as a provision to secure Parliamentary representation." To the contention that neither did these Acts authorise the Unions to provide financial benefits for their members—an omission which had greatly influenced Mr. Justice Darling and Mr. Justice Phillimore in holding that there was nothing to prevent Trade Unions from having a great number of additional objects besides those stated in the Acts—the Master of the Rolls found provisions elsewhere in the Acts to cover the point.

The Court of Appeal found additional reasons to give judgment against the Society in the existence of the Trade Disputes Act of 1906 which, they held, placed Trade Unions in a wholly exceptional position in the eyes of the law. On this ground alone Lord Justice Fletcher Moulton agreed with the Master of the Rolls in holding that it was *ultra vires* for Trade Unions to collect funds for the purpose of maintaining Parliamentary representation by way of compulsory contribution from members. But he went on to state a further reason for his decision, based on considerations of public policy. He said that the rules of the Society prescribed the object of its Parliamentary Fund was to secure the return of Members of Parliament who should be bound to vote in a prescribed manner, and who were required to give an undertaking so to vote. This was a reference to the conditions upon which Unions affiliated to the Labour Party, whose constitution required candidates and Members to abide by the decisions of the Parliamentary Party, to appear before their constituencies as Labour candidates only, to abstain strictly from identifying themselves with, or promoting the interests of any Party not eligible for affiliation. A pledge-bound Party, in the view of the Court, was an anomaly, and such an agreement on the part of its members was void, as contrary to public policy.

Against the unanimous decision of the Court of Appeal the Railwaymen's Society carried the case to the House of Lords. It was contended there, on behalf of the Society, that the section of the 1876 Act, upon which Osborne's case was founded, was an enumeration, not an exhaustive enumeration, of the objects of Trade Unions; moreover, that it was not necessary to maintain that Parliamentary representation was one of the *objects* of a Trade Union, but that it should be enough that it should be one of the *methods*. As to the condition that Labour candidates must sign and accept the constitution of the Labour Party, this only meant that they undertook to be loyal to the Party. Notwithstanding these arguments, the House of Lords delivered their considered Judgment on December 21, 1909, against the Society. Lord Halsbury, a leading conservative lawyer of the time, and an aged one at that, expressed the view that a Union only existed as a legalised combination within the limits of the Statute "whatever those limits are"; and he contented himself by saying that the political contributions collected by the Society was "to my mind manifestly beyond the powers possessed by a Trade Union." Other law lords took substantially the same view, that political organisation was a thing distinct and different from a combination for trade purposes, and the rules governing it were *ultra vires* and illegal.

One of the law lords, however, Lord James of Hereford, founded his Judgment upon one particular fact that he found in the case. He did not regard the relevant section of the Act as an exhaustive definition, and was prepared to hold that it might well be in the interests of Trade Unionism that a Fund should be devoted to the expenses of a Parliamentary Member; but he based his dissenting Judgment on the basis of the rule compelling such a Member to accept the Whip of the Labour Party. Lord Shaw of Dunfermline elaborated this "constitutional" argument. He confessed that he was not clear in his own mind as to payment of Members of Parliament being *ultra vires*, and confessed to some hesitation in so "construing language of statutory recognition as a definition imposing such hard and fast restrictive limits as would cramp the development and energies and destroy the natural movement of the living organism." He went on to discuss the position of a Member of Parliament supported by the contributions of a Society, and expressed the view that such a Member would be under a contract to subject his own convictions to the decisions of the Parliamentary Party: "I do not think that such a subjection is compatible either with the spirit of our Parliamentary constitution, or with that independence and freedom which has hitherto been held to lie at the basis of representative government of the United Kingdom." Having quoted Blackstone, Locke and Burke, he pictured the peril which threatened Parliamentary government "if the public well-being were liable to betrayal at the command, and for the advantage of particular individuals or classes." It is interesting to note that in the course of his Judgment, Lord James foreshadowed payment of Members as a partial solution of the difficulties of representation. But he was emphatic that the Labour Party's "pledge" was both unconstitutional and illegal, and on this ground he based his concurrence with the other members of the Court.

The Osborne Judgment was a capital event in the history of the Labour Party. It convinced trade unionists that they had nothing to expect from "Judge-made law" but obstruction and hostility to their political progress. It taught them the significance of the long struggle that earlier generations of trade unionists had to carry on in order to secure a legal basis for their industrial organisation; only to find that the Acts which protected their Unions could be, and were being, used to frustrate their natural development. Criticism of the Judgment was vigorous and insistent: it was freely stated that the law courts had exhibited an animus and prejudice which the Trade Disputes Act and the rise of the Labour Party had excited. The President of the Trades Union Congress (James Haslam, M.P.) addressing the 1910 assembly, pointed out that the idea of Parliamentary representation for the Unions carried them over nearly fifty years of history, and that from the beginning of the effort to establish a political organisation of the wage earners, right up to the decision in the Osborne case, the Trade Union world had believed that one of their lawful objects could be to maintain in Parliament, Labour men representing the Trade Union forces of the country.

From 1874 onwards (Haslam said) the funds of Trade Unions had been applied to the purpose of returning and paying members of Parliament. Even those who had taken action against the Railwaymen's Union had been for years content to pay for Labour representation, and it was only when, through the formation of the Labour Party, the forces represented in the Trade Union Movement and the Socialist bodies were brought together that objection was taken by these men. In no single case, Haslam declared, had a Trade Union embarked upon political representation without receiving instruction from its members by ballot vote. In almost every case there had been overwhelming majorities in favour of that principle: the Miners' decision was two to one in favour of representation; the Typographical Association nearly four to one; the railway workers five to one; textile workers four to one—and similar figures (he added) could be quoted from many other organisations. He stated his own view emphatically that nothing short of the reinstatement of the Unions' position previous to the Osborne Judgment could be accepted. Matters affecting the workers, organised and unorganised, had received the attention of Parliamentary representatives, and he claimed that the influence of Labour in Parliament had been for the good of the community. "Without these representatives of the labouring classes there, it is not possible to give full and fair discussion to economic and social problems, as well as to those of a purely Trade Union character."

Whatever may have been the correct view of the law as thus defined in the Osborne case, there can be no doubt that the legal decisions inflicted a heavy blow on Trade Unionism. It was supplemented by a later decision that the Osborne Judgment covered local as well as Parliamentary representation. Injunctions were subsequently obtained against twenty-two other societies. It was clear that unless the law was altered there was an end to the political activities of the Unions, and to every other activity except those sanctioned by the narrow definition of the 1871-76 Acts. It was explicitly stated in the course of the legal proceedings in the Osborne case that Trade Unions could not carry on a newspaper. All their educational work was *ultra vires*. Their association in Trades Councils, and even in the Trades Union Congress, was of extremely doubtful legality. It should be noted, too, that the unanimity of a Union's decision to carry on such activities made no difference to the legal position. As the authors of the "History of Trade Unionism" defined the situation: "A distinct challenge was thereby thrown down to the Trade Union world. Not only were the activities of their Unions to be crippled, not only was their freedom to combine for whatever purposes they chose to be abrogated, they were to be expressly forbidden to aspire to protect their interests or to promote their objects by Parliamentary representation, or in any way to engage in politics." [1] Another historian of the Labour Movement says: "At one stroke the financial resources of the Labour Party, or of the political activities of the Unions appear to have been cut off." [2]

The National Committees of the Labour Movement, as represented by the Joint Board, took immediate action to make known to the working people the significance of the Osborne Judgment. In its report to the Labour Party's Annual Conference at the beginning of 1910 the National Executive of the Party declared that if the decision of the House of Lords remained unaltered, Trade Unionism would suffer greater impediments in its activities than even the Taff Vale Judgment imposed upon it. In conjunction with the T.U.C. and the General Federation of Trade Unions, the situation was considered and arrangements made for a Special Conference on the basis of resolutions adopted by the Joint Board, to the following effect:

> "That we agree to declare for an alteration in the definition of a Trade Union as given by the House of Lords in the Osborne v. A.S.R.S. case, so as to allow Unions to engage in the political activities they have pursued since 1868 up to the present time, provided that their members agree, and that such activities are specified in the Union's rules as part of their declared objects, as has been the case hitherto."

At the Special Conference convened by the Joint Board early in 1910, David Shackleton, M.P., who presided, said that he was of opinion that those who had set out to damage the Labour Party had a little over-reached themselves. Shackleton said that historically the Labour Movement never had a better case for a Parliamentary Bill to restore its old position. The right of the Trade Unions to engage in political activities had never before been questioned, and he said, without hesitation, that that right must be regained at the earliest possible moment.

The Conference shared its chairman's conviction, and a vigorous campaign was then set in motion to win support for the demand of the Unions for a restoration of their political rights. This campaign interlocked

[1] S. & B. Webb "History of Trade Unionism," page 267.
[2] Max Beer "History of British Socialism," Vol. 2, page 342.

with the general political campaign by which the Liberal Government was seeking a clear mandate to deal with the House of Lords.

Even before the Osborne Judgment an intense political activity had been stirred up by the attitude of the House of Lords towards the Liberal Government's legislation. By the end of the second session of the 1906 Parliament the Liberal Government realised, as we have seen, that the House of Lords stood obstinately in the way of the programme of Liberal Social Reform. Many measures to which the Liberals attached much importance were either wrecked or mutilated in the Upper House: in fact, all the major Liberal policy—education, temperance legislation, land reform, Welsh Disestablishment, Irish Home Rule—roused the destructive passions of the Peers. Some of these measures excited deep feelings because they were an attempt to undo the work of the Balfour Government. But none of them stirred up so much excitement as was aroused by the first Budget introduced (in 1909) by Lloyd George, who had succeeded Asquith as Chancellor of the Exchequer, when the latter became Prime Minister on the retirement of Sir Henry Campbell-Bannerman.

In comparison with later war-time budgets the demands made upon the taxpayer by the 1909 Budget hardly justified the political convulsion that followed its introduction. It increased income tax from 9*d.* to 1*s.* 2*d.*, imposed a supertax beginning at £3,000 on incomes over £5,000, and death duties up to 10 per cent. on fortunes of £200,000. But it also proposed a tax on "unearned increments," in the form of a tax on land values, a duty of one-fifth, or 20 per cent. of the increased value of land when it passed from one owner to another, an annual duty of one halfpenny in the pound upon "undeveloped land," and a reversion duty of 10 per cent. on the value accruing to the owner of a lease when the lease terminated. Provision was also made for a valuation of land, and this was hated by landowners quite as much as the land taxes and the increment duties.

There was a prolonged struggle in the House of Commons over this Budget. Forty-two days were spent on the Committee stage of the Finance Bill which passed, finally, by a House of Commons vote of 379 to 149. Public interest in its progress through Parliament was heightened by the lively attacks which Lloyd George made on the ducal landowners, and their spokesmen's equally lively retaliation. Under pressure of their wealthy supporters, the Conservative Party leaders resisted all efforts to prevent a head-on collision between the Liberal House of Commons and the Tory-ridden House of Lords. Even the King himself (Edward VII) anxious as he was to avoid the threatened constitutional crisis, could not bring the Tory leaders to see reason or the dangers lying ahead. The Peers who trooped forth from the backwoods found the counsel of Lord Milner to go ahead with the destruction of the Budget "and damn the consequences" much more to their way of thinking. Asquith, as Prime Minister, put the issue clearly by saying that there were two ways, and only two ways before the country of meeting the necessities of the nation:

"You may impose, simultaneously and in fair proportion, taxes on accumulated wealth, on the profits of industry, on the simpler luxuries, though not the necessities, of the poor. You may seek, as we are seeking, for new taxes on those forms of value which at present are either inadequately taxed or not taxed at all; values which spring from monopoly; which are not the fruit of individual effort or enterprise—but which are the creation either of social growth, or of the direct activity of the State itself. That is one way—that is the way proposed by this Budget. What is the other, the only other, that has yet been disclosed or even foreshadowed to the Parliament of the country? It is to take a toll of the prime necessaries of life. It is to raise the level of prices to the average consumer of commodities; it is to surround your markets with a tariff wall which, insofar as it succeeds in protecting the home producer, will fail to bring in revenue, and insofar as it succeeds in bringing in revenue, will fail to protect the home producer."

That was the choice to be made, the Prime Minister said, and if to these alternatives there was to be added another, the choice between the maintenance or the abandonment by the House of Commons of its ancient constitutional supremacy over all matters of finance, Asquith declared that there was not a man sitting beside him or behind him who was not ready to join the issue. Nevertheless, on November 30, 1909, the House of Lords rejected the Budget, on second reading, by 350 to 75. There had been no precedent for such action in money matters by the House of Lords for at least 250 years. Rejection of the Budget was a challenge to the constitutional rights of the House of Commons that the Labour Party as well as the Liberals felt it necessary to resist. The resolution by which this challenge was accepted in the House of Commons, as a breach of the constitution and a usurpation of the rights of the Commons, was carried by 349 to 134, and Parliament was forthwith dissolved for a General Election to take place in mid-January of the following year.

The Labour Party's concern with the Lloyd George Budget was overshadowed by its determination to make the Osborne Judgment a capital issue in the General Election. The Liberal Government's taxation policy had Labour's warm, but qualified, support. The Labour Party felt that it could not remain indifferent to the problems of national finance, having regard to the responsibility Labour had taken in urging Parliament to pass schemes of social reform. Moreover, the Party recognised that the Budget was founded upon principles of finance which it had itself advocated. Labour's objection to indirect taxation was strong, but it was firmly of the opinion that the cost of social reform should be borne by socially-created wealth, which was then diverted by the rich in the form of rent, interest and profit. Supertax on large incomes, special taxation of State-conferred monopolies, increased estate and legacy duties, and a really substantial beginning of the taxation of land value were points in the Labour Party's financial policy which found some recognition in the Liberal

Budget. But the Party's main interest in the first of the two General Elections that took place in 1910 was to recover for the Unions the political rights of which the Law Courts had deprived them in the Osborne case.

The General Election which began in mid-January resulted in the return of the Asquith Government with a reduced majority of 124, counting 82 Irish Members as on its side; but it involved for the Liberals a loss of 104 seats. For the Labour Party the results were much more satisfactory. The Party put forward 78 candidates and secured the return of 40. It was the first time that the Party fought unitedly under one banner, as on this occasion the official miners' candidates were elected under the Party constitution. Tribute was paid by the Party Executive after these elections to the magnificent solidarity of the Trade Union Movement behind the Party. The separate Trade Union Group of M.P.s in the House merged their identity with the Party (with two or three "Lib-Lab" exceptions); and though the Party actually lost eight of the seats it held in the 1906 Parliament, it gained three new seats, and on balance was all the stronger as a result of the first of the two General Elections of 1910.

CHAPTER VIII

FOUNDATIONS OF FREEDOM

By Herbert Tracey

Between the two General Elections of 1910 the attention of Parliament was almost exclusively concerned with the quarrel with the House of Lords, and its attendant political consequences. The question of amending the law under which the Osborne Judgment had been made receded somewhat into the background, as the Liberal Government unfolded its policy for dealing with the situation produced by the use made of their powers of veto by the House of Lords. Yet it was in this short lived Parliament of 1910 that the foundations of democratic freedom were to some extent relaid and strengthened. Three measures were framed, in the midst of a good deal of confusion, which, upon their enactment later, provided firmer guarantees that the will of the people would prevail over the obstructions which the forces of wealth and privilege put in its way. These three measures were the Parliament Act of 1911, the Act providing a Parliamentary salary for Members passed in the same year, and the Trade Union Act of 1913.

Although many people thought that the Liberal Prime Minister should have obtained from the King, before the General Election of January 1910, assent to the proposal that new Peers should be created in sufficient numbers to override the Lords' veto on the Budget, it was soon realised that this would have been no fundamental solution of the constitutional problem. In March 1910 three resolutions were laid before the House of Commons, embodying the Liberal proposals. The first, dealing with Money Bills, declared it to be expedient that the House of Lords should be disabled by law from rejecting or amending a Money Bill, and that any such limitation by law was not to be taken as diminishing or qualifying the existing rights and privileges of the House of Commons. The second resolution declared it to be equally expedient that the veto of the House of Lords as respects Bills other than Money Bills should be restricted by law, so that any such Bill having passed the House of Commons in three successive sessions, and being sent to the House of Lords at least one month before the end of the session, if it has been rejected by that House in each of these sessions, shall become law without the consent of the House of Lords on the Royal Assent being declared. The third resolution considered it expedient to limit the duration of Parliament to five years. These resolutions were adopted by the House of Commons with majorities varying from 98 to 106. They constituted the substance of the Parliament Bill which was read a first time on April 14, 1910.

To carry the Parliament Bill, it was necessary, of course, to overcome, in a constitutional way, the resistance of the House of Lords. For that reason, to give proper statutory effect to the measure, the Liberal Prime Minister had to seek from the King a promise to exercise his prerogative in creating a sufficient number of Peers to assist its passage through the Upper House. What the decision of King Edward VII would have been on this point is a matter of inference only; for the King died in May 1910, and the problem was left to his successor, King George V. The political situation for the time was transformed by this event. Emotions excited by the King's death, and the wish to prevent undue embarrassment to the new King, led to a Conference between Party leaders—but not including the Labour Party—on the constitutional questions that divided them. Many meetings were held, without arriving at any definite conclusion. One big obstacle in the way of agreement was the division of opinion on Irish Home Rule, which was becoming more embittered. On the failure of the Conference the Liberal Government decided upon an immediate dissolution of Parliament, on the understanding that if the General Election renewed their mandate, the King would be ready to exercise his constitutional powers (involving the creation of new Peers) if necessary, to give effect to the will of the people. It is on record that King George V assented to the Government's decision, and to the advice the Liberal Cabinet gave him as to the exercise of his Royal prerogative. The second General Election of 1910 was accordingly held in December.

In this General Election the Labour Party contested fifty-six constituencies. The result was a net gain of two seats, which was regarded, in the circumstances of the election, as satisfactory, in view of the fact that the Party was heavily handicapped financially by the effect of the Osborne Judgment upon political activities and resources of the Trade Unions. Arthur Henderson, who was the Party's fraternal delegate at the Trades Union Congress, held in the autumn of 1910, told the assembly that no less than half of the Labour M.P.s were in a serious predicament. Injunctions had been obtained (he said) against Trade Unions represented in the Party by twenty out of its forty members. The Bill which the Party had prepared in consultation with the T.U.C., to undo the ill effects of the Osborne Judgment, could not be brought forward in the 1910 Parliament because none of the Labour M.P.s secured a place in the ballot; and the Government declined to give any Parliamentary time to consideration of the Party's Bill. As a measure of relief in the situation the Party had urged the Government to introduce legislation providing payment of Members; but Henderson made it clear to the Congress that this was not put forward as a substitute or alternative to amendment of the law affecting the Trade Unions. To meet one of the points raised against the Trade Unions' association with the Labour Party, the Party Conference in 1911 altered the Constitution with a view to removing the objection that its members in Parliament were pledge-bound. It was provided that Labour M.P.s were no longer required to *abide* by the decisions of the Parliamentary Party, but were to *maintain* the constitution and "accept the responsibility established by Parliamentary practice." In this way it was sought to make it quite clear that it would be as disloyal for Members to associate themselves with other political Parties as it was before the constitution of the Party was thus amended: what it was sought to do was to put the Party on precisely the same footing as the Liberal Party and the Conservative Party insofar as their loyal support and acceptance of the obligations of membership were concerned. Just before the dissolution, Asquith announced the Government's intention to introduce legislation providing payment of Members. He foreshadowed also "legislation empowering Trade Unions to include in their objects and organisation the provision of a fund for Parliamentary and municipal action and representation and kindred objects, and to combine for such purposes, provided that the opinion of the Union is effectively ascertained, and that there should be no compulsion on any member to contribute to this fund."

With the Government majority of 126, counting the Irish members, the Liberal Government proceeded to carry into effect the proposals embodied in the veto resolutions and incorporated in the Parliament Bill. In form, the resulting Act was a temporary solution of the problem, since it purported (in its preamble) to define the relations between the two Houses of Parliament, pending the establishment of a new Upper House constituted on a popular basis. The Bill went through all its stages in the House of Commons, between February and May, against such resistance from the Opposition as appeared to make it inevitable that the King would have to create new Peers to overcome the deadlock between the two Houses. Amendments were made in the House of Lords which the Government regarded as destructive of the principle and purpose of the Bill both in regard to finance and to general legislation. The Labour Party was not enthusiastic about the measure and, in fact, had contended during the Parliamentary debates for the abolition of the House of Lords. Out of the conflict of views, and in a tempest of political passion, the Liberal solution was ultimately adopted, without the flooding of the Upper House by the creation of new Peers. The compromise, for such it was in fact, has remained a workable one from 1911 to the present time: the hereditary principle upon which the Upper House rests has not been modified by the creation of life peerages, an innovation which the House of Lords has resisted; successive Labour Governments have contented themselves with redressing the balance of Party forces in the Upper House by making a number of their supporters Peers; but legislation to reduce to twelve months the duration of the Lords' veto has been framed by the Third Labour Government.

Almost simultaneously in the first session of the 1911 Parliament, payment of Members was enacted, providing a salary of £400 a year for M.P.s, subject to income tax. This measure implemented one of the six points of the Charter which eighty years previously the agitators for Parliamentary Reform had put forward as the means by which political democracy was to be extended and fortified. By the payment of salaries to Members of Parliament, public service was no longer confined to men of means. A seat in the House of Commons ceased to be one of the privileges of wealth. The enactment of this law helped the Labour Party, at a critical stage, to develop its position as an independent political force.

Neither the Parliament Act, nor the Act providing payment for Members, however, lessened the determination of the Trade Unions to regain their freedom of action in the sphere of politics. Continuous pressure was brought to bear by the Parliamentary Party to secure legislation for amendment of Trade Union law, but it was not until 1913 that the Government finally decided the question with a measure which the Trade Unions and the Labour Party reluctantly accepted, though it did not give them all they sought. The Government Bill, referred to in the records of the time as the Trade Unions (No. 2) Bill, secured a second reading by 234 votes to 134, and was amended in Committee, by the influence of Labour members, without bringing it into full conformity with what the Trade Union and Labour Movement demanded. A Special National Conference was therefore summoned by the Joint Board to decide the attitude of the Movement and the action of the Parliamentary Party on the Government's proposals. The Labour view was that the Bill gave only a qualified right to a Trade Union to engage in politics, to nominate Parliamentary candidates, and maintain them. The Bill provided that "the fact that a combination has under its constitution objects or powers other than statutory objects *shall not prevent* the combination being a Trade Union." This met the Judges' interpretation of existing law which laid it down that objects not stated or defined in the Trade Union Acts were beyond the powers of a Union. The obvious intention and meaning of the first clause of this Bill was to permit a Union to add other objects to its statutory objects, and still remain within the four corners of the law. It followed that the addition of political objects to their other objects would not be unlawful. But before this could be done a ballot of the members had to be taken, and a majority of those voting must be obtained in favour of the Union taking political action. The Bill gave a Trade Union which followed this procedure power to apply its funds for "any lawful objects or purposes for the time being authorised under its constitution"; another clause of the Bill restricted the application of the funds of a Trade Union for political purposes. It required a Trade Union to alter its rules so as to provide:

(*a*) That any payments for the political objects specified in the Act must be made out of a separate fund;

(*b*) That any member of a Union must be exempt from any obligation to contribute to this separate fund if he gives notice of his objection to contribute in accordance with the terms of the Act;

(*c*) That no member who is exempt from the obligation to contribute should be either directly or indirectly penalised by reason of such exemption; and

(*d*) That contribution to the political fund of the Union is not to be made a condition of entry to the Union.

It should be noted that so far as political activities not involving charges on the Trade Union funds are concerned, they are unaffected by anything contained in the Act. In terms the Act provides: "The funds of a Trade Union shall not be applied either directly or in conjunction with any other Trade Union, Association, or body, or otherwise indirectly, in the furtherance of the political objects to which this section applies (without prejudice to the furtherance of any other political objects), unless the furtherance of those objects has been approved as an object of the Union by a resolution for the time being in force passed on a ballot of the members of the Union taken in accordance with this Act for the purpose of this Act by a majority of the members voting." It is important in view of subsequent events to understand the scope and purpose of the 1913 Act, since it is the legislation which again governs the political activities of Unions. The Act did not fully restore to Trade Unions the right to engage in political action in the way they thought they were entitled to do before the Osborne Judgment. Up to the time of the Osborne case, Trade Unions believed that they were entitled to spend their funds on political objects as on other lawful objects involving the interests of their members. No distinction was drawn between the general funds of a Union and its political funds. But the 1913 Act made this distinction, in the process of giving Unions the legal right to add political objects to their other objects, and to take contributions from their members for the furtherance of these political objects. What the 1913 Act authorises is the expenditure of money:

(*a*) On the payment of any expenses incurred either directly or indirectly by a candidate, or prospective candidate for election to Parliament or to any public office, before, during, or after the election, in connection with his candidature or election; or

(*b*) On the holding of any meeting or the distribution of any literature or documents in support of any candidate or prospective candidate; or

(*c*) On the maintenance of any person who is a Member of Parliament or who holds a public office;

(*d*) In connection with the registration of electors, or the selection of a candidate for Parliament or any public office; or

(*e*) On the holding of political meetings of any kind, or on the distribution of political literature or political documents of any kind, when the main purpose of meetings or of the distribution of the literature or documents is the furtherance of statutory objects within the meaning of this Act.

The "public office" to which reference is made here, means office or membership of any public body which has power directly or indirectly to raise money by means of a rate. A combination of Unions (e.g. the Miners' Federation) can function as a Trade Union for the purpose of giving effect to the provisions of this section—that is, a ballot for political action must be taken for the whole of the component membership and decided by a majority of the whole vote.

Another provision is made for the conduct of a ballot for the purposes of the Act. Ballots must be taken in accordance with the rules of the Union, provided that the Registrar of Friendly Societies is satisfied that these rules give every member an equal right, and, if reasonably possible, a fair opportunity of voting; and that the secrecy of the ballot is properly secured. Model rules for the ballot required by this legislation were framed and approved by the Registrar.

Express provision is made in the Act to enable a member of a Trade Union to give notice that he objects to contribute to the political fund of the Union. Control of the Union's political fund is obviously the responsibility of those alone who have contributed to it. On the adoption of a resolution approving the furtherance of political objects as an object of the Union, the law requires that notice must be given to the members acquainting them that each member has a right to be exempt from contributing to the political fund, and that a form of exemption notice can be obtained either by personal application, or by post, from the Head Office or any Branch Office of the Union, or from the office of the Registrar of Friendly Societies. This notice must be given in such manner as is approved by the Registrar, having regard in each case to existing practice, and to the character of the Trade Union.

In the years immediately succeeding the passing of the Act, trade unionists were given, by Party organisations opposed to the Trade Unions in politics, ample opportunities to exercise their right to exemption. Forms were printed and distributed by the hundreds of thousands by these outside bodies after 1913, as they were again in 1946 after the repeal of the 1927 Act which brought back into full force the 1913 Act. When a member gave notice, in accordance with the Act, of his objection to contribute he remained exempt as long as his notice was not withdrawn, nominally starting from the following January. Under the Act a method is also prescribed for giving effect to exemption from contributions to a political fund. This can be secured either by a separate levy of contributions to such funds on the members of the Union who have not claimed exemption; or by relieving any members who are exempt by payment of a proportionate part of any periodical contributions made by the members towards the upkeep of the Union. If the latter method be adopted, the rules usually provide that the relief is given as far as possible to all members who are exempt on the occasion of the same periodical payment, and also that members should know whether or not any such periodical contribution is intended in whole, or in part, as a contribution to the political fund of the

Union. Model Rules for the political fund have also been issued by the Registrar.

The three legislative measures summarised in the foregoing pages had an obvious bearing upon the position of the Labour Party's future development. They did not stand alone in the record of the Parliament elected at the end of 1910, the life of which was prolonged beyond its natural term by the outbreak of World War in 1914. Before the war came, Liberal social reform reached its maximum development in the establishment of the National Insurance system. National Health Insurance was enacted in 1911. It brought into compulsory insurance against sickness and disablement all workers between the ages of 16 and 70, on the basis of a contributory scheme which divided the costs between workmen, employers, and the State, and provided weekly cash benefits along with medical attendance in respect of sickness, disablement and (for women) a maternity benefit. Connected with the National Health Insurance scheme were the beginnings of Unemployment Insurance. When the Labour Exchanges Act was passed in the autumn of 1909, one of its purposes was to enable the Government to measure the extent of unemployment and to operate a system of compulsory and contributory unemployment insurance, as well as to serve the purpose of bringing together employers in need of labour and workers in need of employment. On the basis of the Labour Exchange machinery and the statistics it made available Parliament passed the legislation, embodied in Part II of the 1911 Insurance Act, which provided compulsory insurance in seven selected trades, namely: building, constructional engineering, shipbuilding, engineering, vehicle building, ironfounding, and sawmilling, and about 2½ million workpeople, about one-sixth of the adult workers then engaged in industrial employment were covered by the scheme. It was extended to cover practically all the industrial population in 1920, when about 12¼ million people were compulsorily insured against unemployment, the unemployment fund being sustained by contributions from employers, workpeople and the State in equal thirds, in the original scheme.

Included in the Liberal Government's social programme were embryonic measures of wage regulation, including the Trade Boards system set up by the Trade Board Act of 1909. Labour was responsible for the introduction of the Trade Board principle in Parliamentary debate, and the Bill was introduced by Arthur Henderson in 1908. The Government's measure which became operative in January 1910, established Trade Boards for four trades: tailoring, paper-box making, machine-made lace finishing, and chain making; provision being made to bring in other trades to which the Board of Trade considered its application necessary, where the rate of wages was exceptionally low. By the time war came, (in 1914) there were about a dozen Trade Boards with power to determine legal minimum rates of pay for approximately half a million male and female workers.

Minimum wage legislation was also enacted by the Liberal Government for the mining industry. This legislation, however, came under duress. It arose out of the first national strike of mine workers in 1912. To protect them, the various miners' associations represented by the Miners' Federation of Great Britain, put forward a claim for the fixing of a minimum rate of 5*s.* per shift for adult workers underground, and 2*s.* for boys. The claim had special reference to miners working in "abnormal places," where a living wage could not be earned, on the piece-work basis, on account of technical difficulties. The mine owners refused to concede this claim and a National Strike was called which lasted for about three weeks, when the Asquith Government reluctantly yielded to the Labour Party's insistence upon minimum wage legislation for the mining industry. The Act of 1912 provided for the setting up of Joint District Boards to determine minimum rates of pay, but it did not impose any specific rate of wages in any district or for any grade of worker. Labour members in the House of Commons made every effort to get the miners' claim for 5*s.* and 2*s.* for men and boys written into the Act, but were unsuccessful, and in agreement with the M.F.G.B., the Party opposed the Bill on third reading.

In addition to this minimum wage legislation the Parliaments of 1910 and 1911 enacted some improvements in Factory legislation. But a tremendous industrial convulsion in these years demonstrated the movement of profound social forces in a direction which Liberal legislation could not follow. The strike of the coalfields in 1912 was only one manifestation of the rising tide of industrial unrest which reached its height just before the outbreak of war in 1914. A wave of large-scale strikes revealed the effects of a ferment of new ideas in the Trade Unions, and the existence of new minority movements, which challenged the older Trade Union leadership and the political philosophy upon which the Labour Party was founded.

CHAPTER IX

INDUSTRIAL UNREST AND WORLD WAR

By Herbert Tracey

On the eve of the first World War the Labour Movement was in no easy position. It was in an unsettled state of mind, and by no means sure of its future course of action. The industrial unrest, signalled by a series of strikes involving transport workers, dockers and carters, and later the railwaymen, in 1910-11, marked the impact on the Trade Union Movement of new theories of industrial action. These strikes had an economic justification in the fact that wages were not keeping pace with the rise in prices. Many trade unionists were led to question the traditional policy of the Unions in these circumstances; and to doubt whether the political organisation of the Labour Movement was of any real value to them. A young generation of workers had grown up whilst the battle for independent Labour representation was being fought and won. They adopted a critical attitude towards the Labour Party's programme of Social Reform. They demanded a more militant and revolutionary policy than was represented by the Labour Party's Parliamentary efforts to ameliorate social and industrial evils by way of "Right to Work" Bills, the provision of school meals, or the minimum wage legislation on the lines of the Trade Boards Act and the Miners' Wages Act.

What was described at the time as a "revolutionary and instinctive movement" among the workers found expression not only in widespread strikes, but in an organised propaganda. This embodied both a philosophical theory and a practical programme of direct action with which its advocates sought to inoculate the Trade Union and Socialist Movement. The philosophical theory, whose chief exponent was Georges Sorel, was imported from the European continent in the Syndicalist doctrine of producers' control over the means of production and distribution to be enforced by the General Strike. The programme of "direct action" as a practical method of giving effect to the theories of Syndicalism was taken rather from the militant activities of the section of the American Labour Movement that accepted the doctrines of Industrial Unionism as taught by Daniel De Leon and practised by the I.W.W. (Industrial Workers of the World). The leading British Trade Union exponent of Syndicalism was Tom Mann, who took up the work that James Connolly, the Irish Labour Leader who was later executed (in 1916) for a share in the Easter Rebellion in Ireland, had started in the Clyde district about 1905; but other militant propagandists with anarchist affiliations who joined the Syndicalist Movement gave to it a more pronounced anti-Parliamentary bias.

Into the underlying theories of Syndicalism, industrial unionism, and workers' control, it is not necessary to enter at length. It was particularly influential in the coalfields. One of the earlier publications which attracted a great deal of notice was the pamphlet written for and issued by an active group of the young miners' leaders in South Wales (including Arthur Cook and Noah Ablett), under the title of "The Miners' Next Step." But journals, pamphlets and fly-sheets appeared in great profusion all over the country at this time, all advocating the use of the Trade Unions as the instrument of revolutionary action, not only against the employers, but against the Government as the executive of the possessing class.

Such publications as the *Syndicalist*, the *Transport Worker*, and the *Syndicalist Railwaymen*, expressed the same philosophy of violence and preached the relentless prosecution of the class war by the organised workers. They repudiated the idea of Parliamentary democracy on philosophical as well as practical grounds, insisting that outside the workshop and the factory, workers hold divergent political opinions which render mass action difficult if not impossible: only in the workshop is there a sense of solidarity overriding all minor differences, and capable of animating great masses of workers in concerted action on the industrial field. Moreover, it was contended that the political Party is not and cannot be a purely class organisation: on the other hand, the Trade Union is immune from the corrupting and enfeebling influences of middle-class leaders and can be inspired with the revolutionary *élan* by a militant minority. It was the growing dissatisfaction of the rank and file of the Trade Unions with the somewhat uninspired work of the Parliamentary Labour Party in its earlier days which gave the British Syndicalist leaders their opportunity, and the extent of their influence is to be measured by the multiplication of new organisations brought into existence at that time to further the ideal of workers' control and to quicken the pace of social revolution.

One shortlived experiment in industrial organisation gave rise to exaggerated hopes and fears. The large-scale strikes affecting many great bodies of workers in all parts of the country created a militant temper which found, perhaps, its clearest manifestation in the great Dublin Strike of 1913, under the leadership of James Larkin. To achieve his aims, Larkin sought to win the support of the British workers for a sympathetic General Strike. In the course of the long struggle the militant forces in the organised Movement could not secure the sympathetic action they agitated for. But with the powerful assistance of the then "rebel" *Daily Herald* carrying the vivid and trenchant cartoons of Will Dyson, they succeeded in arousing the whole Labour Movement to a high pitch of activity and brought the whole country to a realisation of the gravity of the industrial revolt. The Asquith Government, compelled repeatedly to intervene in the recurrent disputes, tried to stem the tide with schemes of industrial arbitration and conciliation. Extensive use was made of the services of Sir George (later Lord) Askwith as industrial peace maker. Attempts were made to establish joint consultative machinery representative of both employer and Trade

Union leaders to assuage the conflict. This body, known as the Industrial Council (1911) was the rather feeble forerunner of developments in industrial relations which were pursued with much greater vigour and with clearer vision after the National Strike of 1926, and during the second World War.

But for the time being, organised Labour was in no mood for compromise. The trend was all the other way. Without conscious appreciation of the argument of Georges Sorel, who insisted that the direct actionists were the real Marxists, and that the basic principle of Marxism was not surplus value but the class struggle, many British trade unionists at this time believed wholeheartedly that the strike weapon was the source of their salvation. "The idea of a General Strike," wrote Sorel,[1] "has such power behind it that it drags into the revolutionary track everything it touches. In virtue of this idea Socialism remains ever young: all attempts made to bring about social peace seem childish: desertions of comrades into the ranks of the middle class, far from discouraging the masses, only excite them still more to rebellion: in a word, the line of cleavage is never in danger of disappearing." It was Sorel also who pointed out that the idea of the General Strike destroys all the theoretical consequences of every social policy: that is to say, its partisans look upon even the most popular reforms (he said) as having a middle-class character: so far as they are concerned nothing can weaken the fundamental opposition of the class war.

Theoretical arguments of this nature were translated by the British Syndicalists into strike propaganda. "We most certainly favour strikes," wrote Tom Mann:[2] "We shall always do our best to help strikes to be successful, and shall prepare the way as rapidly as possible for the General Strike of national proportions. This will be the actual Social and Industrial Revolution. The workers will refuse to any longer manipulate the machinery of production in the interests of the capitalist class, and there will be no power on earth able to compel them to work when they thus refuse." When the capitalists get tired of running industry (Mann added) the workers will cheerfully invite them to abdicate, and through and by their industrial organisations will run the industries themselves in the interests of the whole community.

As a concrete result of the industrial unrest of the period in which such propaganda was rampant, the miners, transport workers and railwaymen decided to form the Triple Industrial Alliance. This step was taken at a conference of the three bodies, the Miners' Federation, the National Union of Railwaymen, and the National Transport Workers' Federation, in the spring of 1914. The initiative had been taken by the Miners' annual conference in the previous year, by instructing the M.F.G.B. Executive to approach the Executives of other big Trade Unions "with a view to co-operative action and the support of each other's demands." In theory

[1] In his "Reflections on Violence."

[2] In the *Industrial Syndicalist*, March 1911.

the Triple Industrial Alliance was created for the purpose of drawing up and enforcing a common programme of reforms in the related industries. It constituted a formidable combination, as the membership of the three bodies constituting the Alliance numbered considerably more than 1¼ million—800,000 miners, 270,000 railwaymen, and 250,000 transport workers at that time.

As a matter of history, the theoretical purpose of the Triple Alliance was never tested in practice. Its declared aim was to enable the three bodies to formulate simultaneously a programme of advance, each in its own group of trades. Its method was to be concerted action to secure the acceptance of this programme. All three groups were to present their claims to the employers at the same time, accompanied by a notice to terminate existing agreements. Notices to cease work were to be handed in and timed to become operative in the three related industries on the same date. A simultaneous withdrawal of labour was implied if the employers resisted the demands. War came before this scheme of organisation was ratified by the constituent bodies. Nothing was done during the war years to create an administrative organisation to serve the purpose of the Alliance. The plan required each partner to submit its programme to the other two partners; and upon joint proposals it was intended that joint action should be taken. Preoccupation with war issues prevented anything like this being done. The Triple Alliance hardly made its existence felt during the war. When trouble arose after the war in the mining industry the attempt to use this formidable engine of direct action failed completely. In a later chapter a full account is given of the circumstances in which the mining industry's troubles led up to the General Strike of 1926. This was a pivotal event in the history of the Trade Union and Labour Movement which had far-reaching political consequences, and these require further elucidation. It will suffice here to anticipate those later developments only to explain the inglorious exit of the Triple Industrial Alliance from the field it was to have dominated.

In the summer of 1920, the M.F.G.B. put forward a claim for an increase in miners' wages. They linked with it a demand that the price of coal should be reduced, not only to benefit home consumers, but also to assist the economic recovery of European countries who were having to pay heavily for their coal imports. British coal exporters were in a position, after the war, to charge what the traffic would bear, and had no scruples about doing it. The miners' leaders argued that their wage claim could be met from the coal owners' surplus profits. The Government refused to take this view of the question and a strike ballot was taken in the coalfields. An attempt then made to set in motion the machinery of the Triple Alliance failed. Neither of the other two organisations could decide for a stoppage of their own industries in support of the miners.

Clearly, the original purpose of the Triple Alliance was not being furthered in a dispute affecting only one of the three industries. There were practical difficulties, arising from the fact that the other two bodies had not drawn up any programme to place before their employers. It was found, too, when the question of simultaneous action came to be considered, that railwaymen and transport workers had different rules governing the giving of notice to stop work, and securing authority from the rank and file membership for strike action, from those operative in the coalfields: the miners had to take a ballot and get a two-thirds majority in support of a sympathetic strike, whereas the railwaymen and the transport workers could act on a decision of their respective Executives and delegate conferences in regard to sympathetic strikes. It was realised, also, that the effect of a miners' strike was of a long-term character, whereas a strike in transport and railway services would have an instantaneous effect.

For both these theoretical and practical reasons the Triple Alliance was, therefore, unable to make its weight felt in the mining dispute, when the miners went on to call a strike in the autumn of 1920. The stoppage lasted about three weeks and ended in a truce. Among the militant trade unionists the attitude of the leaders of the transport workers and railwaymen was regarded as a betrayal. But the possibility that the Triple Alliance might yet be used led the Government to secure "Emergency Powers" legislation which was used ruthlessly in the National Strike of 1926.[1]

The truce in the coalfields was of short duration. Trouble arose when the Government brought war-time control of the industry to an end, five months earlier than the date fixed by Act of Parliament. In the ensuing difficulties the coal owners proposed drastic wage reductions and resisted the miners' efforts to maintain the national system of wage regulation which operated during the war. A further effort was made to bring the Triple Alliance into action. But a clear-cut line of policy failed to take shape, although the transport workers and railwaymen were pledged this time to support the miners, and the political influence of the Labour Party was brought to bear in negotiations with the Prime Minister. A split took place between the miners and the transport unions on a vital principle in the miners' programme, and on Friday, April 15, 1921, it became clear that the Triple Alliance had fallen to pieces.

The historical importance of "Black Friday," as it was called at the time, is of minor interest now. What was significant in the whole of the circumstances revolving around the Triple Alliance was the strong trend towards a philosophy and programme of direct action by the Unions, based upon the idea of the class war and the technique of the General Strike. To the political leaders of the Labour Movement such conceptions of working aims and methods were futile and dangerous excesses. They were regarded as subversive of all that the political organisation of the workers was trying to accomplish through the Labour Party. It was not that the political leaders denied the reality of the workers' economic grievances: they

[1] Another important consequence of the events connected with the rise and fall of the Triple Alliance, was the transformation of the old Parliamentary Committee of the Trades Union Congress into the T.U.C. General Council, in 1920-21. This development is dealt with more fully in Chapter XIII.

recognised that the industrial unrest had its roots in the "deplorable insufficiency of wages" which had persisted, "notwithstanding a great expansion of national wealth and a considerable increase in the cost of living." This was the attitude taken up by the Labour Party in a Labour amendment to a Liberal motion in the House of Commons, on Industrial Unrest in 1912. But the political leaders maintained, as we have seen, the closest possible touch with the Union leaders and did their utmost to give expression to Trade Union views whenever the industrial disputes came before Parliament. Thus, when the 1911 railway strike began, before the big transport strikes of that year ended, the Labour Party in Parliament took active steps to effect a settlement in a dispute which really turned upon the refusal of the railway companies to "recognise" the Union; an obstinate and reactionary position which the railwaymen met by refusing absolutely to consider any proposals for a settlement until their Union representatives met the railway management face to face. The Joint Executives of the Railway Unions concerned in this dispute gave their thanks by resolution to the Party leaders in Parliament, Arthur Henderson, G. H. Roberts and Ramsay MacDonald, "for the very painstaking and laborious efforts in bringing about the settlement, feeling confident no better efforts could have been made." The Executive of the Miners' Federation tendered similar thanks for the great assistance the Party had given to them in their endeavours to improve the Minimum Wage Act of 1912. A representative of the Party even served on the Strike Committee which conducted the Port of London dispute—his duties being to keep the political leaders informed of developments, and to convey to the Strike Committee the Parliamentary leaders' view. But the political leaders were, of course, profoundly hostile to the idea of direct action by the Unions as a means of securing the overthrow of the capitalist system and securing the control of production by the workers.

It is beyond question that the wisdom, intellectual ability, and powers of leadership possessed by Trade Union leaders at the head of the political organisation of the workers in this period of industrial unrest prevented an unbridgeable schism between it and the industrial organisation as the latter fell more and more under the influence of the new ideas of Trade Union organisation and policy. On both sides there were intellectual gains from this conflict of doctrine. The political leaders as well as the trade unionists found their views of economic organisation and working-class action sensibly modified by the rise of the Guild Socialist Movement in the years immediately preceding the first World War. The significance of this Movement in the history of organised Labour lies largely in the function of reconciliation it filled between the collectivist and syndicalist schools of thought. It gave to the ideal of workers' control at once a fuller and more practical meaning than either the syndicalists claimed or the collectivists at that time were ready to concede: British Socialism was largely diverted from a narrow and bureaucractic interpretation of collectivism in terms of nationalised industries managed by civil servants, by the educational work carried on in the Labour Movement by journals like the *New Age* and by the influential group of writers who gathered about the *Daily Herald*, among whom G. D. H. Cole was by far the ablest and most scholarly leader. The nature of the controversy is indicated by the change of thought and direction that took place under the influence of the Guild Socialists, in the Labour and Socialist Movement. Not only was the absolute antinomy between political action and direct industrial action thereby prevented from becoming disruptive of the Movement's solidarity, but the way became clear for the harmonious and orderly co-ordination of the two sides of the working-class movement. The state of mind was then created which made acceptable at a later time the organisation of public enterprise under the control of public boards and commissions which has been perhaps the most significant development in the field of political institutions during the present generation. It is enough to say in this connection that the socialisation programme of later Labour Governments, nowhere following the traditional method of organising a socialised service on the lines (for example) of the Post Office, has carried the conception of public enterprise under competent technical management, on the basis of public ownership and democratic control, into wider fields.

But these developments are for later study and elucidation. At the stage we have reached in the history of the Labour Party, other and more menacing developments challenged the capacity and understanding of its leaders. Industrial unrest was not the only disturbing phenomenon of the period. Political animosities were rising to a perilous climax in the conflict between the two older Parties on the question of Home Rule and the control of legislation by the popularly elected House of Commons. The whole country, indeed, seemed at that time to have become a prey to the wildest and most extreme passions that can beset a nation. It was a time in which the King himself was constrained to say, in opening the Buckingham Palace Conference on the Irish question in July 1914, that: "The trend has been surely and steadily towards an appeal to force, and today the cry of civil war has been on the lips of the most responsible and sober-minded of my people."

Relations between the two older Parties, and between the two Houses of Parliament had indeed reached breaking point on the problem of Irish self-government. The Liberal Government's policy of Home Rule for Ireland was being wrecked on the rock of Ulster's resistance. Nor was it merely a political resistance: it took the form of preparations for armed rebellion, organised under the leadership of Sir Edward (afterwards Lord) Carson, F. E. Smith (later Lord Birkenhead), and other politically powerful figures in the Tory Party; there was military mutiny, illegal gun-running, and sporadic outrages and outbreaks of violence, which testified to the depth of the political bitterness that existed. Public disorders excited by the militant suffrage movement, sinking deeper every day into mass hysteria among women who acknowledged no restraint, heightened the sense of crisis in the months immediately preceding the outbreak of war with Germany and Austria-Hungary.

We are concerned with the first World War, in this historical survey, only insofar as it affected the position of the Labour Party, and the relations of the Party with the organised working-class movement. The onset of war revealed divergent tendencies within the ranks of organised Labour, and dissensions amongst its leaders on fundamental issues of foreign policy. The Labour Movement had its international responsibilities, dating back to a much earlier time. It was represented in the International Socialist Congress by the Labour Party, the Independent Labour Party, the Fabian Society and the Social-Democratic Party—and there were uncompromising British Socialists who denied the right of the Labour Party to be inside the Socialist International as it had not openly avowed a Socialist faith and doctrine. Some sections of the Labour Movement held themselves pledged by a resolution adopted at the International Socialist Congress held in Stuttgart in 1907. This resolution bound the constituent bodies in the Socialist International to resist war by every possible means: "If war threatens to break out it is the duty of the working class in the countries concerned and of their Parliamentary representatives, with the help of the International Socialist Bureau, as a means of co-ordinating their action, to use every effort to prevent war by all the means which seem to them most appropriate, having regard to the sharpness of the class war and to the general political situation. Should war nevertheless break out, their duty is to intervene to bring it promptly to an end, and with all their energies to use the political and economic crisis created by the war to rouse the populace from its slumbers, and to hasten the fall of capitalist domination."

Great debates took place in international congresses before 1914 on the Socialist attitude to war, in which commanding personalities of the International Socialist Movement, Jaurés, Bebel, Hardie, Vandervelde, and the rest, contended one against the other. The question was on the agenda of the Congress which was to have assembled in Vienna in August, 1914. But the war came before this Congress could meet, and the several national Parties had to interpret for themselves the policy laid down by the International Socialist Congress. Meetings of the International Socialist Bureau were held in July, after Austria declared war upon Serbia. It was proposed to hold the International Congress earlier, and a call went out for its delegates to meet in Paris in August. Events moved too rapidly, and the Paris Congress was not held.

Meanwhile the British Labour Party acting upon its understanding of International Socialist policy, three days before the British declaration of war, issued a manifesto over the joint signatures of Keir Hardie and Arthur Henderson, calling upon the organised forces of Labour throughout the country to hold demonstrations against war in the hope, that proved vain, of preserving peace. "Whatever may be the rights and wrongs of the sudden crushing attack made by the militarist Empire of Austria upon Serbia," said the manifesto, "it is certain that all countries likely to be drawn into the conflict must strain every nerve to prevent their Governments from committing them to war. Everywhere socialists and the organised forces of Labour are taking this course. Everywhere vehement protests are made against the greed and intrigues of militarists and armament-mongers. We call upon you to do the same here in Great Britain upon an even more impressive scale. Hold vast demonstrations against war in every industrial centre. Compel those of the governing class and their Press who are eager to commit you to co-operate with Russian despotism, to keep silent and respect the decision of the overwhelming majority of the people, who have neither part or lot in such infamy. The success of Russia at the present day will be a curse to the world. . . ."

The voice of Keir Hardie, particularly, sounded in this manifesto. But it did not reflect the actualities of the international situation. Although great meetings of protest were held by the Socialist and Trade Union organisations in all the capitals of Europe, the general protest against war was not made effective by any concerted industrial or political action on the part of the organised workers. On the contrary, the leaders of international Socialism, in their own countries, gave their support to their national governments. Violation of the neutrality of Belgium had a great deal to do with the final determination of organised Labour's attitude towards the Central Powers. An equally influential factor was the decision of the German socialists in the Reichstag to vote war credits to the Kaiser's Government. Vandervelde, chairman of the International Socialist Bureau, could find no reasonable alternative to a decision to enter the Belgian Cabinet, and his socialist colleagues, practically unanimously, endorsed his action. Even Jules Guesde and Gustave Herve, in France, embittered anti-militarists—the latter had once urged French soldiers to desert if war came—Marcel Sembat and Albert Thomas, all of them in their several ways, gave their support to their Government. The Social Democrats in the Russian Duma refused to vote credits to the Tsarist Government, but they too, like the socialists in Austria-Hungary, were unable to withstand the nationalist frenzy. In a word, the International Socialist Movement broke up on the outbreak of war.

In every Socialist Party there were those, at first a very tiny minority, who dissented from the decision of the majority, and who, like Liebknecht, Haase, and Ledebour, in Germany, returned very soon to preach International Socialism and strove to re-establish the solidarity of the working-class movement in opposition to war. From their protest, important consequences flowed. The most far-reaching developments which came later owed their origin to the Russian socialists in exile, who acknowledged the leadership of Lenin and Trotsky: they, with other leaders of minority groups in the international movement, convened conferences, in the Swiss villages of Zimmerwald, (in September 1915) and at Kienthal (in April 1916) at which a new alignment of socialist forces was formed and the rudiments of a Socialist peace policy formulated on the principles of no annexations, no indemnities, and the right of all peoples to self-determination. But the war had to be fought through four weary years before the significance of the Zimmerwald and Kienthal conferences became apparent to the Socialist Movement at large.

For British Labour the onset of war in 1914 brought to a head an inner conflict between the Socialist leaders whose approach to political and economic problems was along the path of theory rather than of practical experience, and the more matter-of-fact Trade Union leaders whose political philosophy was of a more empirical and pragmatic nature. It was the former group who wrote the manifestos and resolutions of the earliest August days in 1914; but it was the latter group whose influence made itself felt when Parliament had to face up to the question of voting war credits and rallying behind the Asquith Government. A special meeting of the National Executive of the Labour Party, held on the two days following the British declaration of war, adopted resolutions which defined the Movement's position more clearly than the Hardie-Henderson manifesto of August 1. These resolutions of the special meeting reiterated the fact that the Labour Movement had opposed the policy which produced the war, and affirmed that the Movement's duty was now to secure peace, "at the earliest possible moment on such conditions as will provide the best opportunities for the re-establishment of amicable feelings between the workers of Europe." But without in any way receding from its attitude of opposition to engagement in a European war, the Executive of the Party went on to advise all the Labour and Socialist organisations in the country to concentrate their energies upon measures to meet the difficulties which war would bring to the working people as long as the state of war lasted.

These war emergency measures had been considered at a national conference of representatives of all the Labour organisations on the day after war began. This conference constituted itself as a National Committee and appointed an Executive body, which came to be known as the War Emergency Workers' National Committee. It was a thoroughly representative body, with Robert Smillie, the miners' leader as its first chairman, and with representatives not only of the Trades Union Congress and the General Federation of Trade Unions, along with the Independent Labour Party, the Fabian Society, and the British Socialist Party (a new name of the S.D.P. which had split on the question of the war), but of the Co-operative Union, the Co-operative Congress, and of the big Trade Unions, such as the M.F.G.B., the National Union of Railwaymen, the Transport Workers' Federation—in fact, all the really strong and well-organised working-class bodies co-operated in carrying on an extraordinarily varied and active programme of industrial and social work in the interests of the working people. Inevitably as the war went on, this machinery developed into one of the means by which the country was enabled to prosecute the war ever more vigorously, and the national committees of the Labour Movement became more closely associated with the country's war effort.

The Parliamentary Labour Party had to face the problem of voting war credits, and lost its chairman (Ramsay MacDonald) as a consequence of its decision to let the first war credit of £100 million go to a vote (on August 7) without any statement of the Party's attitude on the issues of war policy which divided the Movement. Arthur Henderson succeeded MacDonald as chairman. The T.U.C. and the General Federation of Trade Unions united to declare an industrial truce (on August 24). The Labour Party entered into an electoral truce with the other Parties (on August 29), under which no by-elections were to be contested; vacated seats were to be retained by the Party to which the late Member belonged. The Labour Party's machinery was used for the purpose of enlisting recruits for the armed forces. And the Trades Union Congress on September 3, through a manifesto issued by its Parliamentary Committee committed the Movement finally to an all-out war effort against the Central Powers.

The Trades Union Congress should have met in September 1914. This annual meeting was abandoned for the first time in Congress history, but the manifesto of the Parliamentary Committee, addressed to the trade unionists of the country placed its attitude on the war beyond all doubt. It expressed satisfaction with the way in which the Labour Party in the House of Commons had responded to the appeal made to all political Parties to support voluntary recruitment. It expressed the opinion that the prospect of having to face conscription for military service should stimulate the manhood of the nation to volunteer. Trade unionists were called upon to remember that the result of the struggle in which the country had entered would determine the future of free and unfettered democratic government, which would prove to be the best guarantee for the preservation of the peace of the world. It asserted the view that men have a duty to perform in the common interest of the State. Equally the State (the manifesto declared) owed a duty to its citizens who were prepared—and readily prepared—to make sacrifices in its defence, and for the maintenance of its honour: "No single member of the community would do otherwise than uphold a Government which in such an important and vital matter took a liberal and even generous view of its responsibilities towards those citizens who come forward to assist in the defence of their country."

A later manifesto, signed by most of the Labour Members in Parliament, by the T.U.C. Parliamentary Committee, by the Management Committee of the General Federation of Trade Unions, and by other representative leaders of Labour, reaffirmed and underlined this earlier declaration of policy. The outbreak of war was attributed "to the deliberate act of the ruler of the Empire of Germany." If Britain had not kept her pledges to Belgium, a German victory would have been probable:

> "The victory of Germany would mean the death of democracy in Europe. . . . Until the Power which has pillaged and outraged Belgium and the Belgians, and plunged nearly the whole of Europe into the awful misery, suffering and horror of war is beaten there can be no peace. . . . When the time comes to discuss the terms of peace the Labour Movement will stand, as it has always stood, for an international agreement among all civilised nations that disputes and misunderstanding in the future shall be settled, not by machine-guns but by arbitration."

Later the organisations represented in the British section of the Labour and Socialist International were able (in February 1915) to get together representatives of the Labour and Socialist Parties of France, Belgium and Russia. In this, the first of a series of inter-Allied Socialist Conferences which made a significant contribution to the development of Labour's international policy, a resolution was adopted without dissent declaring that:

> "The invasion of Belgium and France by the German armies threatens the very existence of independent nationalities, and strikes a blow at all faith in treaties. In these circumstances a victory for German Imperialism would be the defeat and the destruction of democracy and liberty in Europe."

The resolution went on to state in broad outline the "War Aims" of Labour in the struggle. These were later to be more fully and firmly stated in an important document issuing from the later inter-Allied Socialist Conferences. There was insistence upon the demand that Belgium should be liberated and compensated; that the principle of self-determination of nations should be applied; that Poland should recover autonomy and independence; that all populations annexed by force from Alsace-Lorraine to the Balkans should have the right freely to dispose of themselves in accordance with the principle of self-determination, and that the working classes must re-unite—

> "in order to suppress secret diplomacy, put an end to the interests of militarism and those of the armament makers, and establish some international authority to settle points of difference among the nations, by compulsory conciliation and arbitration, and to compel all nations to maintain peace."

How the Labour Party met the war is sufficiently clearly explained from these citations from contemporary documents. They are significant, too, as containing the essential principles of Labour's international policy. This policy was steadily and consistently applied insofar as Labour influenced the making of the peace at the end of the war, in the building up of the League of Nations and especially the International Labour Organisation connected with the League, in its efforts to rebuild the Labour and Socialist International, and in its attitude on the question of armaments. Consistency does not stand high in the scale of political virtues. It is none the less instructive to see, as will be shown in later chapters, that the Labour Party did not depart from first principles in the War of 1914-18. It continued to follow the same clear line of policy in the two decades that separated the two World Wars; and in the second World War the Party was able to take its stand again with a clean conscience for the principles it sought to uphold in the first World War.

CHAPTER X

LABOUR'S FIRST COALITION

By HERBERT TRACEY

DURING the World War of 1914-18 the Labour Party had its first experience of Coalition Government. It was not a satisfactory experiment. The Labour Party entered upon it, in the spring of 1915, with a divided mind, and with many misgivings. These were shared by those who supported the decision to enter the Coalition Government as well as by those who opposed it. Political dissensions arising out of the agitation to introduce compulsory military service, recriminations over the alleged shortage of munitions, and the controversy excited by the conflict between Winston Churchill and Admiral Lord Fisher over the operations in Gallipoli, forced Asquith, as Prime Minister, to reconstruct his Government on a three-party basis. The Coalition Cabinet he formed comprised twelve Liberal Ministers, eight Conservatives, one non-Party Minister (Lord Kitchener), and one representative of the Labour Party (Arthur Henderson).

The Labour Party's decision to join the Asquith Government was far from being unanimous. It was taken only after a great deal of argument. On May 19, 1915 the National Executive of the Labour Party and the members of the Parliamentary Labour Party met separately to consider whether to accept the invitation from the Prime Minister to join a Coalition with their two historic rivals. Asquith proposed to give a Cabinet seat to Arthur Henderson, and to assign two less important positions in the Government to representatives of Labour. No political principles were at stake, Asquith said. It was to be a union of Parties exclusively for war purposes. But it caused difficulties inside the Labour Movement not merely because an article of the Party's Constitution prohibited it from joining any "capitalist" Government, but because it meant the surrender of the Party's independence and with it the right to criticise both the policy which led up to the war and the method of conducting the great struggle with the Central Powers.

By a vote of nine to three the National Executive in which Henderson's influence and authority as Secretary of the Party was supreme, decided to accept the invitation. The Parliamentary Party, on the other hand, was almost equally divided for and against acceptance, and by nine votes to eight decided to reject the invitation. The deadlock was broken at a joint meeting of the two bodies which decided by 17 votes to 11 that the Party should assist to form the Coalition. In accordance with this joint decision, Henderson became President of the Board of Trade with a seat in the Cabinet; William Brace, one of the Welsh miners' leaders, became Under-

Secretary for Home Affairs, and G. H. Roberts, a politically active trade unionist belonging to the Typographical Association, and at one time a leading propagandist in the early days of the I.L.P., became Junior Lord of the Treasury. In the light of after events, importance attaches to the fact that Henderson retained his position as Secretary of the Party, and had no difficulty in retaining his seat at Barnard Castle when he stood for re-election on his acceptance of a place in the Government.

Broadly speaking, the attitude of various sections of the Labour Movement towards the Asquith Coalition was determined by their attitude to the war. The solid Trade Union centre of the Labour Movement supported the decision, with one or two notable exceptions—J. H. Thomas, the ablest and most active of the railwaymen's leaders, was, for example, opposed to it, although he was a vigorous and resolute supporter of the national war effort. The Socialist bodies were divided: the I.L.P. whose leaders included Philip Snowden (who was on a visit to the United States when war broke out), Ramsay MacDonald, W. C. Anderson, Bruce Glasier and his wife, and others less well known, was practically unanimous in opposition; the Fabian Society was nearly as unanimous in support of it, but again with individual exceptions; and the Marxian Socialists who formed the S.D.P. were divided against it in the proportion of about two to one—Hyndman led one group in patriotic support of the war effort, and left the organisation he had created and, with one-third of its membership, formed the National Socialist Party, whilst the opponents of the war carried on the old organisation under the name of the British Socialist Party.

To the advocates of international Socialism and peace at almost any price, who found their rallying point in the I.L.P. and the B.S.P. the entrance of Labour representatives into the Coalition meant a betrayal of fundamental principles. Henderson and his two colleagues, they said, were nothing more than hostages in the camp of Labour's political enemies. When the war ended and the vital issues of peace and reconstruction had to be faced, the Labour Party would find itself, they predicted, compromised and discredited by its association with the Coalition Government. It might recover its independence but its political influence would be gone, and its leaders would have lost all prestige and authority in the organised working-class movement. The strongest argument they used against joining the Coalition was that the Labour Party would gain more and still be doing its duty in the national crisis, by staying out of the Coalition and continuing its policy of voluntary co-operation—a policy symbolised by the inter-Party agreement to maintain a political truce during the war and not to contest by-elections one against the other. Philip Snowden put the issue clearly and with characteristic brevity and emphasis when he wrote:

> "The whole Labour Movement will be united on one point—namely, that it is the duty of the Movement to help the nation in its present difficulties. But the

> point of difference is that some members think that the Labour Party can be much more useful outside the Government than inside it. The acceptance of office in the Coalition Government will take away the freedom of independent criticism, which at a time like this may often be the most valuable service a small Party can render to the nation." [1]

Apart from such considerations of general political principles there were, too, difficult questions of policy to embarrass the Party leaders who were in favour of joining the Coalition. Compulsory military service was one of the most serious of these questions of policy, but by no means the only one. It came very near to wrecking the Coalition Government early in its career. The whole Labour Movement was strongly and bitterly opposed to conscription. Labour entered the war to defend democracy against Prussian militarism, and conscription was to them the very symbol of militarism. To preserve the voluntary system Labour undertook to join in a joint campaign with the other Parties to recruit men for military service. On the special invitation of the Prime Minister and the Minister for War, the Party undertook a special recruiting effort on Labour platforms in the autumn of 1915. They supported the effort made by Lord Derby, to whom was entrusted the responsibility of justifying the voluntary system by recruiting men for the Armed Forces. In connection with Lord Derby's campaign, Asquith gave a pledge that single men must join first in order to induce married men to attest.

The campaign failed to produce the desired results: it was stated authoritatively that over 600,000 young unmarried men eligible for recruitment had failed to respond to the call. The Government pledge that no married man would be called up until the young unmarried men were brought in was preserved in the Bill which was then introduced imposing compulsory service on young men. This measure aroused strong opposition inside the Labour Movement, and a special National Congress representative of the whole Movement, industrial and political, was called to consider this grave decision. The Conference met on January 6, 1916, this being the first occasion on which the Trades Union Congress, the General Federation of Trade Unions and the Labour Party met in joint session. Delegates to the Conference were aware that the three National Committees controlling the three bodies had tried to find a way out of the impasse on the conscription issue, and had been unable to agree on anything more than a proposal that members of the Labour Party in the House of Commons should be free to vote for or against the Conscription Bill as they choose. The Conference refused to sanction even this compromise. By nearly 2,000,000 votes against rather more than three-quarters of a million, it adopted a resolution recommending the Parliamentary Party to oppose the Conscription Bill in all its stages.

Arthur Henderson and his two Labour colleagues in the Government had then no alternative but to offer their resignation. The Prime Minister

[1] In the *Manchester Guardian*, May 21, 1915.

took the unprecedented step of meeting the National Executive of the Labour Party. He gave an official assurance to this body that nothing in the nature of industrial conscription was contained in or implied in the Bill; that there would be no extension of compulsion to married men; that the Bill was to operate during the war only; that the Tribunals to be set up for hearing appeals by conscripted men would be civilian and not military courts; and that exemption of conscientious objectors to military service would be safeguarded. On these assurances the resignation of Henderson and his colleagues was withdrawn, pending discussion at the next Annual Conference of the Party. In the Parliamentary debates on the Conscription Bill opposition fell to negligible proportions: the Labour vote against the Bill amounted to no more than ten Members, and thirty Liberal Members also voted against it; the second reading being carried on January 12, by 433 votes against 41, including tellers. Henderson, of course, spoke and voted in support of the second reading, and amongst the Party leaders who opposed it were MacDonald, Snowden and J. H. Thomas.

The difficult position in which Henderson and his two Labour colleagues were placed inside the Coalition was further illustrated by the decisions of this Annual Party Conference, which was held in Bristol in January 1916; the Conference which should have been held in 1915 was postponed, and this Bristol Conference was the first opportunity the Labour Movement had had since the outbreak of war to make known its view of the political developments in which the Party had become involved. By the emphatic vote of 1,674,000 against 269,000 the action of the Party authorities in agreeing to join the Coalition Government was endorsed. By nearly as large a vote, 1,622,000 against 495,000, the delegates also agreed that in the best interests of the country the Party should continue to support the Coalition, notwithstanding the Cabinet's decision to introduce compulsory military service. These votes were decisive evidence of the Labour Movement's attitude on the war. But another series of votes was evidence that the Party was far from willing to accept everything that the Coalition Government did, on the plea of war necessity. By as many as 1,716,000 votes to 360,000 the Conference declared its continuing opposition to conscription.

The military fortunes of the country did not favour the opponents of conscription. Four months after the Party Conference had declared so firmly its unwillingness to accept compulsory military service, the Party leaders had to consider whether they would agree to the extension of compulsion to married men. At the Party's instigation a secret session of Parliament enabled the Government to explain the position, with the result that the Labour M.P.'s were given a free hand in deciding how they would record their individual vote. The issue was clarified for most of them by the decision of the T.U.C. Parliamentary Committee and the Management Committee of the G.F.T.U. to support the new proposals, on assurances given by the Government that the legislation would automatically lapse on the coming of peace and would not be used as an indirect means of coercion of the workers in the war industries.

Relations between the Government and the Unions had by then been placed on a fairly stable footing. Credit for this lies equally with Lloyd George on the Government side and Arthur Henderson for the Trade Unions. The two National Committees of the Trade Union Movement—the Parliamentary Committee of the T.U.C. and the Management Committee of the G.F.T.U.—declared an industrial truce soon after the war began, and the trade disputes in progress at the time were very speedily settled. In March 1915, the problem was tackled of placing the relations of the Unions with the Government on a firmer foundation. In the very early months of the war the increasing demands of the Army for recruits came into conflict with the manpower needs of the war industries. There was a serious shortage of skilled labour in the engineering and shipbuilding trades. Efforts that were set on foot to ease the situation by persuading the Trade Unions to relax restrictions and workshop practices of peace-time were not successful until in March 1915, representatives of thirty-three leading Unions came into conference with Lloyd George at the Treasury—he then being still Chancellor of the Exchequer. The summons which went on to all the Unions that were directly concerned with the production of munitions invited them:

> "To consult with the Chancellor of the Exchequer and the President of the Board of Trade in certain matters of importance to Labour arising out of the recent decision of the Government embodied in the Defence of the Realm (Amendment) Act, to take further steps to organise the resources of the country to meet naval and military requirements.

At this Conference the Trade Unions agreed to surrender existing trade practices, rules and customs affecting production in return for a pledge from the Government that any departure during the war from practices ruling in the workshops, shipyards and other industries, should be for the duration of the war only, and would be absolutely and completely reinstated when war was over. This pledge was embodied in the Munitions Act, which also provided that no worker should leave one employer and engage with another for higher wages without a leaving certificate. The Treasury Agreement embodied an undertaking on the part of the Unions to forego stoppages of work on account of trade disputes during the war, and to have recourse to arbitration, whether by a single arbitrator agreed upon by the parties or appointed by the Board of Trade, or by a Court of Arbitration upon which employers and labour were equally represented. An undertaking was given by the Government to restrict the profits of firms engaged in war production as a part of the agreement for the relaxation of Trade Union restrictions.

It was also agreed at the Treasury Conference that a National Advisory Committee of Labour should be set up to facilitate the carrying out of recommendations embodied in the Agreement. To ensure the prompt and most efficient application of all the available productive resources of the country to the manufacture and supply of munitions, a joint committee had already been set up, of which Arthur Henderson was a member. But as the problems of war-time industry multiplied, the need for more effective joint co-operation became urgent, and steps were taken to develop the line of policy laid down in the Treasury Agreement.

At the Annual Trades Union Congress, held at Bristol in the autumn of 1915, Lloyd George, who had then become Minister of Munitions, made a strong and effective plea for the help of the Unions in solving the manpower problem. The T.U.C. responded by calling a Conference of Trade Union Executives to meet the National Advisory Committee, to consider the question of introducing female labour on a large scale in the war trades, and to encourage the policy of "diluting" skilled labour by the upgrading of semi-skilled and unskilled workers. This Conference of Union Executives endorsed the proposal to establish a Joint Committee representing the Unions on the one hand, and the National Labour Advisory Committee and the Ministry of Munitions on the other, with additional members, to advise and assist the Ministry in carrying out its manpower programme. In accordance with that decision a Central Munitions Labour Supply Committee was constituted with Arthur Henderson as its chairman, and composed of representatives of both the skilled and unskilled Unions concerned, with Mary Macarthur representing the women workers, along with representatives of both the Supply Departments and the Labour Department of the Ministry of Munitions. Local Labour Advisory Boards came into existence to assist in implementing the Government's munitions programme.

It cannot be said that this improvised machinery of labour regulation enabled every industrial difficulty to be overcome without serious stoppages of work. The Industrial Truce entered into at the beginning of the war disposed only temporarily of some contentious wage questions, notably the claim put forward by the Clydeside engineering and shipbuilding workers for increased wages. This claim, which fell into abeyance at the beginning of the war, was renewed at the end of 1915, and led to a number of unauthorised strikes in the Clyde area. It produced, among other unfortunate consequences, a rift between the Union Executives and local leaders of their rank and file membership acting as shop stewards. Emergency legislation had been enacted which provided penalties applicable to employers locking out workmen as well as to workmen on strike. Among the regulations under the Defence of the Realm Act was one which gave the competent military authority the right to remove suspected persons from any area and prescribing heavy sentences for persons attempting to cause sedition or disaffection either in the Armed Forces or among the civilian population, or trying to impede or restrict the production, repair or transport of war materials; and such sentences were in fact imposed upon a few people found guilty of instigating strikes.

Such regulations were found impracticable in the case of the strike of 200,000 miners in South Wales who ceased work within thirteen days of the passing of the Munitions of War Act which made strikes illegal. In this case the Government chose rather to negotiate than to use force—a decision with which Arthur Henderson had a great deal to do. A more difficult situation arose in the Clyde area soon after the South Wales dispute was settled, when a body of workers came out on strike in protest against the dismissal of two shipwrights. The local leaders in this Clyde stoppage were brought before a Tribunal, and penalties were imposed upon seventeen of them; some finally agreed to pay the fines and escape imprisonment, but three refused, and their subsequent arrest and imprisonment led to a very serious state of affairs. The Clydeside leaders threatened, in the name of 97,500 workpeople in the Clyde Valley, a stoppage of work unless the three men were released within three days.

Trouble on the Clyde found its focus in the shop stewards' organisation which the Union Executives generally refused to recognise. At the end of 1915 Henderson and other responsible Trade Union leaders prevailed upon Lloyd George to visit Glasgow to meet the shop stewards and explain his Labour policy. The meetings which the Minister addressed were stormy; the shop stewards who had formed themselves into the Clyde Workers' Committee put forward a demand for the complete nationalisation of industry and an effective share in control for the workers as a condition of their co-operation in securing output and dilution. This programme was framed with an eye on the end of the war rather than in the expectation of anything being done about it whilst the war went on.

The Minister's visit did not dispose of the crisis on the Clyde by any means. Defence of the Realm Regulations had finally to be invoked against the leading members of the Clyde Workers' Committee, and six of them were deported from the area and sent to other parts of the country. Unrest died down thereafter to some extent on the Clyde, but there were other disquieting manifestations of the influence exercised by the shop stewards' movement, notably in Manchester. When Lloyd George became Prime Minister he appointed a series of Commissions in mid-1917 to make investigations in various parts of the country and to report upon the industrial unrest with a view to a policy being framed by the Government. This inquiry produced useful material and supplied the impulse to action taken later by the Lloyd George Government in appointing the Whitley Committee upon Relations of Employers and Employed.

The industrial unrest found a parallel in the political crisis which was precipitated towards the end of 1916. The rock on which the Asquith

Coalition foundered was the proposal, sponsored by Lloyd George, that the conduct of the war should be placed in the hands of a War Committee of three members. As originally planned, this Committee was to include the First Lord of the Admiralty and the Secretary of State for War—the third member to be, obviously, Lloyd George himself. This triumvirate was to have full powers, subject to the supreme authority of the Prime Minister, who was to have the right, in his discretion, to refer any matter to the Cabinet. Decisions of the War Committee were to be carried out by the Government Department concerned, unless the Cabinet, on reference by the Prime Minister, reversed a decision of the Committee. Asquith as Prime Minister rejected these proposals. He insisted that the Prime Minister must be chairman of the proposed War Committee: "He cannot be relegated to the position of an arbiter in the background or a referee to the Cabinet."

In the ensuing discussions Henderson was associated with the negotiations that Asquith carried on with his Liberal and Conservative colleagues. In the effort to preserve the Coalition under Asquith's leadership, Lloyd George forced matters to a crisis by the offer of his resignation on the ground that the policy of the Government had shown "delay, hesitation, lack of forethought and vision," for which he could not accept responsibility. A conference of the political leaders at Buckingham Palace, under the chairmanship of the King, failed to solve the crisis. Asquith tried to break the deadlock by securing authority from the King to ask for and accept the resignation of all his colleagues, and to form a new Government. He made this known to Lloyd George on December 4, 1916, and on the following day Lloyd George gave in his resignation, embodied in a long letter setting forth his view of the Asquith Administration in uncompromising terms. Asquith countered this move by resigning himself, and Bonar Law was summoned by the King and given the task of forming a new Government. The Conservative Leader proposed to take Henderson and Arthur Balfour to the Palace to see whether they could preserve national unity by forming a Government under Balfour's leadership. The consultations broke down on Asquith's indignant refusal to accept this solution. He rejected the suggestion that he, who had held first place for eight years, should be asked to take a secondary position. His refusal to serve in an Administration formed by Bonar Law was the main reason why the latter declined to undertake the responsibility of forming a Government. The task then passed to Lloyd George, who took it knowing (as he wrote later in his memoirs) that "at least half of my own Party and more than half of the Labour Party" were bitterly hostile, and a considerable section of the Conservatives—including most of their leaders—were suspicious and distrustful.

Opinion within the ranks of the Labour Movement was unanimous against the methods by which the first Coalition was destroyed and Mr. Asquith deposed. Lloyd George, as he made clear in his later account of these transactions, felt it to be a matter of the first national importance to bring the Labour Party into active co-operation with his Government. He made up his mind (according to his own account) that in addition to Henderson, who was the only Labour Member then in the Cabinet, and who was not suggested as a member of the proposed small War Committee, there must be a more substantial and effective representation of Labour in the new Administration. He also decided that one of the Party's "most prominent and respected leaders" should be a member of the small body which would have the supreme direction of the war.

Lloyd George had to overcome the strong scruples of Arthur Henderson who was brought into the conclave of Liberal Ministers whom Asquith called together at the height of the crisis: all of them (except Henderson) pledged themselves to refuse to serve in any Government of which Asquith was not the chief. Henderson then consulted his own Labour colleagues and found them divided on the question of giving their support to the Lloyd George Government. It was, however, agreed that Lloyd George should be asked to meet the representatives of Labour. He told them that it was obvious that "no Government could be carried on in this country, whether during war or peace, without, I won't say the support of Labour, but the co-operation of Labour." Upon Labour's determination to help to win the war everything depended. He went on to pay a warm tribute to Henderson "who has been my colleague for eighteen months or two years, and let me say at once that I never want a more loyal colleague. He has faced tasks which I thought were difficult, but which were twice as difficult because of his association with Labour: he has faced them with courage and with very true comradeship and I shall always be grateful to him." History repeated itself almost in these identical words before the break-up of the second Coalition formed by Winston Churchill in 1940!

At this meeting with the Labour representatives Lloyd George proceeded to outline his proposal for the inclusion of Labour in the Government he had undertaken to form: "not a subordinate position, but a real share in the War Committee to direct this war; a real share in the Administration by those who are not members of the War Committee." He said it was essential to have a Labour Ministry which would incorporate the Labour section of the Board of Trade and the Labour section of the Ministry of Munitions under one head. This new Department, he declared, would certainly be one of the most important Departments in the Government. He indicated his intention to place the Pensions Department under the control of a Labour Minister, and suggested there should be two Under-Secretaries and a representative of Labour in the Whips Office as well. On other questions of policy he said that he saw only one solution for the problem in the mining industry, and that was that the State should have control of it. He personally thought the same line should be taken in shipping; and he promised to appoint a

Controller to supervise the production and distribution of food. When the time came to make peace he felt (he said) that it was inconceivable that any Minister would make terms of peace without consulting the representatives of Labour.

Following Lloyd George's statement the Joint Conference of the National Executive of the Labour Party and the Parliamentary Party discussed the situation in a debate which was officially described later as "remarkable for its frank facing of the issues involved and the general straightforward and unimpassioned declarations of a large number of the members present." It was finally decided by a majority of five to accept the invitation to co-operate actively in the war direction by permitting some of its leading members to join the Government. Discussion in the Party meeting before the vote was taken reflected the same broad division between those who supported and those who opposed the war. Arthur Henderson, William Brace, George Roberts, George Barnes, James O'Grady, and other influential representatives of the Trade Unions in the Party, were for acceptance of Lloyd George's invitation. They won to their support John R. Clynes, who had been opposed to the first Coalition, and also J. H. Thomas. Philip Snowden and the I.L.P. Group generally were still irreconcilable. But the Party's decision, as Lloyd George admitted later, assured the success of his task in the "formation of a truly National Ministry." It was the deciding factor in the attitude of the Conservative Party leaders. So the first War Cabinet was constituted, with Lloyd George, Lord Curzon, Lord Milner, Bonar Law, and Arthur Henderson as its members in supreme control of the war effort. The new Prime Minister fulfilled his promise to create a Ministry of Labour, and placed in charge of it John Hodge, a sturdy trade unionist who rendered yeoman service in unionising the iron and steel trades. George N. Barnes, a former secretary of the old Amalgamated Society of Engineers, became the head of the newly-created Pensions Ministry. Both of these Ministers were of Cabinet rank. William Brace continued as Under-Secretary for Home Affairs; G. H. Roberts became Parliamentary Secretary of the Board of Trade, and James Parker succeeded Roberts in the position of Junior Lord of the Treasury. Early in 1917 Stephen Walsh, a tough little leader of the Lancashire miners, became Parliamentary Secretary for National Service. When the Food Ministry was set up and Lord Rhondda became Food Controller, John R. Clynes became its Parliamentary Secretary and discharged his responsibilities in the House of Commons with such cool competence and ability that he inevitably became Food Minister on the death of Lord Rhondda in the following year.

The circumstances attendant upon the withdrawal of Labour from the Lloyd George Coalition must be left for another chapter. They were such as to weaken temporarily the electoral position of the Labour Party, under the conditions of the "Coupon" election which Lloyd George hastened to hold as soon as the war was over ; complicated as this General Election was by the new Franchise Act which increased enormously the number of the electors, and gave votes to women. On a long-term view of politics, however, Labour came out of its first experience of Coalition Government with a new-found sense of Party solidarity, and with a programme of national and international resettlement and reconstruction which made it the strongest moral force in the immediate post-war years.

CHAPTER XI

SOCIAL PLANNING AND POLITICAL REORGANISATION

By HERBERT TRACEY

EXPERIENCE of Coalition Government and reflections upon the course of events during the 1914-18 War produced three classic Labour documents. One was a *Memorandum on War Aims*, which was concerned with the problems of the peace settlement from the standpoint of international Socialism. The second document, entitled *Labour and the New Social Order* set forth the principles of Labour policy in terms of the social and economic reconstruction that had to be undertaken after the war. The third document was a new Constitution for the Labour Party which broadened the basis of membership and fortified the constituency organisation of the Party in good time for the General Election which the Prime Minister (Mr. Lloyd George) precipitated in December 1918.

More clearly than any other development of the war years these three documents epitomised the history of the Labour Party's relationships with the older Parties and its rediscovery of its international Socialist mission. Their practical significance lies in the evidence they furnish of the Labour Movement's instinctive sense of the importance of maintaining unity in thought and action, and of broadening the foundations of its political organisation. The resistance of the Labour Movement to disruptive influences, either inside or from without, is one of its most remarkable characteristics.

Not only during the first World War, but in the inter-war years, during the lifetime of the Second Labour Government, and throughout the period of the Churchill Coalition Government in the second World War disruptive tendencies were let loose inside the organised working-class movement.

Deliberate attempts were made from the outside to destroy its solidarity. Rival organisations were called into being with the object of driving a wedge, particularly, between the Trade Unions and the Party. Headstrong and short-sighted members of the Party exercising considerable influence among the Trade Unions embraced policies and theories of political organisation which, if they had had their way, would have wrecked the Party, or at least would have diverted it from the straight and narrow path that led it ultimately to victory at the polls.

Against all these dividing forces, conspiracies and diversions, the Labour Movement has always stood like a rock. How the Labour Party during the first World War successfully withstood disruption from without, and re-established a united and stronger front when the war came to an

[Barratt's

THE LABOUR PARTY AS OFFICIAL OPPOSITION
On the Terrace of the House of Commons, 1923

end, will be seen when the origin and purpose of these three historical documents are explained. They are connected both in time and in the web of political events.

The *Memorandum on War Aims* marked the final phase of the Labour Party's strong effort to secure a democratic and just peace founded upon international Socialist principles. It was a definite step towards the restoration of the International Labour and Socialist Movement since it brought together the Socialist and Labour organisations of the Allied nations on the basis of agreed principles for the making of the peace. When war broke out, the Second International, successor of the First International Association of Working Men, founded by Karl Marx in 1864, which expired in 1873, presented an appearance of massive strength. It was more an illusion than a reality. International Socialist organisation reappeared at the beginning of the present century, after an interval of about a score of years following the collapse of the First International. It comprised, when the first World War came, about twenty-seven Parties with an aggregate membership in excess of 12,000,000. The British Labour Movement was represented in it by the Labour Party, the I.L.P., the B.S.P., and the Fabian Society, these constituting the British section.

The abortive efforts made by the International Socialist leaders to prevent the war have already been described. International Socialism suffered an irreparable loss in the assassination of the leader of French Socialism, Jean Jaurés, on the eve of the war; but even had he lived to exert his immense personal influence, it is more than doubtful whether the International Socialist Movement could have been held together. As it was, it was badly divided. But it did not altogether fall apart. The International Socialist Bureau in the skilful hands of its secretary, Camille Huysmans, continued to function, though it was driven out of its headquarters in Brussels by the German invasion of Belgium, and its contacts with many of its affiliated bodies were broken. Huysmans kept the International Socialist Bureau going, first at The Hague, then in London, and finally in Stockholm, where the Dutch members, in agreement with the Swedish and Danish Socialist Parties, co-operated to form a Dutch-Scandinavian Committee, over which Hjalmar Branting, the leader of the Swedish Party, and one of the strongest Socialist supporters of the Allied nations among the neutral nations, presided as its chairman. This was an important link in the chain of events leading up to the reconstitution of the Labour and Socialist International and the framing of peace terms on the basis of Socialist principles.

Through Huysmans and the organisation he was able to rebuild, communications were maintained with affiliated bodies in both the Allied and neutral countries. Neither was the line of communication broken entirely with the Socialist Movement in Germany and Austria-Hungary. Relations were established with such Socialist leaders as

Liebknecht, Rosa Luxemburg, Clara Zetkin, and a few others in Germany who opposed the war from the outset, reinforced later by contact with veteran socialists like Bernstein, Kautsky, Haase and others, who subsequently ranged themselves in support of the policy of a negotiated peace.

As the war continued, this objective of peace by negotiation found adherence in all the Socialist Parties. Its development was facilitated by the consultations arranged at Stockholm by the Huysmans-Branting Committee with delegates of the various countries involved in the war. The Labour Party and the other bodies forming the British section were invited to participate in the Stockholm consultations. But "peace by negotiation" was a controversial phrase, defining an issue that had divided the British Labour Movement at the outset of the war. The I.L.P. and that section of the B.S.P. which opposed the war made it their policy from the very beginning. They strove to get the British Labour Movement to endorse the policy of peace by negotiation at the earliest possible moment, and sought to obtain the Movement's repudiation of the policy of the "knock-out blow" which Lloyd George in particular proclaimed as the fundamental war aim of the British people. The Labour Party, strongly influenced by the Trade Unions, could not identify itself with a policy that implied no difference in the degree of war guilt between Germany and the Allied nations. The Party was confirmed in its stand against the idea of "peace without victory," by the evolution of the war policy of President Wilson, who translated the Allies' war aims into his Fourteen Points, involving unconditional acceptance of the Allies' terms by Germany.

A resolution was put forward at the 1917 Conference of the Labour Party in Manchester, demanding that the Government should declare "its readiness to enter into immediate negotiations for peace." This proposal was emphatically rejected by 1,697,000 votes against 302,000. The Conference did not consider that the time had come when it was possible to reconstitute the Labour and Socialist International. British Labour, however, felt that it was now necessary to formulate Allied war aims. It undertook the responsibility, therefore, of convening in London conferences of the Labour and Socialist Parties of the Allied nations, including the American Federation of Labour; all sections of the Allied Parties being invited to send representatives for purposes only of consultation and elucidation of their views, on the understanding that no decisions of a binding character would be taken in these meetings. Complications arose when the Russian Council of Workmen's and Soldiers' Deputies, the revolutionary organisation which led the Russian people in the first stages of their revolution, issued a manifesto calling on the Socialist and Labour Parties of all countries to participate in a Conference to secure a working-class peace without annexations and without indemnities. Amidst the confusion and cross purposes of this period of political and social history, the consistency and far-sightedness of the Labour Party leadership was justified by the ultimate outcome. Almost simultaneously the march of events decided the resignation of Arthur Henderson from the War Cabinet, the withdrawal of the Labour Party from the Lloyd George Coalition, and the publication of the *Memorandum on War Aims*. Its publication, following the consideration given to it by the Inter-Allied Labour and Socialist Conferences, led logically to the production of Labour's post-war programme of reconstruction, *Labour and the New Social Order*, and to give effect and force to the Party's claim to national leadership in the post-war years, came also in logical sequence, the new Party Constitution.

The controversy over the proposal to call the Stockholm Conference made a great deal of noise in the world. It had political consequences in this country which were of more far-reaching import than was seen at the time; for, arising out of Arthur Henderson's breach with Lloyd George and the War Cabinet, came the Labour Party's decision to challenge the older Parties for first place in a General Election conducted on a wider franchise than ever before in the country's history, including enfranchised women.

In its declaration of war aims British Labour revealed itself as firmly and consistently opposed to any settlement of the European struggle calculated to prepare fresh conflicts, create new grievances, and subject various peoples to the double plague of armaments and war. It accepted President Wilson's Fourteen Points as guiding principles in the making of the peace. It did not find the Peace Treaties issuing from the Conference at Versailles as conforming wholly to these principles. In essential respects, the Party said, the Versailles settlement was opposed to the declarations of President Wilson, and to those made by the Inter-Allied Labour and Socialist Movement. The settlement was defective, in the Party's view, from the standpoint of world peace, and bore evidence of compromise influenced by capitalist imperialism. The imperfections of the Treaty must be eradicated, and its provisions adapted by the League of Nations to the requirements of a changing European Order, the Party leaders declared: and from its birth the League of Nations, and the International Labour Organisation, received the unwavering and resolute support of the Labour Movement.

So deep was Labour's interest in the League that a Special Congress, representing both the industrial and political organisations, was summoned in London upon the publication of the League of Nations Covenant. This Special Congress welcomed whole-heartedly the publication of the Covenant, but did not accept all its provisions uncritically and without demur. In fact, a series of amendments was proposed, calling for a modification of its main articles. Among other things, Labour wanted the League to admit Soviet Russia to membership, and also the former enemy countries, on their acceptance of the purposes, the constitution, and the obligations of the League. Direct control by the League of the manufacture of armaments, as well as of armed forces for police purposes, was another amendment.

Labour's attitude to the League, indeed, corresponded to its conception of the European Settlement as presented in the *Memorandum on War Aims*. Taking its stand upon the firm ground of principle, the Party found itself more directly in opposition to the policy of the Coalition Government. It challenged very sharply the action of the Allied Governments in relation to Soviet Russia. From the Lloyd George Government it sought to obtain an assurance that it was not the intention of the British Government to interfere with the right of the Russian people to decide for themselves their own form of government, and asked the Government to pledge itself that British armed forces on Russian territory would be withdrawn. No satisfactory answer was given by the Lloyd George Government to the demand for the withdrawal of British troops and the cessation of the aid then being given by the British Government to the operation of counter-revolutionary forces in Russia. Proposals for "direct action" by the organised workers to stop the supply of munitions to reverse the Government policy of intervention, and to enforce its raising of the blockade against Russia, received widespread support; and Councils of Action were formed throughout the country to implement the Movement's demand for non-intervention in Russian affairs. But these controversies merged, at the end of 1918, into the wider argument which the General Election of that year was called upon to settle.

This General Election marked a turning-point in British political history. It involved, in the first place, a direct appeal by the Labour Party to a greatly enlarged electorate of 21,000,000, the great majority of whom were voting for the first time, among them the enfranchised women. Secondly, the electorate was in possession of a clear statement of the Labour Party's programme of national reconstruction, as set forth in *Labour and the New Social Order*. And in the third place, the contest was a clear-cut issue between the Labour Party on the one hand, and a combination of the older Parties under the leadership of Lloyd George. It is true that a section of the Liberal Party, still loyal to the Asquith leadership, made an independent bid for existence in the 1918 Election. But to all intents and purposes the contest was between Labour and a Coalition of Liberal and Conservative candidates, who appeared before the electorate wearing the "coupon" awarded to them by the organisers of the Coalition Parties. Less than 60 per cent. of the electors, however, took the trouble to record a vote. Labour's candidates numbered 361, and their aggregate vote constituted about one-fifth of the total poll for all candidates. If seats had been distributed on the basis of proportional representation, the Party would have had one-third of the representation in the House of Commons; but actually it obtained no more than fifty-seven seats. Yet, in this election the dividing line in matters of principles and practical policy was clearly drawn between the Labour Party and the Parties in the Coalition.

In *Labour and the New Social Order* it was made clear, beyond any possibility of misunderstanding, that the Labour Party was opposed to any patching up of the old economic order. It turned its back resolutely on the conditions of poverty and starvation which were all that capitalist society allowed to millions of workers. It stood for such a systematic reconstruction of industrial and social relations that would give to the workers by hand and by brain the full fruits of their labour. The essence of Labour's policy is in those words. Specifically wide measures of reform were advocated in this classical document. A just and generous provision was claimed for discharged soldiers and sailors, along with reinstatement in civil employment at Trade Union rates of wages with complete security against involuntary unemployment. Complete fulfilment of the nation's pledge to restore to the Trade Unions the conditions and customs of the workshops which the Unions had consented to relinquish in the public interest during the war. Freedom of speech and publication, freedom to travel and choose one's occupation, the abolition of all compulsory military service, and the completion of political democracy by adult suffrage, with equal rights of voting for both sexes, were among Labour's aims. Specific political measures proposed included the fullest possible measure of Home Rule for Ireland. State ownership of railways and canals, and the creation under public control of a national system of transport; nationalisation of the coal and iron mines; the provision and management by the Government, in conjunction with the local authorities, of the new gigantic super power stations which were projected as a means of providing electricity at the lowest possible cost; and the effective maintenance of the standard of life for the whole nation by the suitable amendment and extension of the factories, mines, Trade Boards and similar legislation; reorganisation of agriculture and rural life by the resumption of State ownership of the land and its use as State farms, small-holdings and allotments, or co-operative enterprises; a substantial and permanent improvement in the housing of the whole people as a comprehensive national measure, to be carried through by the local authorities, with grants-in-aid sufficient to prevent any charge on the rates; a national system of education, free and effectively open to all persons, irrespective of their means, from the nursery school to the university; the nationalisation of life assurance; development of the Post Office savings bank into a universal national banking system; and a taxation policy, including a much steeper graduation and increase of the super-tax, the taking of unearned increment by the taxation of land values, the increase of death duties, and the imposition of a carefully graduated capital tax, as Labour's method of placing the financial burden on the broadest backs—these were the main points of the reconstruction policy placed before the electorate in *Labour and the New Social Order* and in the election manifestos.

It was the programme of a political Party which had ceased to regard itself as a class Party. In the political sense Labour has never accepted a simple class definition of its aims and purposes. It has claimed to represent "the people," the working masses, whose political and social interests the older Parties had failed adequately to serve. But the Labour Party in its original constitution limited actual membership to members of Trade Unions and affiliated Socialist Societies, and other recognised working-class bodies. It was not in the literal sense a national political Party, under its original constitution. Arthur Henderson, with customary force and clarity, put the issue plainly before the Special Delegate Conference of the Party in February 1918, which ratified the reconstruction programme and the new constitution.

It was obvious to all, Henderson said, that the great world conflict in which they had been involved, had created for political parties an entirely new situation. Problems of a social and economic character that had been with them in all the years they had been an organised political force had been aggravated and had become much more acute and much more pressing as a result of the experiences of the war. Remedies had to be found which went right down to the roots, and involved a reconstruction of society. It was essential, not only to put their programme before the country, but at the same time to put their own house in order so that there might be behind that programme the greatest and most highly organised social and political force the country had known. When they looked at their present position as an organised Party, delegates would realise, he suggested, that their organisation was altogether inadequate, because of the limitation they inherited from the resolution of the Trades Union Congress, in 1899, which called the Party, as a Labour Representation Committee, into being.

Up to the moment at which he was speaking, the Party existed as a political federation of Trade Unions, Socialist bodies and Co-operative Societies. In recent years local Labour Parties had developed, many of them out of the existing Trades Councils. But the organisation was essentially a federation. The constitution did not provide for individual membership. They were in the position of saying to the electors in 400 constituencies: "You have votes, and we want you to give them to the Labour candidate, but we won't give you membership in the Labour Party." Was that the way to political success? They were faced with two possibilities. They could scrap the whole of the existing machinery and begin again *de novo*, which would mean ceasing to exist as a federation, and building up from a new foundation a political organisation based solely upon individual membership. That was not a practical proposition, in view of the near approach of a General Election.

Keeping in mind all the social and economic problems facing the

Labour Movement, what was proposed as the best thing to do was to stick by the federation, but to graft on to it such a form of constituency organisation, linked up with the local Labour Parties, or Trades Councils, as would remove the restriction on individual membership, and throw the Party open to every person who chose to apply for membership, and subscribe to the constitution and programme of the Party. This accorded with the declared aim of the Party as stated in the new Constitution: "to secure for the producers by hand or by brain, the full fruits of their industry, and the most equitable distribution thereof that may be possible, upon the basis of the common ownership of the means of production, and the best obtainable system of popular administration and control of each industry or service," and "generally to promote the political, social and economic emancipation of the people, and more particularly of those who depend directly upon their own exertion by hand or by brain for the means of life."

The forceful presentation of the case for the new constitution which Henderson made supplied the answer to those who contended that the old constitution was sufficiently broad to let into the Party anybody who wanted to come in. This was obviously not the case, since in order to become attached to the Labour Party it was necessary to join either a Trade Union or an affiliated Socialist Society, or other attached working-class organisation, and the plain fact was, as Henderson pointed out, that these affiliated bodies had not expanded their membership, in correspondence with the broadening of the electoral franchise. The combined membership of the three Socialist Societies in affiliation with the Party at that time was no more than 75,000. There were 6,000,000 new women electors, most of them the wives of working men: but they were not eligible for membership in Trade Unions, except where they were themselves wage earners, and it seemed unlikely that any of the three Socialist organisations, or all together, could gather them in. Moreover, the close political association of workers by hand and by brain, promised a new source of strength to the Party. It opened the door to the reinforcement of the Party's appeal to the electorate, as a Party of the people, and one in which class differences were transcended by a new political unity and a common social purpose.

At the 1918 General Election political conditions did not favour Labour's bid for power, on the basis of this broader conception of its mission. It took time to build up the local Labour Parties. Individual membership grew, however, steadily, if slowly—and, as political time is measured, not so slowly after all. Within four years there was another General Election, and in the 1922 contest the Party put fifty more candidates in the field than in 1918, and nearly trebled its representation in Parliament, doubling its total vote: 414 seats were contested as against 361 in 1918, and 142 members were returned to the House of Commons as against 57 in 1918, the Labour vote rising to nearly 4,250,000 from about 2,250,000 in 1918. This was a substantial advance in four years. It was greatly accelerated in the General Election results of the succeeding year. In 1923 Labour increased its representation in Parliament from 142 to 191, and its total vote showed an increase of more than 100,000. This was evidence of the growing influence of the Party, and of the efficiency of its organisation in the country. The Party machinery, under the supervision of Arthur Henderson, had fallen into the skilled and experienced hands of a new national agent, Egerton P. Wake, who built up a scheme of administration in a very short space of time, which is at once the envy and the admiration of the older Parties. Political organisation among women electors was developed simultaneously in women's sections of local Labour Parties, by the devoted work of women organisers led by Dr. Marion Phillips.

But political circumstances contributed to the rising force of Labour in the country. The Coalition Government played into the Party's hands by refusing to proceed with the nationalisation of the coalmines as recommended by a majority of the Royal Commission it had itself appointed. Questions of finance and taxation also gave the Party its opportunity to expose the Parties on the other side, for they declined to consider the imposition of taxes upon fortunes created as the result of the war, notwithstanding the recommendation made by a Government-appointed committee that this should be done. The Government Parties also made the political mistake of including the surpluses of Co-operative Societies resulting from the operation of mutual trading within the scope of the Corporation Profits Tax. Worse still, they sabotaged the Land Valuation scheme, they decontrolled the mines, which led to serious difficulties in the mining industry and brought about a National Strike of mine workers. The shortlived trade boom of 1919-20 was followed by the first phase of the inter-war economic crisis marked by rising unemployment and a forcing down of wages. By the time the Lloyd George Coalition came to an end in 1922, it was already clear that the social legislation and the promises of fundamental reconstruction the older Parties were committed to, would be carried no further by them.

In the Labour Party's annual report in 1922 the feeling of the country against the Coalition was clearly reflected: "the sooner the record of this Government is submitted to the electors, and the sooner this Parliament is purged, the better for the welfare of the nation," said the Party Executive. And the purging took place at the end of that year. The Conservative section of the Coalition refused to serve under Lloyd George, and in the Election that followed its break-up Labour was returned to Parliament as the second largest Party. This marked a new stage in its history. Up to that time it had always been numerically weaker than either the Conservative or the Liberal Party. But with the relegation of the Liberal Party to the third place, and that Party hopelessly split, Labour found itself the official Opposition. This meant that in the event of the Conservative Government formed by Bonar Law being overturned, the Labour Party would have the automatic reversion of office; though this, of course, was extremely unlikely in view of the huge Conservative majority. The Labour Party, nevertheless, took its responsibility as the official Opposition with the utmost seriousness. Steps were taken to reorganise the Party in Parliament in a manner which was calculated to make it most effective. J. Ramsay MacDonald was elected leader and chairman, with John R. Clynes as deputy chairman and Arthur Henderson as Chief Whip, as well as secretary of the Party. When leadership of the Conservative Party and the premiership passed to Stanley Baldwin, another General Election was precipitated, by his decision to appeal to the country for a mandate to introduce a system of Protection as a remedy for unemployment. The General Election took place in December, and as a result Labour increased its representation from 142 to 191 seats. As the strength of the Conservative Party was reduced to 258, with the Liberals in possession of 158 seats, and eight Independents in the House, there was a heavy majority against the Baldwin Government if the Liberals and Labour could combine. The Labour Party put the issue to a test as soon as the new Parliament assembled, by moving a vote of no confidence in the Government, following the presentation of its programme in the King's speech. This vote was carried by 328 to 256: the Liberal Party, in other words, chose to see Labour in Office rather than to allow the Conservatives to continue, but there were ominous injunctions from the Liberal leaders calculated to restrain the Labour Government. There were those who thought at the time that Labour's acceptance of office in the political circumstances of the time was a risky proceeding. That the first Labour Government in British history was prepared to undertake the responsibilities of office when it was open to defeat, not merely at the hands of the combination of the other Parties, but through the withdrawal of support from one other Party alone, was a testimony to the high political purpose and sense of public spirit of the Party leaders. They knew the country was looking to their Party for a courageous lead, and they took the decision to enter Office after full consideration of all the circumstances, by the Executive bodies of the Labour Party and the Parliamentary Party in conjunction with the General Council of the Trades Union Congress.

CHAPTER XII

THE FIRST LABOUR GOVERNMENT

By J. Vernon Radcliffe

Seen in historical perspective—even the perspective afforded by the lapse of twenty-three years—the brief record of the first Labour Government, which took Office in January 1924, has the character of a trial trip. It was an adventurous and sprightly episode and soon over, but it broke the tradition of a two-Party political system and marked the arrival of Labour at the full stature of a Party ready to undertake the conduct of national affairs at home and abroad. Timorous men would have hesitated; Labour dared. In the Parliamentary position, in the strain of economic circumstances—the reaction from the post-war boom having set in—and in the jarring tone of international relations there were good reasons for holding back, except for the bold. The times were profoundly unsettled and difficult and called for firm, clear policies. Labour had new principles to apply and a fresh attitude of mind to bring to bear on domestic and foreign problems alike, yet it had not the strength to make those principles effective nor its views decisive. It was in Office but not in power. Though the second largest party in the State it had fewer than a third of the members of the House of Commons. With its 191 members it was able, in association with the Liberals, who numbered 158, to overthrow the Baldwin Government which had won only 258 seats in the election of the preceding December. But then, taking up the responsibilities of Government, Labour was itself confronted with the anxieties, the cares and uncertainties of a Party liable on any occasion of moment to be voted out of Office by a combination of the other two. In front, in unqualified opposition, was a watchful and eager Tory Party, roused and alarmed by the portent of Socialists sitting on the Government benches. On the flank, boastfully non-Socialist, was a rather sore Liberal Party, with a sense of dispossession, an opportunist friend for the ousting of a tariff-making Tory Party but a potential opponent tomorrow and rather ostentatiously the arbiter of the Government's fate.

Asquith, the Liberal Leader, had left no doubt of his view of the constitutional position. In the debate on the amendment which brought the Baldwin Government down he had said that "when an administration so situated resigns, the Party which naturally and properly succeeds to the task is the Party that is numerically preponderant in the Opposition . . . and if the Labour Party is willing . . . to assume the burdens of Office in such conditions it has the absolute, undisputed right to claim it." Of the part which the Liberal Party would play with a Labour Government in Office Asquith was equally frank. Liberals were pledged to give no more countenance to a Socialist experiment than to a Protectionist experiment and would keep those pledges. But Labour had a right to the succession in Office—the King's Government must be carried on—and it was the duty of every patriotic man and woman to facilitate their task. In these terms Asquith suggested the possibility of co-operation in the sphere of social legislation.

All this was constitutionally sound and it was benign; but if it was the official policy of the Liberal Party it was departed from by some of its more pugnacious free-lances who quickly showed their intention to embarrass and by no means to assist the Government. Moreover, Asquith himself, in a less judicial and wholly partisan temper, had said that "the Labour Government must eat out of the Liberal hand." The phrase, though not entirely without provocation, did not contribute to an accommodating spirit anywhere, and rank and file relations between Labour and the Liberal Party tended to express a natural antagonism and no affinity. It was the essential antagonism between Socialism and the capitalist system. This was the background against which the political drama was staged in Parliament.

Labour accepted Office as a constitutional right and duty. If, when in Office, it was to be defeated, at once or later, then that must be the responsibility of the other Parties. Labour had put 427 candidates in the field. They received 4,348,379 votes, coming short of the Tory vote by more than a million, but exceeding by 97,000 what the Liberals got. Having won second place, Labour was not ready to surrender it supinely, and when the prospect of the Tory defeat was sure the leaders of the Party decided that when Baldwin resigned and Ramsay MacDonald was sent for, he should undertake to form a Government. Another decision soon followed upon this. Was a Labour Government without the support of a majority in the House of Commons, to proceed with a full red-blooded Socialist programme, and invite defeat, or should it prepare more modest legislative proposals which the Liberals might be expected to support in the main and so be able to face the electorate, when the time came, with a record of solid gains and the promise of more to follow if given the necessary power? This issue was easily settled. Neither the country nor the Party in the country would have tolerated a merely theatrical gesture that would, in effect, have been a renunciation of the opportunity to prove Labour's readiness and fitness for Office and a patent disregard of the fact that Labour had not an adequate Socialist mandate. Nor can it have been absent from the minds of those in the Party's inner councils that a period of Office—even Office without power—would give Labour Ministers an opportunity of gaining administrative experience, a knowledge of the working of the great Government Departments and insight into the methods of conducting the nation's business, its finance, its trade and foreign relations and the multifarious matters comprised in the term "affairs of State."

The Labour leaders had little knowledge of State business. The Prime Minister himself, Ramsay MacDonald, had not previously held office of any kind and besides being Prime Minister he was also Secretary of State for Foreign Affairs. Only one of his colleagues in the Cabinet with a past record of Party service—Arthur Henderson—had before had ministerial experience at Cabinet level though other Labour Members had served in other capacities in the Coalition Government of the first World War. This dearth of experience, coupled with the constitutional requirement that two Secretaries of State must be in the House of Lords, imposed conditions on Government-making. To complete the Ministry MacDonald went outside the Party to make Viscount Chelmsford, a former Viceroy of India, First Lord of the Admiralty and Viscount Haldane, Lord Chancellor. Comparative newcomers to the Party like Lord Parmoor, Brigadier-General Thomson (who was raised to the peerage), Noel Buxton, C. P. Trevelyan and Colonel Josiah Wedgwood, all of them men of proved political or administrative capacity, were available for other posts and the Cabinet as a whole and the other ministerial appointments demonstrated the ability which the Party could bring to the nation's service. The Cabinet of twenty was constituted as follows:

First Lord of the Treasury, and Secretary of State for Foreign Affairs—J. Ramsay MacDonald.
Lord Privy Seal and Deputy Leader of the House of Commons—J. R. Clynes.
Lord President of the Council—Lord Parmoor.
Lord Chancellor—Lord Haldane.
Chancellor of the Exchequer—Philip Snowden.
Secretary of State for Home Affairs—Arthur Henderson.
Secretary of State for the Colonies—J. H. Thomas.
Secretary of State for War—Stephen Walsh.
Secretary of State for India—Lord Olivier.
Secretary of State for Air—Lord Thomson.
First Lord of the Admiralty—Viscount Chelmsford.
President of the Board of Trade—Sidney Webb.
Minister of Health—John Wheatley.
Minister of Agriculture and Fisheries—Noel Buxton.
Secretary for Scotland—William Adamson.
President of the Board of Education—Charles Philips Trevelyan.
Minister of Labour—Thomas Shaw.
Postmaster-General—Vernon Hartshorn.
Chancellor of the Duchy of Lancaster—Josiah C. Wedgwood.
First Commissioner of Works—F. W. Jowett.

The formalities associated with the formation of the Government had some amusing incidents. In conformity with constitutional practice the new Ministers were called to Buckingham Palace to receive their seals of Office from the King. It was the time-honoured practice that Ministers should wear frock coats—a mode of dress already out of fashion and soon to be obsolete—and tall silk hats. But who of the Ministers drawn from the ranks of Labour possessed either a frock coat or a tall hat? Two or three were equal to the emergency but the rest were not. Indeed it was said of some of them, by one of their number, that they only had with them in London the suits in which they stood. This was disturbing to Court functionaries; and Sir Maurice Hankey, Secretary of the Cabinet, was anxious that the

THE FIRST LABOUR CABINET, 1924

new Government should make, as it were, a good first appearance. Time did not permit of the ordering of new suits and perhaps the new Ministers did not know all the resources of London's services for exactly such a circumstance of personal difficulty. When no way of escape from the dilemma appeared the matter was referred to Lord Stamfordham, the King's Private Secretary. It is a duty of a private secretary to the King to ensure the decorum and etiquette of royal occasions, and at first he was nonplussed. Ministers must receive their seals of Office and must receive them from the King himself! This, after all, was more important than the dress they wore and the one thing that could be done was done. Ministers were allowed to wear whatever clothes they had. Those who had frock coats wore them. If a Minister had not a frock coat then a morning coat would do and if he had neither then perforce he might go in a lounge suit. So that little problem was happily settled. There was no need to change the form of the ceremony but it was thought prudent that Ministers should be instructed in its procedure. Sir Maurice Hankey, therefore, conducted rehearsals—not dress rehearsals—in Downing Street and the Ministers, his pupils, went through the simple but trying ceremony without a hitch. But they made a precedent by wearing ordinary dress in the Palace.

The Government took an important step in foreign policy before meeting Parliament on February 12. On February 1 *de jure* recognition was given to the Soviet Government. Of the conditions attached to recognition the two most important were an understanding to settle the claims of each nation against the other and Russian abstention from propaganda against British interests. When Parliament reassembled there was no King's Speech to outline Government policy. The speech from the Throne had been delivered at the opening of the session while the Baldwin Government was in Office and had, of course, no longer any relevance. The Prime Minister, therefore, made a comprehensive statement to indicate the general principles which would guide the Government's policy and certain of the legislative measures that would claim attention. He was studiously moderate and even conciliatory, frankly recognising minority backing for the Government and giving the House latitude for the amendment of Government measures provided that the amendments did not infringe a vital principle. "If the House," he said, "on matters non-essential, matters that do not strike at the root of the proposals that we make and do not destroy fundamentally the general intentions of the Government in introducing legislation—if the House wish to vary our proposition then the House must take the responsibility of this variation. A division on such amendments and questions as those will not be regarded as a vote of no confidence." This was a rational *modus vivendi* and if accepted with goodwill would have ensured the Government of a useful and fruitful period of office. In fact no channels of communication were developed in order to avoid open clashes of opinion and within a fortnight two motions hostile to the Government were brought forward by Liberal members. One was in opposition to a decision to proceed with the building of five cruisers (the Admiralty had demanded eight) in view of the serious state of unemployment in the shipbuilding areas. Two Liberals voted against the Government for every one that voted with them in this critical division and Tory votes prevented an immediate crisis. On the second occasion a division between Liberals and Tories could not be counted upon. The matter at issue this time was the cancelling by the Minister of Health of an Order made years before by Sir Alfred Mond (afterwards Lord Melchett) restricting the Poplar Board of Guardians in the granting of Poor Law Relief. The Government would have gone to defeat if John Wheatley's cogent defence had not convinced the Liberals that in substance they had no case.

It will be seen therefore that from the very beginning the Government's life was precarious. Defeats on minor matters, which were not infrequent, had no particular significance but wily opponents were at work to bring about a combination of forces that the Government could not outvote and yet must resist. The margin of safety was at times very small. Notwithstanding the constant state of suspense the Government did succeed in placing several valuable measures on the Statute Book and in reducing the tension in foreign relations. The most important legislation was the Housing Bill introduced by Wheatley, a bold, far-reaching measure to produce houses in numbers to meet the national need and to be let at rents within the means of the wage earners. This could only be done with the aid of subsidies from public funds and the Bill made provision for a subsidy of £9 a house in urban areas and of £12 10*s*. in rural areas for forty years. It was foreseen that the annual cost to the Exchequer and the local authorities would rise to a peak figure of £34 million. Wheatley had prepared the way for the effectiveness of his scheme by negotiations with the building industry. The building programme was to provide 2,500,000 houses in fifteen years and the industry gave assurances that it would be completed in the specified time. The Party was enthusiastic for the Bill which successfully ran the gauntlet of Tory and Liberal criticism, skilfully piloted and expounded by a Minister whose Parliamentary ability was of the highest order. A second Bill to which both Wheatley and the Party attached great importance was intended to prevent profiteering in building materials. It was impossible to get the Bill through in the summer and, being deferred till the autumn, it was involved in the fate that overtook the Government.

This great housing measure was the outstanding achievement of the session but other useful legislation was also passed. The first of the Government's Bills abolished the gap of three weeks in the payment of benefit to insured persons who had drawn benefit for twelve weeks in excess of the amount due on account of contributions. Unopposed, this easement of the unemployed man's hardships was soon law. It was followed by another measure benefiting the unemployed without insurance rights. Their "uncovenanted benefit" was made statutory and increased in amount and made to cover the whole year. A further mitigation of the unwanted workers' lot was made by a reduction of the "waiting period" between the loss of a job and the commencement of benefit from six to three days. For old age pensioners there was a substantial concession. Under the pre-existing law a pension of full amount was not allowed to anyone with an income from any source of more than 10*s.* a week. A Bill introduced by the Chancellor of the Exchequer provided that income from any form of savings up to £39 a year for a single person and £78 for man and wife should be disregarded. As the existing law made no deduction of pension in respect of an income of up to 10*s.* a week the full effect of the alteration was to allow a single person with sufficient resources from savings to enjoy an income of 35*s.* a week, including the pension, and a married couple (with a double pension) an income of 70*s.* a week. So the "penalising of thrift" was either abolished or greatly lessened and 225,000 persons hitherto disqualified became entitled to pensions.

One of the Bills limited in scope and effect by the opposition of the other parties was promoted by the Minister of Agriculture to establish county agricultural wages committees and a central wages board. A clause to enable the central board to revise the decisions of local committees was defeated, but the Government proceeded with the remainder of the Bill in order to secure valuable machinery for fixing minimum rates. A second Bill to be drastically changed while before Parliament was a franchise measure. In its final form it was limited to the equalising of the franchise for men and women but even so it was left over to the autumn session and therefore lost. This was originally a private member's Bill but the Government were prepared to take it up after the committee stage. A Bill to nationalise the mines and minerals, sponsored by the Miners' Federation and approved by the Party, was rejected on the second reading. It was wholly opposed by the Tories and only five Liberals voted for it. A Bill well forward in preparation would have consolidated and amended the Factories Acts, bringing them into line with modern requirements, but it also was relegated to the autumn session in the opening days of which the Government were defeated.

All through the session the Government were concerned about unemployment. The steps taken to make the circumstances of the unemployed less intolerable have already been mentioned but work-giving projects were also put in hand and in addition the Budget was helpful to national recovery. The Chancellor of the Exchequer was chairman of a Cabinet Committee which recommended a number of large industrial projects and negotiated with public bodies and public utility companies to get them adopted. There was an extension of relief works though the Government were careful to point out that they did not regard relief works as a solution of the unemployment problem. The Unemployment Grants Committee approved schemes of the value of £5,500,000 in the six months from February to July and was then considering other schemes of the value of £3,400,000. To a road programme to cost £13,500,000 the Government was ready to contribute £10,400,000. Export credits to the amount of £10 million were sanctioned and under the Trade Facilities Acts credits for another £10 million. A large scheme of electrical development was also projected involving an outlay of £10 million in three years. Half of the unemployment in the country was attributable to the depression in the three industries of shipbuilding, engineering and cotton. An analysis of the causes of the depression in those industries showed that in large measure it was due to the price level of our exports being 90 per cent. higher than before the war, while the price level of imports was only 50 per cent. higher. The Government had hopes of reducing costs of production by bringing down costs of transport, "one of the main items entering into the price of marketable commodities."

The first Labour Budget was awaited with deep interest and here and there with trepidation. Snowden told the story of a telephone call from a countess who asked him if it were true that the Labour Party intended to cut the throats of all aristocrats and steal their property. Such ignorant fears did not afflict the business world which was nevertheless uncertain of the principles which would direct Labour's financial policy. The Budget reassured them. Snowden was fortunate in having a prospective surplus of nearly £40 million and was, therefore, able to reduce taxation. He turned first to the food taxes. He halved the duty on tea, more than halved the duty on sugar, lessened the duty on dried fruits and abolished the duties on sweetened table waters. The entertainments tax on the cheapest seats was repealed and reduced on other low-priced seats. The inhabited house duty which Snowden abolished is now one of the forgotten taxes. So far the Chancellor of the Exchequer was not in the area of acute Party controversy; but he proceeded to abolish the McKenna duties—a series of duties introduced as war taxes in 1915 but definitely protective in character. They included the duties on motor cars and motor cycles, musical instruments, clocks and watches and cinema films. On the other hand, the withdrawal of the corporations profits duty, another war tax, was acclaimed everywhere. It was the most costly of all the budget changes. One effect of Snowden's proposals was to improve the relations between Labour and the Liberals in the House of Commons. The proposals won the complete assent of the Liberals and put good heart into the Government's own supporters. Only the repeal of the McKenna duties was seriously challenged by the Tories and Liberal support gave the Government a majority of sixty-five in the division.

In the field of foreign affairs the Government had to take up the negotiations on German reparations. The Dawes Committee, composed of international financial experts, had prepared a new scheme of payments. The Committee had faced the technical problems of reparations and though the associated political problems were outside its terms of reference it had indicated that the proposed plan assumed that political and military guarantees which hindered Germany's economic recovery would be eventually withdrawn. France's continued occupation of the Ruhr was thus called in question and the Inter-Allied Conference, which met in London in July to consider the report, could not evade the sharply contentious political issues. MacDonald and Snowden were the leading British members of the conference. Before it assembled MacDonald had a meeting at Chequers with M. Herriot who had become Prime Minister of France more recently than MacDonald had become Prime Minister of England. There was much interest in the meeting of the two Socialist leaders and hope that they would be able by personal understanding to find a way to a reconciliation of the opposing views of the two countries. Immediately after the conversations MacDonald sent a despatch to the British Ambassador in Rome which mentioned Herriot's agreement to the calling of an Inter-Allied Conference and then stated the British view of a suggested protocol to be signed by the Allies and Germany. Through misunderstanding it was publicly inferred, and notably so in France, that the British Note, coming so soon after the MacDonald-Herriot meeting expressed the French Government's views and Herriot's position as head of the French Government was shaken. MacDonald saved the situation by going at once to Paris, spending a week-end with Herriot and reaching agreement which was definite enough to frame in a long memorandum. With that danger past, the conference assembled, but the conflicting views on sanctions remained though France's policy was modified. The negotiations were tough, France being deeply preoccupied not only with reparations but also with security. At one point failure was imminent, but France accepted an obligation to withdraw from the Ruhr within twelve months and the conference came to a happy conclusion, though the Dawes plan itself did not achieve its purpose and only four years later was abandoned for another. MacDonald was chairman of the conference and his tact and ability in steering its deliberations contributed greatly to its success.

The Government's prestige rose, but just before Parliament adjourned for the summer recess ominous portents of trouble appeared and during the recess two damaging blows were struck at the Government's credit, one of them aimed unworthily at the Prime Minister's personal reputation. Signs of a heavy storm appeared with the publication of the draft treaty with Russia on which discussions had begun in April. On the British side, Arthur Ponsonby was in charge of the negotiations. By August 4, three days before the adjournment of Parliament, a treaty had been drafted though not approved. There was deadlock on the question of compensation for the repudiated Russian debts and the confiscated private property of British subjects. When the Foreign Office announced the breakdown of the discussions a group of Labour Members and trade unionists made urgent representations to Ponsonby of the unfortunate consequences they apprehended from the failure to agree and next day they suggested a formula to bridge the gap. The formula was regarded by Philip Snowden—a Member of the Government with a strict sense of financial proprieties—as innocuous and indeed as mere face-saving. It sufficed, however, to save the negotiations (which were resumed that day, August 6) from a confessed collapse. The House of Commons was thereupon informed that a preliminary treaty had been concluded and would be ratified after it had been laid on the table of the House in the customary way for twenty-one days in which the House was sitting. Next day the draft treaty appeared as a White Paper and it was seen that the matters of deadlock were to be referred to an Anglo-Russian Committee. The apprehension that the Government might guarantee a Russian loan even though these matters were unsettled provoked a storm. Critics ignored or overlooked the safeguards in the preliminary conditions. Political tempers interfered with calm and dispassionate judgment.

Presently tempers were more highly inflamed by an incident in the law courts, the notorious Campbell case. A prosecution was started against an acting editor of the *Workers Weekly*, a Communist paper, for alleged sedition in a "Don't Shoot" article addressed to men in the Forces with reference to strikes. The prosecution was withdrawn. This incident brought the Government down, but the blow was not struck till after the reassembly of Parliament in October. Meanwhile, a personal attack had been made on the Prime Minister. He had accepted the gift of a motor car and shares to provide an income to run it, with the understanding that the shares would eventually revert to the donor of the car or his heirs. The gift had been made in March and the King's Birthday Honours in June announced a baronetcy for the giver. Malice seized on these facts and put them together to convey the insinuation of political corruption. In fact the giver's name had been placed in the suggested list of baronetcies during the period of Office of a previous Government and his well-known public benefactions and services in Scotland were alone the occasion of the original nomination for the honour and its conferment. No imputation whatever was made by responsible politicians or newspapers but slander did evil work, though MacDonald was free from reproach. His sensitive mind was deeply injured and perhaps this contributed to his readiness to demand a vote of confidence or to face a General Election when the Campbell Case was raised in the House of Commons on October 8.

The Tories moved a direct vote of censure. A Liberal amendment called for a Select Committee "to investigate and report upon the circumstances leading up to the withdrawal of the proceedings recently instituted by the Director of Public Prosecutions against Mr. Campbell." MacDonald told the House that the amendment, like the motion, was regarded by the Government as a matter of confidence. The accusation against the Government was that Party political reasons had interfered with the normal course of legal procedure. Neither in all respects nor at all times had the Government's attitude to the political aspects of the case been made as clear as it might have been, but the statement of the Attorney General in justification of his decision to withdraw the prosecution was precise. Campbell had fought in the 1914-18 war; he had been decorated for gallantry and been lamed in both feet. Should the Attorney General put in the dock at the Old Bailey such a man as the most dangerous Communist he could find? Moreover, the Attorney General had doubts whether the prosecution could succeed. Before deciding to withdraw the case he saw the Prime Minister and also met the Cabinet. All this, of course, did not appear at the time of the withdrawal of the case and between then and the debate there were some unclear statements that allowed the Opposition unnecessary latitude in attack. To bring about the end they desired and to prevent a divided vote the Tories voted against their own motion and supported the Liberal amendment which was carried by 364 votes to 198.

In these tragic circumstances the first Labour Government decided to appeal to the country and was confronted there by the Zinovieff letter—whether a spurious fabrication or authentic was never established with complete certainty though Labour had no doubt of the perpetration of an Election fraud. The letter made reference to underground Communist interference in British politics and was a powerful instrument to stampede the electorate. There was a heavy poll. Labour put forward 514 candidates, an increase of 87 over the number nominated in the preceding year, and altogether received 5,487,620 votes, an increase of 1,139,241, but the number of members returned was 42 fewer. The Tory vote increased by 2,265,000 and 413 Tory Members were returned. The Liberal vote was 2,982,563, a decrease of 1,230,000 and only 40 Liberal Members were returned. The Tories took Office.

CHAPTER XIII

FROM POLITICAL TO INDUSTRIAL ACTION

By Herbert Tracey

Labour held in the new Parliament forty-two fewer seats on a much increased total Labour vote. Growing public support for the Labour Party was reflected in the increased Labour vote in the 1924 General Election. But the circumstances of that election left the Labour Movement in a state of confusion and unsettlement. For a time, once again, the repressed tendency of the industrial elements in the Labour Movement to doubt the wisdom of relying too exclusively upon political action in the furtherance of its narrower aims, influenced the relations of the Unions with the Party. Though they maintain an independent existence side by side, the Unions and the Party constitute one organised Movement, and cannot be separated. Their activities are closely interwoven. Connected as they are by a common membership in their affiliated organisations neither the Labour Party nor the T.U.C. can move in an isolated orbit: the motions of the one disturb the other.

But the history of the Labour Movement as it has been recorded in the earlier chapters of this work attests the truth of the statement that the organised workers tend to turn alternately from political or industrial action as events appear to demonstrate the weakness and inadequacy of the one or the other method of attaining their ends. This "swing of the pendulum" from political to industrial action was illustrated in the industrial unrest which marked the years immediately preceding the first World War. There were at that time an unprecedented number of large-scale strikes. Coincident with them was a systematic propaganda carried on by the advocates of industrial Unionism which decried Parliamentary methods and exalted the theory of direct action. A similar reaction carried the organised workers over to the preparation and prosecution of a general stoppage of work of hitherto unparalleled scope in the months that followed the fall of the Labour Government in 1924.

The propaganda of direct action made its influence felt again after the first World War when the Labour Movement registered its resolute opposition to the Coalition Government's policy of intervention in Soviet Russia. The establishment of Councils of Action signalled qualified recognition by the Movement's political leaders that considerations could arise which might be held to justify the use of the Movement's economic strength for political purposes. This point of view was never formally ratified. Labour's political leaders were profoundly uneasy about the implications of the decision to use industrial action, by way of boycott and stoppages of work, to prevent the supply of munitions to the anti-Soviet forces in Russia. It is on record, in fact, that the National Executive of the Party felt that industrial action was a matter that remained within the sphere of Trade Union responsibility.

The initiation of a General Strike for the purpose of achieving not industrial but political objects was a new precedent. It was imperative, the Party Executive said, that the Trade Unions, whose members would be called on to fulfil the obligations implied in the new policy and whose functions would be involved, should realise the responsibility such a strike movement would entail, and should themselves determine the plan of any such new campaign.

The Trade Unions, for their part, were being drawn more and more in the direction of organising their resources for purposes of self-defence in a period of industrial crisis. The growth of unemployment and the beginning of what looked like a concerted attack upon the wage standards attained by the Trade Unions during the war produced a militant temper amongst the industrial leaders. They began to consider the necessity of establishing something in the nature of a defence mechanism, of a purely industrial kind. There was much talk at the time of bringing into existence a Trade Union General Staff to co-ordinate the action of Unions in the industrial field. In the circumstances surrounding the Labour Government's defeat and the conditions in which Labour fought the election of 1924, Trade Unions discovered further reasons for developing their economic power and preparing once again, if necessary, to resort to the use of industrial weapons. They applied themselves deliberately to the task of framing a policy aiming at the accomplishment of purely industrial objects under unified leadership, and although nobody probably foresaw it, the result in due course was the general stoppage of work in May, 1926. The necessity for a strong industrial organisation and a definite industrial policy was proclaimed by Trade Union leaders, even whilst the Labour Government was in Office. It was unfortunately the fact that neither the composition of the Labour Government nor the policy it pursued commanded the entire confidence of the Trade Unions. There had been criticism of Mr. MacDonald's action as Prime Minister in choosing so many ex-Liberals as Ministers, whose places many Trade Unionists thought would have been more fittingly and not less efficiently filled by tried and experienced leaders of the working-class movement, with a lifetime of service to both the Labour Party and the Trade Unions standing to their credit. The omission from the Government of some of the ablest and best known of the industrial leaders disposed Trade Unionists to examine more critically the tendency of the Labour Government's policy, particularly in relation to industrial affairs.

Industrial policy was a matter of great importance to the Trade Union leaders: they expected to be consulted about it; they even felt they had some claim to determine its direction and results. And they were disappointed to find that the Labour Ministers directly concerned with industrial affairs dealt with them very much as other Governments had done, giving their views full consideration, but not inviting that direct co-operation with the Trade Union leaders or definitely associating them with the working out of the Government's industrial policy in the manner they expected.

Evidence of the determination of the Trade Union leaders not to allow political activities to absorb the whole strength and thought of the organised Labour Movement was supplied at the Trades Union Congress at Hull, in 1924, a month before the Labour Government fell from Office. Amongst the resolutions adopted was one defining the Trade Union demand for radical changes in the social, economic, and political system, including public ownership and control of natural resources and essential services, with participation of the workers in control and management; the establishment of a legal maximum working week of forty-four hours; a legal minimum wage for each industry or occupation; work or maintenance for the unemployed; adequate housing accommodation; fuller educational facilities; compensation for all forms of industrial accident and disease; State pensions for all at the age of 60, with a proper system of pensions for widowed mothers and dependent children.

This declaration of policy was significant as an indication of the intention of the Trade Unions to have a programme of their own, which was not merely an echo and reproduction of the Labour Party's programme: a definite goal towards which the Unions would expect Labour Governments to move. It showed that the Unions did not mean to be docile and inarticulate supporters of any Labour Government that might achieve power, offering an uncritical acceptance of everything such a Government might propose to do; the Unions were laying down, in this Industrial Charter, the criteria of a Labour Government's policy, and demonstrating their determination to assert the right of judging it independently, without regard to their relations with the Labour Party.

Still more significant as a revelation of the new orientation of the Trade Unions was the resolution of the Hull Congress investing the General Council with extended powers in dealing with industrial disputes. This resolution imposed upon the affiliated Unions the obligation of keeping the General Council fully informed with regard to matters arising as between the Unions and employers, as well as between one Union and another, particularly where such matters may involve directly or indirectly large bodies of workers. The General Council claimed power to disseminate the information to all the Unions in the industry concerned, and assumed the right to intervene, in the interests of the organised Movement as a whole, in the event of negotiations breaking down or of a deadlock arising of such a character as to involve other bodies of workers affiliated to the Congress, or such as to imperil standard wages, hours or conditions of employment. As long as there was a prospect of an amicable settlement of disputes by the machinery of negotiation existing in the trades concerned, the General Council would not intervene; but failure thus to settle would bring the Council into action, the first step being to call the representatives of the Unions involved in the dispute into consultation with the Council, which would use all its influence to effect a settlement. The Council was empowered by the constitution to make full inquiry into the facts and to offer its advice to the Unions, and refusal of such assistance by any Union was to be reported to Congress. Further, where the Council intervened and its help was accepted, and still no settlement was secured, with the result that the policy of the employers enforced a stoppage of work, either by lock-out or strike, the General Council was instructed by the resolution to take steps forthwith to organise on behalf of the Union or Unions concerned all such moral and material support as the circumstances of the dispute may appear to justify.

Upon its acquisition of these powers and responsibilities, the General Council began to develop the policy which led, twenty months later, to the organisation of a National Strike in support of the miners. In the working out of this policy the Trade Union Movement took up a more detached position in relation to the Labour Party than it had previously occupied. Joint administrative departments, which had been established at the headquarters of the Trades Union Congress and the Labour Party, were wound up, and separate departments—for research, publicity, and international affairs—were created by the Trades Union Congress for the furtherance of its own distinctively industrial work; similar arrangements being made by the Labour Party for maintaining corresponding departments for political work. These changes did not, of course, signify any severing of the bonds between the Unions and the Party; they marked rather the development of a more independent policy on the part of the Trade Unions through their Congress.

This did not mean any slackening of the Labour Party's activities in Parliament or in the country. Whilst the Trades Union Congress filled a larger space than the Labour Party in the history of the period between the General Election and the General Strike, the Party continued to make remarkable progress and carried on a vigorous campaign in opposition to the Government. As the outcome of the General Election, when the new Parliament assembled in November 1924, the Parties grouped themselves as follows:

Conservatives	413
Labour	151
Liberals	40
Independents	5
Constitutionalists	6

By-elections added four seats to the Labour total; the Conservative majority at the General Election in Stockport, Darlington, East Ham North, and

Hammersmith being converted by an extraordinary turn-over of votes into Labour victories. The by-election results, especially those that occurred just after the national stoppage—at Hammersmith and Wallsend—testified to the energy of the Labour Party in the political field and to the recovery of its forces after the set-back of the General Election.

But interest had shifted, not only in the organised Labour Movement, but in the country at large, from political to industrial concerns, and especially to the slow maturing of the crisis in the mining industry. The mining problem produced the National Strike. The question of miners' wages and working conditions dominated the thoughts of both the industrial and political leaders of the Labour Movement almost from the beginning of 1924, when the Miners' Federation of Great Britain gave notice to terminate the national agreement, which had regulated wages by a complicated formula for dividing the proceeds of the industry, since 1921. The development of the crisis then set in motion was retarded, whilst the Labour Government was in Office, by the appointment of a Court of Inquiry under the chairmanship of Lord Buckmaster. On the basis of his report, a temporary settlement was reached in negotiations between the mine owners and workers, providing (*a*) that the amount of the standard profits should be 15 per cent. of the amount of standard wages instead of 17, as in the original agreement of 1921; (*b*) that the minimum percentage payable on basic rates should be 33⅓ per cent. instead of 20; and (*c*) that the surplus of the proceeds remaining after payment of standard wages and standard profits should be divided into the ratio of eighty-eight to wages and twelve to profits, instead of the ratio of eighty-three to seventeen, as in the original agreement. An increase of one-eighth in subsistence wages was granted in certain of the districts, and the settlement also provided that no wage was to fall below an amount equal to 40 per cent. on the standard wage of the lowest paid class of workmen in the district.

This agreement was accepted, to remain in operation for twelve months, terminable thereafter by one month's notice from either side. It ran for the full term. Then the mine owners reopened the wage question by giving notice on June 30, 1925, of their intention to terminate the agreement. Negotiations and inquiries followed, the Government setting up another Court to investigate "the causes and circumstances of the dispute in the coal mining industry and to report thereon." The Court, composed of Mr. H. P. Macmillan, K.C., Mr. Will Sherwood, and Sir Josiah Stamp, reported in favour of the miners' claim that any wage agreement they were asked to accept should provide for a minimum wage, the amount of such wage to be settled by negotiations between the owners and the men. Whilst the discussions proceeded the General Council of the Trades Union Congress appeared on the scene in the capacity of mediator.

At a joint meeting between the miners' leaders and representatives of the General Council, the miners' case was fully explained and placed unreservedly in the Council's hands. The Council unanimously endorsed the miners' attitude, and pledged the support of the organised movement in their resistance to the owners' terms. The Council appointed a special committee to maintain contact with the miners and to organise material and moral support, as a result of which plans were drawn up for laying an embargo on the movement of coal in the event of the dispute leading to a stoppage of work in the coalfields. This was the germ of the General Strike, which came to maturity nine months later. The immediate crisis was averted by the action of the Government in offering financial assistance to the industry to enable the existing wage agreement to continue in operation pending a full inquiry into all the facts and circumstances of the industry. The operation of the subsidy was limited to a period of nine months.

Within this period the Coal Commission, under the chairmanship of Sir Herbert Samuel, with Sir Herbert Lawrence, Sir William Beveridge, and Mr. Kenneth Lee, conducted an extensive inquiry and produced its report. By common consent, the report embodied a serious and important contribution to the solution of the mining problem. It was presented on March 6, 1926, and on March 24 the Prime Minister met representatives of the miners and mine owners to inform them that the Government was prepared to carry out such measures as the State was required to undertake in order to give effect to the Commission's recommendations, on the understanding that those responsible for carrying on the industry would agree to accept the report. The Prime Minister also stated that although the Commission definitely recommended the discontinuance of the mining subsidy on the appointed date, the Government was prepared, provided an agreement could be reached by May 1, to consider the question of granting further temporary assistance in order to ease the position in those districts, chiefly engaged in producing coal for export, where considerable wage sacrifices would have to be accepted by the miners.

As an earnest of the Government's intention to give effect to the report, the following list of the Commission's recommendations, involving Government action, was drawn up and presented to both parties:

(1) Further assistance by the Government in the investigation of processes of low temperature carbonisation;
(2) Establishment of a National Fuel and Power Council;
(3) Provision for research to be largely extended by the industry with the support of the State;
(4) Promotion of desirable amalgamations by provision for the compulsory transfer of interests under existing leases where such amalgamations are prevented by the dissent of some of the parties or their unreasonable claims;
(5) State purchase of royalties;
(6) Provision for a contribution from royalties to the Welfare Fund;

(7) The granting of power to local authorities to engage in the retail sale of coal;
(8) The establishment of a Standing Joint Committee of the Ministry of Transport and the Mines Department to promote measures to secure the use of larger mineral wagons on the railways and a greater concentration of ownership of wagons;
(9) Statutory provision for profit-sharing schemes, providing for the distribution to workmen of shares in coal mining undertakings;
(10) Provision for such modification in the law governing hours of labour as the owners and men might agree;
(11) Provision by the Government of facilities for the transfer of displaced labour, and the provision of funds for such purpose;
(12) Consideration of the regulations governing the qualifications of mine managers;
(13) Provision for compulsory pithead baths to be financed from the Welfare Fund;
(14) The establishment of Joint Pit Committees.

These fourteen points constituted the Government's contribution to the effort to place the mining industry on an assured foundation. Had all the parties shown the same frankness and readiness to face the issues raised by the Coal Commission's report an amicable settlement might have been reached. But in fact, in the discussions that followed between representatives of the owners and the miners the broad constructive proposals of the Coal Commission were obscured by the dispute that arose concerning the form and contents of the new wage agreement. It became evident quite early in the discussions that the owners took a totally different view of the situation from that held by the miners' leaders.

On April 1 the owners issued a statement defining their attitude towards the whole problem. They declared their willingness in general to conform to such measures as Parliament might enact, and expressed their desire to do their utmost to give effect to the objects aimed at in the recommendations which called for action by the owners. But they stated with great bluntness their view that there was no possibility of re-establishing the prosperity of the industry without a longer working day. They also affirmed their conviction that only the districts themselves were competent to deal with the wage question and to fix the minimum percentage additions thereto: this being a reversal of the method of settling wages and conditions by national negotiation to which the miners attached the utmost importance as one of the gains they had won during the war. The owners were prepared to agree that the rates so determined might be brought before the National Board for approval, but that the Board would not be competent to modify or reject any local wage agreement thus reached. In detail the owners also expressed their dissent from some of the most important recommendations of the Commission, including those relating to royalties, amalgamations, co-operative selling, municipal trading, and other points, which they held to be matters either outside the scope of their responsibility, or such as only the individual coal owners could deal with.

Meanwhile the miners' leaders had been active in defining the policy of the Miners' Federation, and in getting into touch with the leaders of the Trade Union Movement. On March 25 they sought an interview with the Industrial Sub-Committee of the Trades Union Congress General Council, and informed them of the Government's statement and the owners' attitude. The Industrial Committee reaffirmed their intention to "support the miners in their efforts to secure a favourable settlement." But the prospects of a happy termination of the dispute receded when the owners insisted that the first step towards the framing of a new wage agreement must be taken in the districts. Upon the disclosure of the owners' policy a deadlock arose, the nature of which is clearly enough indicated in the resolution adopted at the national delegate conference of miners held on April 9:

> "That this conference, having considered the report of the Royal Commission, and the proposals of the coal owners thereon, recommend the districts as follows:
> (*a*) That no assent be given to any proposal for increasing the length of the working day.
> (*b*) That the principle of a National Wage Agreement with a national minimum percentage be firmly adhered to.
> (*c*) That inasmuch as wages are already too low, we cannot assent to any proposals for reducing wages."

These recommendations were referred to the districts for ratification or otherwise, and, as everyone anticipated, they were endorsed by the coalfields with practical unanimity, and thus became the official policy which the Federation pursued with extraordinary tenacity throughout the crisis. The policy was expressed in popular form in the slogan: "Not a minute on the day, not a penny off the pay," and it remained unaltered through the longest industrial conflict this country has yet known.

Following its formulation, however, the situation hardened into a deadlock which no mediation could break. The policy which the Industrial Committee of the General Council of the Trades Union Congress had decided to follow, in endeavouring to narrow down the issues of conflict between the miners and owners, was frustrated by the refusal of the owners to negotiate a national agreement embodying the principle of a uniform national minimum percentage. Thus, on April 13, after meeting the miners' leaders, the Industrial Committee issued a statement protesting against the action of the owners in abandoning national negotiations, and in attempting to open negotiations with the districts; they reiterated their previous declaration in support of the miners, pledging the fullest resistance to the degradation of the miners' standard of life, and the utmost help in obtaining "an equitable settlement of the case in regard to wages, hours, and national agreements." The quoted phrase was carefully chosen in view of the terms in which the miners' delegate conference had embodied the Federation's policy. The Trade Union leaders were not, in fact, committed to the slogan, "Not a minute on, not a penny off"; they were, however, resolute in their insistence upon the necessity of opposing the owners' attempt to settle the dispute with a high hand on the basis of district agreements embodying both wage reductions and extensions of hours.

There were almost continuous meetings between the Industrial Committee of the General Council and the miners' leaders on the one hand, and between the Committee and the Ministers in charge of the negotiations on the other, from the middle to the end of April. On April 26 the Prime Minister was obliged to tell the Industrial Committee that, acting upon their suggestion, he had seen the miners' and owners' representatives separately, but had been unable to get agreement. He asked the Committee to use their influence to bring about real negotiations, and suggested that two or three of the Committee should be associated with the negotiating committee of the miners. Mr. (later Sir) Arthur Pugh, the chairman of the General Council, who acted as chairman of the Industrial Committee, stated at this meeting the firm view of the Trade Union leaders that the whole question had been wrongly handled by the Ministers. The question of wage reductions, he said, was raised far too early; it had been put in the forefront of the discussion, and the whole effort of the Ministers appeared to have been to get from the miners an undertaking that they would agree to wage reductions before there had been any real attempt to ascertain what the position of the industry would be when the Commission's recommendations for its reorganisation were accepted and applied. He thought the first step should have been "to get down to the report."

A further effort on the part of the Prime Minister drew from the owners, on April 27, the statement that if he invited both parties to meet him together, they (the owners) would not impose any limitations or reservations at all upon the conference, but they were unwilling to adopt the Prime Minister's suggestion of associating either some or all of the members of the Industrial Committee of the T.U.C. in their discussions with the miners. The conference was held, and there were subsequently a series of separate conferences between the Prime Minister and his colleagues and the various committees representing the owners, miners, and Trade Union leaders involved in the work of negotiation. Nothing came of these meetings, inasmuch as in various forms the issue which arose again and again to block the path to a settlement was the question whether the miners would agree to the principle of wage reductions as a preliminary step to the consideration of the larger issues raised by the Commission's report.

On April 29, therefore, when the Industrial Committee faced the conference of the executives of the Trade Unions, which had been summoned, as the highest authority with power to act in such a matter, to consider the situation and decide upon the policy which the Trade Union Movement would pursue in relation to the dispute, all they could do in the first session was to state the facts about the deadlock and explain their own action in trying to mediate a settlement. The conference, after hearing these statements, passed the following resolution, which defined the position of the Trade Unions on the eve of the mine owners' lock-out notices taking effect:

> "That this conference of Trade Union executives affiliated to the Trades Union Congress endorses the efforts of the General Council to secure an honourable settlement of the differences in the coal mining industry.
>
> "It further instructs the Industrial Committee of the General Council to continue its efforts, and declares its readiness for the negotiations to continue, provided that the impending lock-out of the mine workers is not enforced.
>
> "That this conference hereby adjourns until tomorrow, Friday, and agrees to remain in London, to enable the General Council to consult, report, and take instructions.

This resolution signalled the near approach of the climax of the mining dispute. It contained, for those who were able to read between the lines, a clear warning of what lay ahead. Tired and anxious, the negotiators met again on the following day, April 30, to make a supreme effort to find a way out. From Downing Street the Prime Minister sent at midday to the miners' leaders and the Industrial Committee, waiting at the House of Commons, the final proposals of the owners. What they proposed was a reduction of wages to the level of the 1921 agreement, and the extension of working hours to eight per day; that is, a national minimum of 20 per cent. above the basic rates of the districts on a uniform eight-hour basis, with corresponding hours for surface workers. The Prime Minister, in transmitting these proposals, stated that the Government would undertake to set up a Commission not later than December 31, 1929, to decide whether the coal industry had sufficiently improved to justify a reversion to the seven-hour day. On these terms a national agreement could be framed, on the lines of the draft agreement presented by the owners, providing for the retention of the principle of a national overriding minimum percentage addition to wages.

The presentation of such terms, at a moment when the owners' lock-out notices were already taking effect and thousands of mine workers were already on the streets, came as a bombshell to the Trade Union leaders. Whilst the Prime Minister's letter was being considered by the miners' executive and the national delegate conference—its rejection was a foregone conclusion—the Industrial Committee sought to obtain from the Prime Minister a favourable answer to the resolution of the previous day's conference of Trade Union executives, asking for the withdrawal of the lock-out notices. That conference was still in being, adjourned from hour to hour, awaiting the outcome of these discussions. But the Prime Minister declined to consider the suggestion of withdrawing the lock-out notices until he had received from the miners their reply to the owners' offer. This reply, delivered by letter, unceremoniously rejected these terms as unworthy of consideration; and the later meetings in the evening of April 30, were concerned with the Government's attempt to extract a pledge that the miners would accept wage reductions as a preliminary condition of the suspension of lock-out notices and the continuation of negotiations. No such pledge could be given.

Thus, on the eve of the national stoppage, the position was one of complete deadlock. Following the rejection by the miners of the owners' offer, involving both wage reductions and extension of working hours, the Government put to the Trade Union leaders this question:

> "Will the Trades Union Congress Committee obtain assurance that, if further time were available for negotiation, the miners' representatives would enter into negotiations accepting the Commissioners' recommendations on this point" (i.e., wages) "printed at the top of page 236 of the report?"

The reference here is to the Commission's declaration that "If the present hours are to be retained, we think a revision of 'minimum percentage addition to standard rates of wages' fixed in 1924 at a time of temporary prosperity is indispensable. A disaster is impending over the industry, and the immediate reduction of working costs that can be effected in this way, and in this way alone, is essential to save it." Here the Government took its stand. But the miners also were firm in their attitude. The Trade Union leaders brought back to the Prime Minister the miners' answer to the question he had put, and it was in the following terms:

> "In reply to the Government's memorandum, the miners say they are not prepared to accept a reduction in wages as a preliminary to the reorganisation of the industry. They reiterate that they would be prepared to give full consideration to all the immediate difficulties connected with the industry when the scheme for reorganisation has been initiated by the Government."

In the view of the Trade Union leaders this statement was sufficient to warrant a suspension of the lock-out notices, and they urged the Government to accept it and act upon it. They pointed out that the miners' president, Mr. Herbert Smith, had declared the miners' executive were not shackled by decisions of the delegate conference, and that he was prepared, when he saw the Government and the owners meant to carry out the reorganisation of the industry as recommended by the Commission, to put a value on it and make a recommendation to his executive. But the Ministers insisted that Mr. Smith's assurance that he was willing to discuss a reduction of wages was valueless, since it did not bind him to *accept* a wage reduction during the period of the reorganisation. As the Prime Minister put it, the Government was not convinced that there was a better chance of progress at the moment in pursuing negotiations. There was no assurance that they would lead to any fruitful result, and they feared that a continuation of the negotiations might end again in a second deadlock, which would lead them into a worse position than the one they were in at that moment.

By this time, moreover, the Trade Union leaders were persuaded that the Government had made up its mind that a conflict was inevitable. In the course of the discussions in these closing hours of April 30—the real "zero hour," though the stoppage did not actually start until midnight on May 3—the Trade Union leaders displayed a poster of the "O.M.S.," or "Organisation for the Maintenance of Supplies," an unofficial body created for the purpose of assisting the Government, announcing that the Government had declared a state of emergency and calling upon "all loyal citizens" who were able and willing to undertake any public service to enrol their names at the local centres of the organisation. This poster the printers refused to print, and the Trade Union leaders warned Ministers that an incident of this kind showed the dangers of the situation that had arisen. The Prime Minister assured the Trade Union leaders that he and his colleagues knew nothing of this particular announcement, though he admitted that the proclamation of "a state of emergency" was ready and would be issued when the Government was certain the crisis could not be averted. And it was with this knowledge that the weary and harassed members of the Industrial Committee of the Trades Union Congress General Council went at midnight to tell the conference of Trade Union executives waiting for them at the Memorial Hall that negotiations had broken down.

At that conference the negotiators explained the whole course of events leading up to the breakdown. The draft scheme for a national stoppage of work, which had been prepared by a sub-committee of the General Council, was circulated to the representatives of the Unions with instructions that they were to be considered by each executive and decisions taken prior to the reassembling of the conference at noon on the following day. The proceedings, upon the resumption of the conference on May 1, were charged with dramatic feeling. One by one, as the names of the Unions were read out by the chairman, Mr. Arthur Pugh, the officials of the Unions signified their support of the General Council's policy and programme of action. Representatives of Unions with an aggregate of 3,653,000 members thus declared their readiness to strike, and there were only a few small organisations, with a total membership of less than 50,000, which returned a negative answer to the chairman's summons. By the decision then taken the Unions invested the General Council with full authority for the conduct of the strike. The national delegate conference of miners, before they adjourned, likewise decided to hand over to the General Council the conduct of negotiations in connection with the dispute. The plan of action framed by the General Council's sub-committee provided that the following trades and undertakings should cease work as and when required by the General Council:

> "Transport, including all affiliated Unions connected with transport, i.e. railways, sea transport, docks, wharves, harbours, canals, road transport, railways repair shops and contractors for railways, and all Unions connected with the maintenance of, or equipment, manufacturing, repairs, and groundsmen employed in connection with air transport.
>
> "Printing Trades, including the Press.
>
> "Productive Industries: (a) Iron and Steel; (b) Metal and Heavy Chemicals group,

> including all metal workers and other workers who are engaged or may be engaged in installing alternative plant to take the place of coal.
> "Building Trade, all workers engaged on building, except such as are employed definitely on housing or hospital work, together with all workers engaged in the supply of equipment to the building industry.
> "Electricity and Gas, the Unions connected with the supply thereof to co-operate with the object of ceasing to supply power, the executives of the Unions concerned being required to meet for the purpose of formulating a common policy.
> "Sanitary Services were to be continued.
> "Health and Food Services were not to be interfered with, and the Trade Unions concerned were instructed to do everything in their power to organise the distribution of food and milk to the whole of the population."

Instructions were also framed by the General Council for the supply of food, milk, medical and surgical supplies to hospitals, clinics, sanatoria, convalescent homes, infant welfare centres, maternity and nursing homes, and schools. The Unions were instructed to keep a register of their members, and to see that no one who was called upon to cease work should leave his district, and by following the same or another occupation in another district become a blackleg. It was arranged that the actual calling out of the workers should be left to the individual Unions and measures were suggested for enabling the local trades councils to organise the workers in the most effective manner for the preservation of peace and order. It was also laid down by the General Council that the executives of the Unions should definitely declare that in the event of Trade Union agreements being placed in jeopardy, there would be no general resumption of work until those agreements were fully recognised. A warning was also made against incitement to disorder by spies and *agents provocateur*.

But although matters had gone so far, the Trade Union leaders had not abandoned hope of securing a settlement without resorting to these desperate measures. Up to the breakdown of negotiations on April 30, they had failed to obtain from the Government any positive proposals for a settlement, except those put forward through the Prime Minister by the owners. They still believed an honourable peace could be made if the Government would withdraw its demand for an undertaking from the miners' leaders to consent in advance to a reduction of wages, and the lock-out notices were cancelled. Accordingly, the Industrial Committee of the General Council returned to Downing Street on the Saturday evening, May 1, and met the Prime Minister and his colleagues—Lord Birkenhead, Mr. Neville Chamberlain, Mr. W. C. Bridgeman, Sir Arthur Steel-Maitland, and Colonel Lane Fox. As a result of these renewed discussions the following formula was drawn up:

> "The Prime Minister has satisfied himself, as a result of the consultations he has had with the representatives of the Trades Union Congress, that if negotiations are continued" (it being understood that the notices cease to be operative) "the representatives of the Trades Union Congress are confident that a settlement can be reached on the lines of the report within a fortnight."

This formula was framed in the early hours of Sunday, May 2, but no progress could be made in discussing its meaning and intention until late on Sunday night, owing to the absence of the miners' leaders, who had returned to their districts. Pending their return to the scene of the negotiations, the Trade Union leaders met once more at Downing Street on Sunday evening, and resumed conversations with the Prime Minister and his colleagues, with the object of reaching a clear understanding of what the Prime Minister's formula implied. This talk led to the scribbling down of still another formula, in which the Ministers embodied their view of what the Trade Union leaders were undertaking to do. It was in these terms:

> "We would urge the miners to authorise us to enter upon discussion with the understanding that they and we accept the report as a basis of settlement, and we approach it with the knowledge that it may involve some reduction in wages."

Considerable dispute arose later concerning this formula. It was contended by spokesmen of the Government that the Trade Union leaders accepted it, and were thus committed to the position of having to urge the miners to agree to it. The Trade Union leaders, on the other hand, declared that it had not been taken by them as anything more than a rough summary of the issue they were discussing, a tentative form of words jotted down by one of the Ministers as a statement of the position reached in the discussion. It had no binding effect. In any case it had no practical importance, by reason of the fact that the Trade Union leaders had no opportunity of discussing any formula with the miners' leaders. For when the latter reached Downing Street shortly before midnight, and were beginning to consider with the Trade Union leaders the position of affairs, they were interrupted by a messenger from the Prime Minister. He asked the General Council's representatives to see him, and to them he handed a document which has been quite rightly described as an ultimatum. It declared that the Government, before it could continue negotiations, must require from the Trade Union leaders a repudiation of "overt acts" that had taken place, including "gross interference with the freedom of the press," and an immediate and unconditional withdrawal of the strike instructions.

Why the Government so abruptly decided to break off the conversations, without giving the Trade Union leaders even the opportunity of saying whether they accepted or denied responsibility for the "overt acts"—of which they then heard for the first time—was never explained. The action of the printing-trade workers employed in the offices of the *Daily Mail* in stopping the publication of the night's issue by ceasing work in advance of the Union's instructions, hardly justified the brusque decision of the Government. There was, however, a strong group in the Cabinet, headed by Mr. Neville Chamberlain, who thought the Government was displaying a dangerous weakness in continuing negotiations under the threat of the General Council's strike instructions. Faced with the possibility of half a dozen resignations from the Cabinet, the Prime Minister yielded to the demand of his colleagues that negotiations must be broken off, unless the strike instructions were immediately cancelled; and the Trade Union negotiators, when they went down from the conference room at Downing Street to deliver their reply to the ultimatum, found that the Ministers had gone home and there was nobody to receive their reply. A reasoned statement of the Council's position was issued an hour later from their own headquarters.

On Monday, May 3, at midnight, the strike instructions took effect. No effort was made on that day to avert the stoppage of the nation's activities. Both sides busied themselves in preparation for the strike. Newspapers, with the one exception of the *Daily Mail*, appeared as usual on that day, but evening papers were stopped, and on Tuesday the "shut down" was almost complete. Trains, trams, and buses ceased to run, except where they could be kept going with volunteer labour, and productive industry came to a standstill as if smitten with a sudden paralysis. To describe the day-to-day development of the strike is not the purpose of these pages. It must suffice to say that the stoppage in the case of transport was practically universal, and that large numbers of workers in the iron and steel and other metal trades, the printing and paper trades, and the building and allied industries obeyed the strike instructions. The stoppage in the gas and electrical power industries was not so complete, although a large number of operatives ceased work; many of the technical staffs remained at their posts, and with the help of volunteers and naval ratings the supply of electricity was maintained fairly fully throughout the stoppage. Even the newspapers contrived to appear in a much attenuated form, and the public was able to get about without much difficulty through the agency of a multitude of private cars which picked up passengers at all points. No serious outbreak of disorder marked the course of the struggle. The spectacular display of armed force in some parts of the country was little more than a demonstration. The Government's emergency transport organisation, the outcome of long preparation initiated by the Coalition Government of 1919, proved very effective. The scheme had been carefully worked out by the Government Departments concerned, in conjunction with the Civil Commissioners, who had been appointed to supervise matters in the various areas; lists of volunteers, owners of vehicles, and centres of distribution had been prepared; routes, relays, and depots were all arranged beforehand. On May 5, the Government started to issue a daily newspaper, the *British Gazette*, and on the following day the Trades Union Congress began the publication of its official strike organ, the *British Worker*; both journals appeared each day until the strike ended.

Official figures estimate the number of workpeople who took part in the strike at approximately 1,580,000; in addition there were 1,075,000 workpeople involved in the mining lock-out. Some of the Unions who were included in the General Council's scheme of strike action were not brought out. Thus the Unions in the engineering and shipbuilding trades received instructions by wire on May 10 to cease work on May 12, the order not to apply to men in the Royal Dockyards, Admiralty, and Government engineering establishments. Before this instruction took effect the strike had been brought to an end. There were several incidents of the strike period upon which extended comment might be made did space permit. For example, the speeches of Sir John Simon, in which he sought to prove that the strike was unconstitutional and illegal, caused a great deal of uneasiness, which was heightened by the judgment of Mr. Justice Astbury in the action brought to restrain officials of the National Sailors' and Firemen's Union from calling out its members without the prior authority of the executive of the Union, a ballot of whom was in progress. In the course of this judgment the Judge expressed the view that the national strike was illegal and contrary to law, and those persons inciting to or taking part in it were not protected by the Trade Disputes Act of 1906. Trade Union leaders, however, inclined to the view that these legal opinions were based on a misreading of the Trade Disputes Act, under the provisions of which sympathetic strikes are not illegal.

Whilst the strike went on efforts were made, not only by the Trade Union leaders, but by public men of all parties, to find a way of bringing the conflict to an end. Officially, neither the Government nor the mine owners made any movement towards a settlement. In fact, on May 8, in a speech broadcast by wireless, the Prime Minister declared that the Government was resisting an attempt of the Trade Unions to force Parliament and the community to bend to their will. "I wish to make it as clear as I can," said Mr. Baldwin, "that the Government is not fighting to lower the standard of living of the miners or any other section of the workers. That suggestion has been spread abroad. It is not true. I do not believe that any honest person can doubt that my whole desire is to maintain the standard of living of every worker, and that I am ready to press the employers to make a sacrifice to this end consistent with keeping the industry itself in order." But the Prime Minister added that the Government must insist upon the strike being called off, "absolutely and without reserve." For their part, the Trade Union leaders maintained with equal firmness that they were not engaged in an attempt to overthrow the Government; they denied that the strike was unconstitutional or illegal; and they insisted that withdrawal of the lock-out notices against the miners was as much a condition of the resumption of negotiations on their side as the Government's demand for the withdrawal of the strike orders.

Matters were thus at a deadlock. Religious leaders, headed by the Archbishop of Canterbury, on May 5, endeavoured to frame the basis of a possible *concordat* involving a return to the *status quo* prevailing before the strike. This proposal, they suggested, was to be interpreted as involving simultaneously and concurrently:

(1) Cancellation on the part of the T.U.C. of the General Strike.
(2) Renewal by the Government of the offer of assistance to the coal industry for a short definite period.
(3) Withdrawal on the part of the mine owners of the new wages scales recently issued.

This suggestion was not taken up. But on May 9, more promising *pourparlers* were opened by the intervention of Sir Herbert Samuel, who returned hurriedly from a continental holiday to assist in the settlement of the dispute. The Government, it is true, declared that Sir Herbert Samuel acted entirely on his own responsibility, and was in no sense an official mediator or plenipotentiary. But it was known that he had discussed the situation with the Prime Minister, and it was believed—at any rate by the Trade Union leaders—that the suggestions he put forward for a settlement were favourably regarded by the Government as the basis of a possible armistice with the Trade Unions.

It was with this idea in mind that the negotiating committee of the Trades Union Congress pursued their conversations with Sir Herbert Samuel. On Monday, May 10, proposals were drafted embodying his suggestions for a settlement. They were considered by the miners' leaders, who wished to amend them. Further discussions took place, there were meetings between the miners and Sir Herbert Samuel, and between the negotiating committee and the miners; and on May 11 the Trade Union leaders took the momentous decision to terminate the strike, satisfied by their conversations with Sir Herbert Samuel that the mining dispute could be settled on the basis of the proposals embodied in his memorandum. How far they were entitled to believe that the Government was a party to the conversations, and what guarantees they had received that if the strike was terminated the lock-out notices would be withdrawn, and the whole of the strikers reinstated without victimisation, can be only a matter of speculation and inference. The letter written by Sir Herbert Samuel conveying the memorandum of his proposals for a settlement, formally disclaimed any suggestion that he had acted with the Government's authority. This letter, dated May 12, was in the following terms:

"Dear Mr. Pugh,

"As the outcome of the conversations which I have had with your committee, I attach a memorandum embodying the conclusions that have been reached. I have made it clear to your committee from the outset that I have been acting entirely on my own initiative, have received no authority from the Government, and can give no assurances on their behalf. I am of opinion that the proposals embodied in the memorandum are suitable for adoption, and are likely to promote a settlement of the differences in the coal industry. I shall strongly recommend their acceptance by the Government when the negotiations are resumed.

"Yours, etc.,

HERBERT SAMUEL."

In an equally formal letter the chairman of the Trades Union Congress and its acting secretary stated the position of the General Council:

> "Dear Sir,
>
> "The General Council having carefully considered your letter of today, and the memorandum attached to it, concurred in your opinion that it offers a basis on which the negotiations upon the conditions in the coal industry can be renewed. They are taking the necessary measures to terminate the General Strike, relying upon the public assurances of the Prime Minister as to the steps that would follow. They assume that during the resumed negotiations the subsidy will be renewed, and that the lock-out notices to the miners will be immediately withdrawn.
>
> "Yours, etc.,
>
> Arthur Pugh (Chairman),
> Walter M. Citrine (Acting Secretary)."

The Trade Union leaders, according to the terms of this letter, placed their reliance not upon private assurances received during the Samuel conversations, but upon the *public* declarations of the Prime Minister. He had said that the Government was not fighting to reduce the standard of living among the mine workers, and that he was ready to press the employers to make a sacrifice so that the standard might be maintained. But he had insisted, as he was bound to do, upon the unconditional termination of the strike. The Government, by representing the strike as unconstitutional and illegal, and as an effort on the part of the General Council to "force Parliament and the community to bend to its will," had made it impossible for the Prime Minister and his colleagues to enter into negotiations, or to countenance negotiations on their behalf, for a termination of the strike on terms: they had made it impossible to bargain with the General Council, because they had represented the General Council as a body of revolutionary conspirators engaged in an attempt to overthrow ordered Government and the established institutions of the country. The General Council, on the other hand, if it continued to insist upon cancellation of the lock-out notices and other conditions before terminating the strike, would have forced matters to an absolute deadlock, which nothing under heaven but the employment of force could have broken. Sir Herbert Samuel's intervention enabled both sides to withdraw from an impossible position: since neither side could contemplate without horror the thought of having to decide the issue by force, the work of the mediator was undoubtedly welcomed by both sides. If at this stage the Trade Union leaders had insisted upon assurances from the Government, the latter's insistence upon unconditional withdrawal of the strike orders would have become an insurmountable obstacle to peace, for the Government could not have given way on that without gravely weakening its authority and prestige, and admitting that a co-equal power had arisen to challenge control of the State. The patriotism and good sense of the Trade Union leaders, not less than their courage and firmness in facing criticism from their own followers, prevented such an impasse being created. Fundamental issues, affecting the very foundation and structure of organised society, were allowed to sink back into obscurity, and the Government emerged from the conflict nominally the victor in a dispute with a new organised power represented by the massed millions of trade unionists, who acknowledged loyalty not to the elected Government, but to their own chosen leaders.

These considerations, however, were not publicly debated at the time when the strike was terminated. The Trade Union leaders had other preoccupations. The most difficult of them was the position of the miners. Before the Trade Union leaders went to Downing Street, on the morning of May 12, to inform the Prime Minister of their decision to terminate the strike, the miners' executive met in session to consider the position in which they stood as a result of the General Council's action. The miners' leaders, on the previous night, had already made it known that they did not regard the Samuel memorandum as an acceptable basis of settlement. At midnight their view had been conveyed to the General Council in the following resolution:

> "The miners' executive have given a careful and patient consideration to the draft proposals prepared by the T.U.C. negotiating committee and endorsed by the General Council as representing 'the best terms which can be obtained to settle the present crisis in the coal industry.'
>
> "They regret the fact that no opportunity for consideration was afforded the accredited representatives of the Miners' Federation on the negotiating committee in the preparation of the draft or in the discussion of May 11 leading thereto.
>
> "At best, the proposals imply a reduction of the wages rates of a large number of mine workers, which is contrary to the repeated declarations of the Miners' Federation, and which they believe their fellow trade unionists are assisting them to resist.
>
> "They regret, therefore, whilst having regard to the grave issues involved, that they must reject the proposals. Moreover, if such proposals are submitted as a means to call off the General Strike, such a step must be taken on the sole responsibility of the General Council."

Efforts were made to induce the miners' leaders to reverse this decision, and at their meeting on May 12, they discussed the position afresh with representatives of the General Council—Messrs. Pugh, Purcell, Walker, Bevin, Turner and Rowan. At that meeting the miners were informed that the General Council would be seeing the Prime Minister to announce their intention of calling off the strike, and the miners were urged once more to accept the Samuel memorandum and agree to this step. The miners' leaders, however, adhered to their earlier decision, and stated their position in the following terms:

> "That having heard the report of the representatives of the T.U.C., we reaffirm our resolution of May 11, and express our profound admiration of the wonderful demonstration of loyalty as displayed by all workers who promptly withdrew their labour in support of the miners' standards, and undertake to report fully to a conference to be convened as early as practicable."

Thus the Trade Union leaders when they went to Downing Street to meet the Prime Minister were aware that the miners were not with them in the decision to terminate the strike. But the General Council, having been invested with full authority not only for carrying on the strike, but for the conduct of negotiations—an authority which the miners themselves had recognised by the decision of their own national delegate conference on the eve of the strike—acted in what it conceived to be the best interests of all concerned, and faced the obloquy and criticism that it knew to be inevitable in the circumstances attendant upon the termination of the struggle.

Those circumstances were such that for the next few days the whole Labour and Trade Union Movement was in a state of confusion and bewilderment. Much of this was due to the action of the Government's organ, the *British Gazette*, in proclaiming the result as a complete victory for the Government; the General Council, it was said, had unconditionally surrendered, having made no bargain either about the withdrawal of the mining lock-out notices or the reinstatement of strikers, or the renewal of Trade Union agreements. The Government had won outright. This was the burden of the newspapers when they appeared—and it was also very much the view taken by the rank and file of the Trade Unions and by the employers. The settlement, in fact, was gravely imperilled within the next few hours by the action of employers in trying to dictate the terms upon which work was to be resumed. It was necessary for the Prime Minister to state firmly in the House of Commons on May 13, that the Government would not countenance any attempt on the part of any employers to use the occasion for trying to enforce wage reductions, or to alter the terms of existing agreements. Victimisation of strikers was attempted. But the Trade Union leaders were firm in their attitude. They issued a statement declaring that the Trade Union Movement was not broken. It was not beaten. It was as united and as resolute as ever, and would resist all attempts of employers to take advantage of the situation. New agreements, indeed, had to be negotiated, and in many of them the employers insisted upon the inclusion of clauses by which the Unions admitted that the strike was a wrongful act, and undertook in future not to call a strike until the procedure for the settlement of disputes by negotiation had been exhausted. But on the whole, industry soon settled down, and there was a minimum of friction in setting the wheels in motion again.

From the General Strike the Trade Unions emerged in a very weakened condition. Funds that had been accumulated over years of careful administration were heavily depleted, and there was in the case of many Unions a decline in membership, caused in part by the defection of a minority of members, who were dissatisfied with the decision of their officials to support the strike policy, and in part by the dissatisfaction caused among a section of the more militant members by the circumstances in which the strike was brought to an end. Cases were reported of the formation of "breakaway Unions," and in the printing and paper trades the employers in some establishments began the formation of "house unions," membership of which was limited to their own employees, and the objects of which were confined largely to the payment of friendly benefits. These aberrations did not, however, affect very seriously the mass organisation of the workers: the Movement rather was injured by the failure of the strike to attain its declared objectives.

Politically the Labour Party suffered much less than the Trade Unions by the course of events in this disturbed period of working-class history. The political leaders were not directly involved in the National Strike. Throughout the negotiations, told in detail in the preceding pages, the Labour Party was required to play the passive role of spectator. The Trade Union leaders admitted the Parliamentary representatives of Labour into their counsels for purposes of information only, and they were given very little opportunity of influencing the march of events, even to the extent of initiating Parliamentary debates. It was treated as a purely industrial dispute, and was kept firmly in the hands of the Trade Union leaders from first to last.

Although the National Strike naturally excited against the Unions a considerable amount of public resentment, it was not, curiously enough, reflected in the by-elections that took place in the months immediately following the settlement of the dispute. At Hammersmith and at Wallsend the Labour candidates materially increased the Labour vote. In the General Election of 1924 the seat at Hammersmith was won by the Conservatives by 12,925 votes to 10,970 polled by the Labour candidate; in the by-election in that division in May 1926, a few days after the strike ended, the Labour vote was increased to 13,095 and the Conservative vote fell to 9,484. At Wallsend, in the by-election caused by the retirement of Sir Patrick Hastings from political life, the seat was held by Miss Margaret Bondfield by an increased majority of 9,027 votes, as compared with a majority of 1,602 votes at the General Election. In the whole of the by-elections that took place in the period dealt with in these pages, the Labour Party candidates polled a total of 197,902 votes, against a total of 184,341 votes cast for the Government candidates; and in no fewer than five cases the Liberal candidates forfeited their deposits through their failure to obtain the requisite one-eighth of the votes. If these results had all been signalled before the National Strike took place, it might have been possible to say that nothing in the figures showed how the country felt about the great industrial upheaval of 1926. But two of the by-elections, and not the least significant, occurred so closely after that event that the figures can fairly be taken as a disclosure of the judgment of the electors upon the part played by the Labour Party and the Conservative Government respectively in relation to the national stoppage and the mining dispute.

CHAPTER XIV

THE WAY BACK TO OFFICE

By Herbert Tracey

The final judgment of the electors upon the events of the 1926 General Strike as they affected the position of the Labour Party was not delivered until 1929. The way back to Office of the Labour Party resembled, in some respects, the path it trod in the earlier years, when its hold upon trade unionists was strengthened by its handling of the situation created by the Taff Vale Judgment in 1902 and the Osborne Judgment in 1909. The organised workers were once again rallied to the Labour Party's standard by the action of the Conservative Government in launching a dangerous attack upon the legal rights of the Trade Unions. No sooner was the National Strike at an end than the Government's draughtsmen were set to work upon the framing of a Bill to illegalise strikes of a general character, to limit the practice of the Unions in picketing, to break the connection of the Civil Service Unions with the organised Movement, and to try to raise new obstacles to the development of the organic relations of the Unions with the Labour Party. The Trade Disputes and Trade Unions Act, passed in 1927, was naturally interpreted by the leaders of organised Labour as a new and more determined attempt to cripple both the industrial and political organisation of the workers, and to strike from their hands their principal defensive weapons.

In resistance to this attack, inspired as they believed by motives of class and partisan hostility, the leaders of organised Labour set on foot a national campaign. It did not succeed in frustrating the Government's resolve to legislate against the Unions; but it did arouse the great mass of the working people, at any rate, to a realisation of the issues involved.

The May Day manifesto issued by the Trade Union committee conducting this vigorous campaign struck the note which was calculated to evoke the right response.

More than ever before (ran the manifesto) it is necessary for the workers on this May Day to reaffirm their unity and their devotion to Labour's cause :

> "Long established rights and legal powers, won by the Trade Unions by years of struggle and sacrifice, are imperilled by the Government's Trade Disputes and Trade Unions Bill.
>
> "A dangerous attack has been launched upon the workers' organisations by the powerful employers' associations and reactionary class influences which control the Tory Government.
>
> "Their aim is to deprive the workers, by Act of Parliament, of their strongest weapons of defence against exploitation and oppression. The Trade Unions are to be fettered by legal restrictions upon the right to strike, the right to picket, the

right to use Union funds for Union purposes, the right of trade unionists to associate with one another and to act together in pursuit of a common policy by lawful means.

"The blow is aimed at the fundamental principle of Trade Unionism—the principle of combination by the workers who share a common experience of toil and hardship, exposed to the risks of unemployment, of wage-cuts, of unjust and oppressive conditions of labour, no matter in what industry or trade they are employed.

"Those who have grown wealthy and powerful by exploitation of the producers, hate and fear the unity and discipline of the Trade Union Movement. They know that the strength of the organised workers is their solidarity, their loyalty and devotion to the organisations they have created. They seek to destroy these organisations, not by frontal attacks which the mass of wage earners can understand and repel, but by mean and malicious attempts to undermine the spirit that has united the workers.

"The Government's Bill offers incitement and encouragement to trade unionists to betray their fellow members, and to bring divisions and dissensions into the Unions.

"It exposes to the peril of criminal prosecution, to fine or imprisonment, those who take part in any strike or stoppage of work which can be declared illegal within the meaning of the Bill.

"It places in the hands of the police, of magistrates, of judges, the power of deciding whether workmen who cease work in protest against injustice or unfair treatment from employers are to be punished as criminals. It disables the Trade Unions from using their funds or their power of effective action to defend their own members when such legal decision has been given.

"Remember the Taff Vale Case!

"Remember the Osborne Judgment!

"Remember the pronouncement of Mr. Justice Astbury!

"In countless instances it has been proved that the law can be twisted to penalise the workers and to paralyse the action of their organisations when industrial disputes arise. This Bill increases these legal dangers for the Trade Unions a thousandfold.

"The Bill denies to workers in the Civil Service, freedom of association with their fellow workers outside the service. The Civil Service Unions are not to have the assistance of other Unions in their efforts to improve conditions of employment under the Crown, and are not to be allowed to assist their fellow trade unionists outside the service, although conditions in other employment are used as an argument against Civil Service workers.

"The Bill strikes a heavy blow also at the political rights of the Trade Unions. It is intended to injure and impoverish the Labour Party by making it difficult for the Unions to collect political contributions from their members. It does more. It strikes at the whole of the political activities of the Trade Unions.

"To disable the Labour Party the rich men who have dictated the terms of the Bill are attempting to prevent the Unions from collecting the political contributions their members have, by ballot, decided to make for the lawful political objects the Unions are entitled by Act of Parliament to pursue.

"The Party of the rich is trying to cripple the Party of the poor.

"A rich Party, financed by secret funds derived from the sale of honours and from large subsidies subscribed by wealthy men, is trying to disable a poor Party which carried on its work by modest contributions from Trade Unionists.

"The Trade Unions make no concealment of their political funds.

"The Labour Party collects its funds in the light of day.

"The Parties opposed to the Trade Unions and the Labour Party are financed from secret sources they dare not reveal.

> "They have millions at their disposal.
> "Are the adversaries of Labour to have the right of obstructing the collection of political funds by the working people, to interfere with the arrangements of the Unions for gathering the pennies of their members in order to maintain the Labour Party, whilst rich men may make large secret contributions to the organisations engaged in fighting the Labour Party and to disable the Trade Unions?
> "Workers! Your enemies use every unfair weapon against you. Meet their unscrupulous, mean, and malignant attack by resolute and united opposition! Rally round your leaders! Your loyalty to your Party is the Party's guarantee of defeat for your enemies and triumph for your cause."

This document merits reproduction in full because it sets out concisely, yet fully, Labour's case against the 1927 Act.

In its final form this legislation imposed serious disabilities upon the Trade Unions involved in industrial disputes. It struck simultaneously at the power of the Unions to act in concert for objects which appealed to the workers' spirit of solidarity; at the relations of the Unions with the Labour Party; and at the association of Unions of Civil Service workers with their fellow trade unionists in affiliation with both the Labour Party and the Trades Union Congress.

What gave the National Strike of 1926 its deepest significance was that it was a demonstration of working-class solidarity under a responsible leadership. It was, moreover, a demonstration of the tremendous power that resides in the working-class organisation permeated by such a spirit. It had shown that the leaders of organised Labour could depend upon the loyalty and self-sacrificing spirit of the millions of trade unionists when they felt that they were being called upon to act in a just cause (notwithstanding the misrepresentation of their action as an unconstitutional attack upon the Government and against the interests of the community). A conspiracy to weaken the solidarity and discipline of organised Labour, to divide its forces, and to deprive it of some at least of the resources upon which its leaders depended for the attainment of both their political and industrial objectives may not have been a deliberate aim of those who framed the 1927 Act: but these were almost exactly the results it was calculated to achieve.

It imposed, in the first place, a limitation upon the right to strike, by illegalising any stoppage of work which had any object other than the furtherance of a trade dispute within the trade or industry in which the strikers were engaged. This provision was aimed at the sympathetic strike. It was intended to prevent workers not directly involved in a trade dispute from taking strike action in support of their fellow workers who called a strike. It illegalised, too, any strike with a political object by forbidding any strike that was calculated to coerce the Government or to intimidate the community by inflicting hardship or suffering upon it or any considerable section of it; and it became an offence to begin or continue or to apply any money in furtherance or support of any such stoppage of work. Penalties of fines or imprisonment were provided against any person who declared, instigated, assisted, or took part in such illegal strikes—a provision manifestly aimed at Trade Union leaders and officials. Rank and file members of a Union who acted simply in obedience to the instructions of their officials in ceasing work were not penalised. But on the other hand, the Act laid it down that any member of a Union who refused to cease work should not be penalised in any way by the loss of any rights of membership—which was putting a premium upon disloyalty among the rank and file to majority decisions and responsible leadership.

Rights of Trade Union picketing were severely curtailed. It imposed a serious disability upon Civil Service workers who were required to withdraw from any association which maintained affiliations with national organisations outside the Civil Service. This meant that half a dozen Civil Service Unions inside the Trades Union Congress, with a combined membership of 137,500 were compelled to cease their membership; their delegates were no longer able to appear in Congress and the seats held on the General Council by representatives of these Civil Service Unions had to be vacated. Similarly, the political affiliation of these Unions with the Labour Party was terminated, and Labour Members in the House of Commons, whose candidatures were sponsored by Civil Service Unions were supposed to withdraw from membership of the Party; though actually more than one of them retained their active contact with the Party, and at least one of them became a member of the Labour Government in 1929.

But the provision of the Act which gave rise to the strongest suspicion about its political motives was the alteration made in the procedure laid down by the Trade Union Act of 1913, concerning the political action of the Unions and their relations with the Labour Party.

Under the 1913 Act the Unions were entitled to take a ballot of their members on the question of adding political objects to their other objects, and to create a political fund for the furtherance of these political objects. Provision was made in the 1913 Act for members of a Union who did not wish to contribute to its political fund to "contract out"; and the Act stipulated that the General Funds of a Union must not be used for political objects, but only the political fund, built up from the contributions of members who had not "contracted out." The 1927 Act deliberately reversed this contracting-out procedure, with the clear intention of making it more difficult for trade unionists to contribute to the maintenance of a political Party of their own making. The 1927 Act, instead of throwing upon dissident members the right to "contract out" of the payment of political dues, required the consenting members who had voted for the setting up of a political fund, to confirm their vote by an individual application in writing to be allowed to contribute to the Union's political fund.

No other organised body of citizens had to submit to humiliating restrictions of this kind. It was not illegal to contribute to political funds. Why trade unionists should be required to signify in writing their wish to do so in the case of contributions to the Labour Party was only too obvious.

If there were vexatious and inconvenient conditions of this kind imposed upon trade unionists, many of them might be expected to thrust the matter aside impatiently and say that they would not be bothered to "contract in." But there were deeper issues involved even than this.

The president of the Trades Union Congress in that year (George Hicks) said that sooner or later the complete futility of the Act would be made apparent. But "there are forces in society stronger than ourselves," he said; "those very forces which brought our Trade Union Movement to birth and caused its growth in spite of oppression, which shaped its destiny and transformed it into the powerful, widespread, and all-embracing Movement that it is today—these forces cannot be shackled by legislation. They are stronger than the Government, stronger than the powers of the capitalist State, and they will be certain to find expression no matter what attempts are made to check and crush them."

There was no menace in this presidential utterance. On the contrary, it was at this Congress, and in this presidential address, that the gesture was made from the Trade Union side that brought about what came to be known as the Mond-Turner Conferences. It was not merely in the political sense, the T.U.C. president said, that the Movement must press forward. The Trade Unions had not reached the limit of their development. Rather he would say that they were just at the beginning of the constructive period of Trade Unionism. More and more the workers were aiming at obtaining a share in the control and administration of industry through the Trade Unions. They all knew, employers as well as trade unionists, he went on, that they were passing through a transitional period:

"Much fuller use can be made under these conditions of the machinery for joint consultation and negotiation between employers and employed. We have not reached the limits of possible development in this direction. It is more than doubtful whether we have seen the fullest possible development of machinery for joint consultation in particular industries. And practically nothing has yet been done to establish effective machinery of joint conference between the representative organisations entitled to speak for industry as a whole. There are many problems upon which joint discussion would prove of value at the present time.

"Such a direct exchange of practical views between representatives of the great organised bodies who have responsibility for the conduct of industry and know its problems at first-hand would be of far greater significance than the suggestion which has been made in certain quarters for a spectacular national conference under the Government or other auspices to discuss a vague aspiration towards 'industrial peace.' Discussion on these lines would bring both sides face to face with the hard realities of the present economic situation, and might yield useful results in showing how far and upon what terms co-operation is possible in a common endeavour to improve the efficiency of industry and to raise the workers' standard of life. It is important that our Movement should frame a clear-cut and coherent policy on practical lines. We should not be deterred by allegations that in entering into such discussions we are surrendering some essential principle of Trade Unionism. On the contrary, they will lead to a much clearer understanding on the part of our own organised Movement of the immediate practical objectives at which we ought to aim and for which we are entitled to use the influence and power with which this Congress is invested."

This pronouncement was readily interpreted as an invitation to the national organisation of employers, then known as the National Confederation of Employers' Organisations, to enter into consultation with the T.U.C. General Council on the problems of industrial relations and other aspects of industry in which both sides had a common interest. But it was also interpreted, and equally rightly, as an indication that the Trade Union Movement, under the guidance of the T.U.C. General Council—which had just then acquired, in the person of Walter Citrine, a new general secretary of very great ability—was deliberately planning a change of policy and direction.

Under the influence of Sir Alfred Mond (later Lord Melchett) a representative and responsible group of employers came into contact with the Trades Union Congress General Council at the beginning of 1928. In a letter on behalf of his fellow industrialists, addressed to the T.U.C., Lord Melchett said that there seemed to be general agreement that a useful purpose could be served by a consideration of fundamental factors in industrial reorganisation and industrial relations. On their side the industrialists for whom he spoke realised that industrial reconstruction could be undertaken only in conjunction with, and by the co-operation of those entitled and empowered to speak for organised Labour. "The necessity of every action being taken to achieve the fullest and speediest measures of industrial reconstruction, therefore, impels us to seek the immediate co-operation of those who are as vitally interested in the subject as ourselves. We believe that the common interests which bind us are more powerful than the apparently divergent interests which seem to separate us."

Following meetings between the General Council and the representative group of employers, who were acting in a purely individual capacity, a Joint Committee was brought into existence. On the employers' side this was constituted as follows: Lord Melchett (then Sir Alfred Mond), Lord Ashfield, Lord Londonderry, Sir Hugo Hirst, Sir David Milne Watson, Lord Weir, Col. The Hon. Vernon Willey, with Dr. A. E. Humphries as a substitute, and with J. Conway Davies as secretary. The Committee representing the T.U.C. General Council included Ben Turner (then its chairman), Ernest Bevin, Walter (now Lord) Citrine, J. H. Thomas, Arthur Pugh, Tom Richards, Will Thorne, with George Hicks as substitute member, and the late Walter Milne-Bailey, as secretary.

A great deal of good work was done by the Mond-Turner Committee. Amongst other things it proposed the establishment of a National Industrial

DEMONSTRATION AGAINST THE TRADE DISPUTES AND TRADE UNIONS BILL, 1927

Council composed of the members of the T.U.C. General Council on the one hand, and of representatives of the employers' bodies in equal numbers, namely: the Federation of British Industries, and the National Confederation of Employers' Organisations (now the British Employers' Confederation). It was agreed that the three main functions of this joint body would be to hold regular meetings, at least quarterly, for joint consultation on the widest questions concerning industry and industrial progress; to establish a joint standing committee to promote joint conciliation boards for the settlement of industrial disputes, and to create machinery for continuous investigation into industrial problems,

The significance of such proposals in their historical setting is that they marked the first step towards the organisation of joint consultation and advisory machinery representing both sides of industry on the one hand, and capable of being brought into close association, as it was during the second World War, with the Government and Government Departments.

Against this background of sane and constructive Trade Union leadership, the organised working-class movement moved towards the 1929 General Election which was to place the Labour Party in Office once again, though still without a majority in Parliament. The identity of aims between the Trade Unions and the Labour Party received unmistakable emphasis in the Trades Union Congress manifesto issued on the eve of the General Election. The case against the Conservative Government was stated in uncompromising terms in this document. Under Mr. Baldwin's administration the position of the unemployed workers had become definitely worse, said the manifesto. Rigorous administration of the unemployment insurance had deprived many thousands of benefit they had paid for, and forced them to seek Poor Law relief. Decent hard-working men and women who cared deeply for their homes and the welfare of their children had been humiliated when they applied for what was sneeringly called the dole. In despair they had turned to the Guardians for help and found their way to adequate relief barred by the unsympathetic policy of the Government. And the Liberal Party was, in this matter, no better than the Conservative Party (said the manifesto), they had claimed to be able to conquer unemployment in a year. Every practicable proposal for decreasing unemployment was embodied, said the T.U.C., in the Labour Party's scheme for the development of the nation's resources. A Labour Government would put into motion their Employment and Development Board, and a National Economic Committee composed of competent authorities, including the representatives of Trade Unionism, to consult with the Government for the preparation of sound, constructive plans for creating useful public work. Reference was made, too, of course, to the blow struck at the Trade Unions in the Act of 1927. No previous Government for a hundred years (said the manifesto) had been guilty of such reactionary legislation against Trade Unionism. It rested with the workers to meet this challenge by placing in power a Party which was pledged to remove it from the Statute Book. The

Trade Unions had proved their concern for the nation's welfare. They had worked unceasingly to protect and improve the people's standard of life. Industry today could not be carried on without their active co-operation. They stood for rational and ordered progress. This was shown, the manifesto emphasised, by the readiness with which the T.U.C. had accepted the request of responsible employers to enter into discussions with the object of establishing industrial prosperity and improving the status and conditions of the workers. These discussions had already led to proposals for dealing with unemployment and for fuller recognition of the Trade Unions and co-operation with them in promoting the progress of industry. Support was urged for the Labour Party on the ground that a Labour Government would assist in the realisation of these aims.

There was enthusiasm and unity of spirit in the Labour Movement in the General Election of 1929. No premonition of the crisis that was to overthrow the Government and weaken the Party for the time being by the defection of a few of its respected and trusted leaders, assailed the Movement during the election campaign. It was conducted, however, under the shadow of economic difficulties which reached their climax in this period. It seems, in retrospect, that Labour Governments are fated to take over the responsibility of Office under abnormal conditions affecting the political and economic life, not only of our own country, but of the world.

CHAPTER XV

THE YEARS 1929-31

By The Rt. Hon. J. R. Clynes

During the stirring and sometimes perplexing period covered in the title to this Chapter, there were scores of subjects which can, without loss, remain undiscussed in these pages. Three outstanding matters dominated the rest. They are: (1) unprecedented unemployment; (2) finance in relation to unemployment; and (3) the amazing conduct of the Leader of Labour in procuring the break-up of the Labour Government and leading the one which displaced us. The first two will require only a few figures from official sources of the time and the third will be presented through the medium of the undisputed statements revealed in the written records which cover the period.

The truth could be modified in order to lessen the impact between some of the characters concerned, and their accusers. But that would be tampering with history and by softening the evidence the reader would be misled. It will be right, therefore, to let the facts speak for themselves. The facts could not be heard in the roar and tumult of the 1931 Election and some of the evidence and the circumstances of that time were so contrary to popular confidence in their Leaders and to common political experience that evidence was heard with resentful unbelief. Time has so completely justified the line taken by the Labour Party during an interval of a manufactured crisis that both adherents and students should have the records as a signpost for future guidance and as material for any further discussion which might arise.

Government by Consent—of Others.—The year 1931 was one of much uneasiness for the Government. We were defeated once or twice early in the year, and an Economy Debate wasted time without reaching any useful conclusions. We had great difficulty in passing necessary legislation to borrow £20 million to meet unemployment payments.

Mr. Baldwin himself moved another Vote of Censure on the Government "for its failure to carry out its election pledges." Yet we had successfully carried into operation eight of the eleven points we promised to the electorate; while two others had been frustrated by the Tories themselves!

We struggled on, handicapped by Tory criticism, crippled by opposition in the Lords, and unable to introduce any other substantial reforms because we were outnumbered in the Commons by the Tories and Liberals, who had by this time joined forces in all but name.

Slum clearance went steadily forward, and thousands of new houses were built. By this time the house shortage due to the first World War was under control, almost entirely due to Labour measures in 1924 and in 1929 and 1930.

Britain was also developing a system of arterial roads, forming some of the finest in Europe. We had planned these roads with an eye to the future, making generous bridges, fine widths of surface, and lasting foundations. They were planted with young trees, and lighting in towns was to be brought up to date. The vast increase of motor traffic with consequent choking of town streets and danger to pedestrians gave us a good deal of concern, and various proposals to improve conditions were considered by the Cabinet. The rumblings of impending trouble, however, could be sensed if not heard and the feeling increased that our lease of Parliamentary life was under review.

It was a harassing fate for Labour to win its first considerable success in a General Election when Party defeat would have been the better fortune. There was no escape from the course which rival plans, political craft and design marked out for us from the starting-post of crushing and uncontrollable unemployment to the bitter and distressing finish hastened by the bewildering unfaithfulness of our Leader and a few of his colleagues. Before reaching the stage of these unhappy results the Government had, however, established a record of good deeds done which justified the labours of Ministers working under the unconcealed threat of dismissal as soon as Liberals and Tories cared to act together. This work covered more than minor and secondary matters, for several of the questions raised issues of great human interest and substance. I need give here only just the names to indicate the range and value of the subjects which occupied our time: Pensions, unemployment insurance, mines, education, housing, land drainage, agriculture, problems of transport, cotton industry, workmen's compensation and annual holidays. Of course, many of the large-scale subjects of the world relating to German reparations, Russia, India, and our Dominions were handled repeatedly. Any student will find in every Annual Report of the Labour Party a separate record of Parliamentary activities for the year and he may there see an adequate answer to the frequently ill-informed question: What is the Labour Party doing?

Warnings and Admissions.—Outwardly the life and work of the Government proceeded on normal lines, until about the middle of 1931, though qualified, of course, by the restricting absence of a majority to sustain our policy and decisions, and by the enfeebling advance of rising waves of trade depression and unemployment the world over. There had been one or two warnings by the Chancellor of the Exchequer concerning burdens of finance and of the airy manner in which demands for expenditure were made by our critics and often by our friends.

At times there were frank and fair admissions by men who were not of our Party of the underlying causes of both our industrial and financial troubles, but these were in the earlier stages and before the scheme for

[Barratt's

THE LABOUR CABINET, 1929

Front Row, left to right: J. R. Clynes, Lord Parmoor, J. H. Thomas, Philip Snowden, J. Ramsay MacDonald, Arthur Henderson, Sidney Webb, Lord Sankey, Wedgwood Benn

Standing: George Lansbury, A. V. Alexander, Charles Trevelyan, Margaret Bondfield, Lord Thomson, Tom Shaw, Arthur Greenwood, Lord Noel Buxton, William Graham, William Adamson

upsetting the Labour Government had taken definite shape. Feeling against us was hardened by a new line of attack in the Press and on platforms in the country.

The last day of July 1931 was black for our prospects. It was the concluding day of the Parliamentary session, and after discussion in the Cabinet it was decided that the Chancellor of the Exchequer should make in the Commons a serious statement on the economic troubles that had been threatening for months. He said:

> "I tell the House quite frankly that the outlook for the Budget of next year, unless very considerable economies can be effected, is a very grave prospect indeed."

It was necessary to make this disclosure. But on the same day, a report was issued by the Committee on National Economy, of which Sir George May, the insurance and finance expert, was chairman. This Committee had been set up by Cabinet decision on a motion of the Liberals, backed by the Tories, when it became obvious that abnormal methods might have to be used to meet demands on the nation's purse.

The Committee's report stated that the new grants to the Unemployment Fund were dangerously straining our financial resources, and that the next Budget, instead of showing a surplus would have to meet a serious deficiency.

Private individuals can apparently live on credit beyond their means for years and suffer no ill effect, but if nations attempt to do so they are told they must face bankruptcy and ruin.

It was unfortunate that the May Report was issued on the day that the House adjourned for the holidays. Before any action could be taken, the details of our national peril, as it was termed, were deliberately distorted into something monstrous by men who saw in it a new mint for Party capital. Thus the Labour Party was made a scapegoat for a condition of world affairs which was no more our responsibility than a thunderstorm might be.

We have in the history of the Party suffered no greater misfortune than that of being obliged to take Office on the threshold of the worst world depression since the first Great War. It rolled over Europe and reached America. That vast country, which had laughed at European unemployment and economic distress, suddenly found herself burdened with 15,000,000 out of work, and a staggering dislocation of economic life.

The Root Cause and Restraints.—Mr. Churchill himself described the Government at this time as "having to face an economic blizzard." Faster than our best plans could put an unemployed worker in a job, half a dozen were thrown out by world trade stagnation. Every week the figures went up, and every day the Tory Party made capital out of that melancholy result. When we argued that the depression was the inevitable result of the war, they laughed uproariously, though Mr. Runciman himself admitted:

> "The prime financial difficulties of all Europe are due to the war, and chiefly to the continuous payment of excessive reparations."

Our political opponents said that the fault was ours, and that we were driving the country to bankruptcy. They said it so often that, in the end, foreign investors listened and believed them. The cry intended to embarrass a Party nearly wrecked a nation's credit.

The basis of the trouble was that we, while in Office, borrowed £120 million for use as Unemployment Benefit. This policy of borrowing was not started by us. The Tories themselves began it years before, and we could not stop it. The risks of upheaval and the intensity of assured suffering were too great for that, even if our predecessors did leave the Unemployment Benefit Fund heavily in debt by the loans they had borrowed.

We promoted schemes for public work that provided employment for about 400,000 men. But meanwhile swiftly shrinking foreign trade threw far more than that number out of work. It was like trying to stop an incoming tide with a sand barrier. Any attempt at a drastic course to provide money by other means than loans without some genuine agreement among the Parties in the House, would have meant instant defeat. Such a blow would not terrify us but it would dismay the hungry unemployed. The Minister of Labour, Miss Bondfield, had the thankless task of piloting motions through the House of Commons for unemployment loans and did the work with great effect and skill.

The Chancellor and Our Chances.—Meanwhile, our borrowing was held up as a more dreadful and vicious thing than Tory borrowing. The terrors of a national money collapse were vigorously paraded, and a few million people were deluded to the length of believing that the comparatively small debt of £120 million due to beneficent social aid would ruin a country that had shouldered the debt of thousands of millions which the first Great War had cost, and had not then been in the least perturbed!

The Cabinet sat day after day. During this critical time two men counted for much in our meetings—MacDonald as Prime Minister and Snowden as Chancellor of the Exchequer. I would not question the sincerity of Mr. Snowden, however bitterly he later on fought against us. He was usually unafraid in any kind of political encounter and had, for House of Commons service, gifts of exposition and advocacy which were rare. At times, however, during these very troubled days he seemed scared by the power which Bankers could wield and knew that they could prevent or permit many acts of Government policy concerning loans, and finance, if they thought that national credit was being shaken and might not retain the solid position it had always had. We saw great danger in the tendency of privileged personages who could influence or control large loans stipulating for certain economies and even wage reductions before the loans were arranged. If such a weapon in the armoury of finance were used, as had been whispered, to lessen even the low pay of the unemployed who were near destitution, the prospect would be grim indeed.

We never quite fathomed the mind of our Chancellor at this time on some of these newly revealed aspects of finance. He was an extremely able Minister and unlike his Leader he rarely said anything which was obscure or left one in doubt about his meaning. His task was very embarrassing but he had usually such a reserve of skill that it was common for him to be greater than his difficulties and overcome them. He was also proud of being both prompt and explicit when circumstances demanded. Recording some experience with the French delegation at a Hague Conference he wrote that Mr. Tardieu had said to the French Press: "After my talks with Mr. Snowden I see no obstacle with the Conference. I was much impressed with Mr. Snowden. I always like a man who can say 'Yes' or 'No'."

If now a loan was to be made conditional upon low-paid workers and unemployed men receiving still lower sums as part of a national economy would Mr. Snowden say "No"? That was a matter at the moment of high policy and of great substance to people so poor that a few shillings weekly made all the difference in the home. Would Mr. Snowden be as stern with British and foreign financiers as he had been with foreign statesmen involved in reparations settlements? We could not be sure; for though on occasion it was not a novel thing for Snowden to take a new line, he had in him on financial questions much of the orthodox, as his critics often told him. But a guiding principle governed Snowden's duty and knowing that his Socialism was the robust sort we hoped for the best though not without fear.

Conspiracy Reveals Itself.—Events were now moving fast. Arrangements not revealed, though made, were afoot leading to a point where the word "crisis" would reach its maximum meaning and the background of make-believe give it effective setting. Signs which, being unusual, themselves conspire to make known what it is intended to conceal. Strange groupings, Press comments, abandoned holidays and other uncommon activities led to questions and these led to evasive answers—or worse. One fact clearly emerged: That the Labour Prime Minister was busy in the high affairs of Mr. Ramsay MacDonald. MacDonald was visited by his new companions, Baldwin and Samuel, who no doubt received from him a dramatic account of the day's changes. Soon after, he went to the King to speak of the formation of a new Government with himself still at the head.

When later on we went to the Palace to hand in our seals of Office to George V the atmosphere was solemn and Ministers silent. We entered His Majesty's study carrying our seals. The King stood beside a table; his face looked grey and lined. I placed my seal on the table, bowed, and silently took my leave.

Baldwin, Samuel, and the echo that was MacDonald, got to work at once to form a new Cabinet. It was called "National," but the Tories themselves soon shook off their pretence with their own laughter at it.

MacDonald was deposed from his position as Leader of the Labour

Party, and I was asked to succeed him. I did not wish it, and we persuaded Arthur Henderson to accept the post.

Within a day or two, the names of the new Cabinet Ministers were announced. No one who had changed sides with MacDonald had suffered as a result of his new convictions. He was, of course, Leader of the new Administration.

Observe that all these high and far-reaching changes were completed without, at any stage, the slightest consultation with the people who had the first claim to be approached. MacDonald was repeatedly pressed to meet the members of the Parliamentary Party who had made him Prime Minister. He refused; scornfully saying that he "was not going to be shot at by those fellows." In his first steps towards desertion it was made known that he expected about 100 Members to follow him. When he knew more of the truth he would not face a meeting. If twice the number had taken his side, that would not have made his own conduct less revolting and unfaithful.

Lord Sankey was the only Minister who attended a Party meeting to state his reasons for retaining his post and we knew that he had particular obligations and duties just then concerning the position in India. He did not convince the meeting but we admired his frankness and courage and our respect for him as a man of honour has never been lowered.

Mr. J. H. Thomas did not think it in the national interest that he should resign.

Mr. Churchill, one of MacDonald's new colleagues on the Government side, said more damning things of him than any Labour man. He termed him: "The boneless wonder," and the phrase was not regarded in the House as being offensive but as a just, if acrobatic, description. When he added that no man could pack such a number of words into so small a space of thought, the allusion was received with approving mirth, and was not deemed to be unjust.

On September 8, Parliament reassembled under the new Government. It was a very bitter moment for many of us who had refused to run away from our Labour duties at a period of greatest trial. We had to look across the table and see opposed to us the faces of some men who for a quarter of a century had been our colleagues. MacDonald was directing the attack upon us, but he did not meet our eyes.

Henderson, in his speech, outlined our position. He said that it amounted to this: That we were not prepared to support an economy campaign that cut unemployment pay for a man with a wife and two children from thirty shillings a week to twenty-four shillings a week. Our opponents wished to do this. When he sat down, a vote of confidence in the new Government was carried by 309 votes to 250—a majority of only 59 votes. The change of Government was not the means of a miraculous saving of the pound. Steadily and simultaneously, foreign countries continued to withdraw their money from us. They were entitled to demand this money from the Bank of England in gold bullion, and they did so.

History Afresh, and A Burlesque Election.—This narration together with later occurrences present "the most remarkable happening in British political history." I take that phrase from the record written by a man renowned for testing affairs by facts and qualified by experience and personal knowledge to state what happened in 1931. Sidney Webb (Lord Passfield) writing at length in the *Political Quarterly* after the events said: "It may be worth while putting on record a recital of what will rank as the most remarkable happening in British political history. The fall of the Labour Government after two-and-a-quarter years' troubled existence; the instant formation overnight of a new National Government under the same Prime Minister purporting to contain within itself all three political Parties; and finally, at the earliest practical date, a hurried General Election in which an unprecedented combination of 69 per cent. of the voters elected all but 9 per cent. of the entire House of Commons, thus replacing Parliamentary Government by what is in effect a Party Dictatorship—the whole unfolding within sixty-three days of a single drama, in all its development foreseen in advance, it is safe to say, only by the statesman who was at once its author, its producer, and its principal actor—finds no parallel in anything in the Parliamentary annals of this or any other country. Why did Mr. Ramsay MacDonald, after thirty years' upbuilding of the British Labour Party, decide to do his best to smash it, going over with a couple of his principal colleagues, and a mere handful of his Party to a Coalition of Conservatives and Liberals? How did he manage to create such a Coalition, and to place himself at its head? What caused an electoral landslide of such unexampled magnitude? Lastly, what is the significance in British political history, and its consequences to the world, of this unique island drama?"

These lines and questions merely register the amazement of a life-long acquaintance at the astonishing conduct of the Party Leader.

The financial position raised by the condition of the workless presented difficulties which we could have overcome by exactly the lines followed by the Tories when they took our places. But they shouted cries of crisis, downfall and bankruptcy. They alarmed large masses of the poor by telling them that their savings were to be taken to provide unemployment money. They said so often that we were on the brink of a bankrupt nation that other countries believed them and requested repayment of their money stored in our banks. When by acts which many men described as fraudulent they got a huge majority in the Election, they raised taxation, used the Sinking Fund and imposed some economies. These and like measures we were ready to use but *we would not lower the pay of the unemployed or lessen the wages of low-paid workers. They were below subsistence level.* So out we had to go! The polling soon followed. It was more like a stampede by a scared and perplexed public than a General Election. The desertion of a few of our leaders increased the confusion and, as time showed, the Election settled nothing whatever.

The troubles of the world grew in succeeding months, and the economic blizzard threw men out of work many times faster than they could be put into work. All the same, the General Election made everything ready for the victorious hosts of the Conservative Party to set things right. After two years of it the Tories found the unemployed figures had jumped to nearly 3,000,000. A few hundred thousand, though out of the lists, were also out of a job, and 250,000 more than in 1931 were thrown back upon Poor Law Relief.

In the period of the Labour Government we sometimes asked a mocking House of Commons to face the truth of the situation and to look at the facts. We told them of the world causes of unemployment—and how they laughed! Their stock retort is again in use. Labour incompetence, muddling and lack of foresight! It is not now so effective as formerly; security is greater, status is higher and fear is less.

It has been a maxim of the Conservative Party that if they can create even a little terror in the minds of electors, they are sure of a majority. Spectres of various sorts have been raised again and again, but never one more gruesome than that of 1931. We could not in my area lay the bogey. Facts were of no avail against fears.

The election, all over the country, was the most shameful and bitter I have ever known. One of the venomous weapons used against us was Mr. Runciman's statement, foolishly echoed by Snowden, that the Labour Party had considered raiding Post Office Savings Bank accounts in order to find money to meet the crisis. No such step had even been mooted, and there was not a word of truth in the story. But it lost us thousands of votes.

When it was all over, the results were found to create something of a record. Labour lost 213 seats, and suffered the defeat of every House of Commons Member of the Cabinet except George Lansbury. Not a single Tory seat was lost. Fifty-six National candidates were returned unopposed; more than the Labour total in the new House. Government supporters finally numbered 556, against an Opposition of 59. It was grotesque! After the election, the *Manchester Guardian*, a Liberal newspaper respected the world over for its impartial and accurate reports, declared that: "The shortest, strangest and most fraudulent Election campaign of our times is over!"

The Tories hilariously declared that the Labour Party was done for. Yet, in about a year, we were winning by-elections. Those renegades who had run into the enemy's camp could not help noting some cause for Labour content on two counts! The fall in the total Labour vote was only 6 per cent., but in our system of single member divisions it meant the loss of 213 Labour seats; and the loyal response from hundreds of the local Parties, which was almost unanimous. The Liberals fared so badly that Sidney Webb in his record wrote:

> "Curiously enough it was the Liberal Party itself that unwittingly brought on the fateful crisis. Regardless of the Party's previous requisitions on the Government for

enormous expenditure on public works to employ the unemployed, the whole Party chose suddenly to demand of the Government the immediate appointment of a non-political Royal Commission of business men, which, in order to lighten the burden that heavy taxation was declared to be pressing on industry, should summarily suggest drastic reductions in public expenditure. The Conservative Party, eager to join in a defeat of the Government on any issue, promised unanimous support."

The Failure of the Faithless.—Before the autumn of 1931, I never felt disturbed by what the Labour Prime Minister might do in a crisis. It had never occurred to me that any living man at the head of a British Labour Government could step aside from his own people to lead the opposite forces. Mr. Baldwin was the chief of our opponents, but if one had read that he had done such a thing, one would have disbelieved the evidence of one's own eyes.

My first feeling of complete disquiet took root only when I saw the content shown by the Prime Minister after our resignations were signified. He did not conceal evidences of his satisfaction when he returned from the Palace to tell us that everything had been completely transformed—except himself. He remained the Leader, no matter that the army he led was another.

Mr. Snowden was more suspicious than some of us about the meaning of Cabinet differences. He wrote in his autobiography:

"When the final disagreement occurred, it was evident that the Prime Minister had anticipated such a development, and had made his plans to deal with it."

Snowden even asked MacDonald for an assurance that the new Government would exist only to deal with the temporary emergency; that it would not be a Coalition, and that no Party legislation would be attempted. He received these assurances. How swiftly they were all broken was emphasised bitterly by Snowden when he resigned to release himself from an intolerable position.

After our Prime Minister turned renegade, he submitted to many humiliations and apparently abandoned every shred of the political faith his Party had accepted and he himself had formerly preached.

There were a few who said that the Party would never survive MacDonald's departure from it. But it was he who did not survive the betrayal.

Later, in 1931, he said:

"It may be the Conservatives will try to put something over on us. If so, I am not their man."

No, he was not—he had become their slave. He was no longer coherent, no longer understood. He was now the Leader of a group said by a political writer to "consist of two men and a boy."

In middle life, this strange man was vigorous and lucid enough. He did great things, and filled positions of high responsibility. Later, his courage seemed to decline, and he developed a deplorable obscureness. In Cabinets, he was in these days of trouble less a Leader than a medium for collecting opinions. He searched for safety, and rarely advised us towards policies which were based on honest convictions and in keeping with Party policy.

Up to that time he had given much to the building up of the Labour Movement. But he always owed to it more than he gave. The highest place, the greatest praise, and an authority which was almost absolute, had been surrendered to him.

When he deserted his side he talked of standing by the nation. Such a claim was idle. His whole life had been spent trying to prove the wisdom of Labour doctrine and the worthlessness of Liberal or Tory programmes. He should have faced the 1931 "crisis" by the application of the principles to which we could all have been faithful. But to do so might have lost him his position as Premier. It might; but of what importance was he afterwards?

Those of us who had to look on impotently after the fall of the Second Labour Government saw enough political chicanery during the next few months to make us deeply resentful that our work for Britain should be so swiftly undone, and that such a deadly tangle should be created.

After the so-called "National" Government took charge, sensation followed sensation, and intrigues and emergencies became almost monthly affairs. MacDonald, the shadow Prime Minister, was easily edged out of the limelight into the political obscurity of Lord President of the Council, so that a Tory of the Tories could take his place as Leader of the House.

The humbug of pretending to avoid Party politics, which the Conservatives used when they covered their blunderings with the cloak of Nationalism, was soon openly abandoned.

The use of the word "National" as a title for that Government was worth hundreds of thousands of votes to the Tory Party. It was an adroit Party move because it made sincere people think they were voting for a nation, not a group. With consummate skill they exploited the audacious fiction that we had run away when the nation was in danger. The truth is we resigned our posts to stick to our principles and defend the bread line of the poor. The Tory Party appropriated nearly all the offices. In the Cabinet of twenty, only a few Ministers were not official Conservatives, and a like proportion was maintained in minor Government positions. Men were not selected on any national ground, but within the limits of a Party claim.

That a Tory Party, masquerading as a National Government, could ever hope to remedy the defects of a Capitalism in which they believed was absurd from the beginning. Yet they went on blindly believing that Protectionist plans, which had never succeeded anywhere, would succeed here.

After years of it the position was worse than ever, and the massive Tory majority could not do anything on a large scale or do anything new. They had frightened a suffering people who were silent and numb.

Even the "silver lining" stage was soon to end, and the melancholy message of Mr. Chamberlain was that in ten years' time unemployment figures may be substantially reduced, and to this end we must "keep pegging away." So that from the period of brag in which we were told of the blessings to result from Tory policy and Tariffs we had moved to the period where Chancellor and Prime Minister spoke to their disheartened followers in the tone of a funeral oration.

The dismay which had spread among men, who recently had exulted in a power acquired by such evil means, may be read in the message at the time of the Parliamentary Correspondent of the *Observer*:

> "The grim announcement which Mr. Chamberlain, as Chancellor of the Exchequer, felt compelled to make on Thursday that the only sure cure for unemployment is the revival of trade, and that but little relief is to be expected for ten years, visibly staggered the House of Commons. Members gasped at each other with consternation. It was so wholly unexpected. Members had met, as they supposed, to hear the much-talked-of plans of the Government for a determined frontal attack on the solid mass of unemployment, only to have this disheartening prospect held out to them. Ten years, in the circumstances, seemed an interminable time."

The device of the "Red Letter" in one election had been excelled by the duplicity practised on that class of the poor who got poorer because they had to remain idle. The drained Fund used to hasten our downfall has now a balance of about £500 million (five hundred million pounds). That reserve has accrued after repaying the borrowed money and clearing the debt on the Unemployment Fund. Apart from the war years which explain most of the balance, this enormous reserve shows how the credit of a nation can safely be used to provide our needs in times of great depression if used without a sordid Party purpose. Sound insurance backed by national credit, though not involving heavier cost, could have been made to cover exceptional depression and the Fund would rise, as it did, to levels of affluence in a period of full employment.

The Parliamentary Party acted in complete harmony with the wishes and principles of its allies in the Trade Union and Socialist forces in the country. Parts of a public statement issued at the time may be given here. It shows how every responsible and representative voice on the side of Labour acclaimed the action of the Party as absolutely right.

MANIFESTO

> of the Trades Union Congress General Council, the National Executive Committee of the Labour Party, and the Consultative Committee of the Parliamentary Labour Party.
>
> "A financial crisis, the true causes of which have not been publicly explained, has brought about the sudden resignation of the Labour Government. Forces in finance and politics made demands which no Labour Government could accept.
>
> "The new Government seeks to enforce a complete change in national policy; not because the Nation's resources have suddenly diminished, not because the Nation cannot afford to provide for its unemployed, not because the Budget cannot

be balanced, but primarily because financial interests have decided that this country is setting a bad example to other countries in taxing the rich to provide for the necessities of the poor.

"Fundamentally, it is an attempt to reverse the social policy which, in this country, has within limits provided for the unemployed, the aged and the sick, the disabled, the orphaned, and the widowed.

"The new Government is irrevocably committed to serious cuts in unemployment benefits, cuts in wages and salaries, in national and local services, a curtailment of expenditure on work which is at present providing employment for thousands of wage earners, and cuts in Public Health and Education.

"Four thousand millions of British capital are invested abroad. Great Britain is still one of the greatest creditor countries. We are still adding to our capital assets. The taxable capacity of the country has not been exhausted. The immediate situation can be met without further depleting the slender means of the poor and without restricting national and local expenditure directed to the development of the country's resources. If the will were present we could overcome the immediate difficulty by mobilising the country's foreign investments, by a temporary suspension of the Sinking Fund, by taxing fixed-interest-bearing securities and other unearned income which has benefited by the fall in prices, and by measures to reduce the burden of war debts."

Should anyone still think that in 1931 there was a financial crisis on account of the indebtedness of the Unemployment Benefit Fund let him reflect on the thousands of millions of debt rightly incurred for the necessities of war in recent years. None dared talk of ruin and bankruptcy when that colossal burden was being shouldered and the nation with massive credit faced its obligations and remained composed. The comparatively trifling sum of £100 million or so could have been raised with ease to enable poor unemployed people to spend it in our shops and stores on their pressing needs. Party motives, however, raised false issues by cries and pleadings even more false. By a manœuvre without example in our history a mighty Party success was secured, but nothing was settled except the fate of a few of the leading figures. That success was submerged in the overwhelming Labour victory of 1945.

Should any reproach in this chapter be viewed as inconsiderate, harsh or unfair let the reader turn to the second volume of Mr. Snowden's autobiography and there read the stinging letter of resignation sent to his partner, Mr. MacDonald in September, 1932. They had acted together in forming the new Government but a stage was reached when Mr. Snowden could no longer endure the duplicity, evasion and betrayal which he had long witnessed, and sent the most pungent and upbraiding letter ever written by one colleague to another. And not without proven cause, if only, as he wrote, to save his own self-respect. Other commentators have in comparison shown themselves quite mild and restrained. Even now the records cannot be read without wonder.

CHAPTER XVI

FROM NATIONAL TO ALL-PARTY GOVERNMENT

By Herbert Tracey

The Government formed by Ramsay MacDonald in the circumstances described in the preceding chapter called itself a "National" Government. Its creator denied that it was a Coalition Government. On the day he formed it, August 24, 1931, MacDonald issued from Downing Street an announcement in the following terms:

> "The specific object for which the new Government is being formed is to deal with the national emergency that now exists. It will not be a Coalition Government in the ordinary sense of the term, but a Government of co-operation for this one purpose. When that purpose is achieved the political Parties will resume their respective positions."

The formation of this "National" Government left the balance of Parties in Parliament undisturbed: that is to say, the Labour Party which was originally the largest single Party in the House of Commons, with 289 members sustained the defection of no more than a dozen members, whilst the Conservative Party's original 260 members were strengthened in numbers by this accretion and had, in addition, the support of the two factions of the Liberal Party which formerly held the balance between the two larger Parties. Neither were the economic and social problems that brought down the Labour Government solved by the *coup d'état* by which MacDonald became head of a new Administration which was strong enough, by a combination of Conservative and Liberal votes, to outnumber the Labour Party. When the House reassembled after the summer recess (in 1931) the Prime Minister, on a formal motion, made a statement of Government policy and explained the reasons which had caused him to form the new Government; and this motion was treated under the Rules of the House as a vote of confidence, which was carried by 309 to 250 votes. Twelve Members who, before the debacle, were reckoned as members of the Labour Party, voted with the majority in this Division. But the "National" Government majority did not avail to avert the dreaded calamity of a departure from the Gold Standard about which the leaders of the new Government had made such dire predictions. In less than a month of the Labour Government's downfall (on September 21) a Bill to suspend the Gold Standard was pushed through all its stages in a single day by the votes of those who had combined to "save the £."

The Labour Party was strong enough, and certainly in the right temper, to offer unrepentant and relentless opposition to the new Government's policy. In blind obedience to the instructions of the three-party commission of bankers, accountants, and industrialists, which decreed drastic cuts in the National expenditure, Philip Snowden as Chancellor of the Exchequer, brought in a new Budget which increased taxation, both direct and indirect, and coupled with it a series of "economies" that included reductions in the salaries of Ministers and Members of Parliament, the judiciary, and the Civil Service; reductions in the pay of the Army, Navy and Air Force, the police forces, and the school teachers; cuts in the expenditure on public health, including the remuneration of panel doctors; and reductions in unemployment benefit, combined with increases in contributions, limitation of the benefit period, and the imposition of a Means Test for transitional benefit. There were a number of other "economies," too. They were all embodied in a separate Bill which the Labour Party vigorously opposed, but which was rushed through Parliament under the "guillotine." On its second reading the Labour Party moved an amendment which challenged the whole basis of the Economy Bill. Its proposals, the Party amendment said, would deprive masses of the people of necessities of life whilst leaving others in the enjoyment of luxuries, and would aggravate unemployment by restricting the purchasing power of wage earners. The Bill was criticised also as one that abrogated Parliamentary control by authorising the making of Orders in Council designed to supersede existing Acts of Parliament or to reverse settled national policy without the previous specific assent of the House of Commons. This strong attack upon the basis of the "National" Government's policy was only repulsed by a narrow margin of votes, the motion being defeated by 310 to 253.

It was not, in these circumstances, surprising that the leaders of the anti-Labour Coalition decided to strike another blow at the Labour Party. The Party's solidarity had not been undermined by the events of 1929-31. The whole organised Movement had reacted resolutely against the attempt to destroy it. Three days after the "National" Government was formed the three National Committees of the Labour Movement—the T.U.C. General Council, the National Executive of the Labour Party and the Consultative Committee of the Parliamentary Party—decided in a joint meeting that the new Government must be vigorously opposed both in Parliament and by the Movement throughout the country. A manifesto was issued repudiating all responsibility for the MacDonald Government, which it described as "a Government of persons acting without authority from the people." It denounced the new Government's purpose, which was (said the manifesto) to "enforce a complete change in national policy: not because the nation's resources have suddenly diminished, not because the nation cannot afford to provide for its unemployed, not because the Budget cannot be balanced, but primarily because financial interests have decided that this country is setting a bad example to other countries in taxing the rich to provide for the necessities of the poor." The three National Committees, in their manifesto, interpreted the formation of the "National" Government as fundamentally "an attempt to reverse the social policy which, in this country, has, within limits, provided for the unemployed, the aged and the sick, the disabled, the orphaned, and the widowed. Unemployment benefit is attacked on the ground that it strengthens resistance to wage reductions. These are the motives which impel the new Coalition Government in its policy of drastic cuts in national expenditure."

As the three National Committees anticipated, the unfolding of the new Government's policy roused the entire Labour Movement to determined opposition to the serious cuts in unemployment benefit, in the wages and salaries of workers in national and local government services, the curtailment of expenditure on work which was providing employment for thousands of wage earners, and cuts in public health and education. All this served to convince the Labour Movement that the country was in the grip of reaction, and that this had still further to go. In the light of later events it is beyond question that the Conservative elements in the Coalition were determined not only to control it, but to make it the instrument of the full Conservative policy. The Government was hardly more than a month old before the Conservative Party organisation was actively engaged in forcing the issue and preparing to bring about a General Election in which, it was believed, the Labour Party would be finally and utterly destroyed. That this was contrary to the agreement upon which the "National" Government was founded mattered not at all. Definite public pledges had been given that the Government would deal only with the existing financial emergency, and that when this purpose was accomplished the political Parties would resume their freedom and independence. In a nation-wide broadcast on the evening of the day he formed his new Government, Ramsay MacDonald reiterated the statement that it was not a Coalition Government. "I will take no part in that," he said; "it is not a Government which compels any Party to change its principles or to subordinate its individuality. I should take no part in that, either. It is a Government of individuals formed to do this work. If the work takes a little time the life of the Government will be short. When that life is finished the work of the House of Commons and the general political situation will return to where it was last week, and those who have taken risks will receive either our punishment or our reward. The election which will follow will not be fought by the Government."

But this was not the Conservative Party's reading of the situation. The powerful "1922 Club" which guided the policy and action of the Conservative rank and file in Parliament made short work of MacDonald's pledges. It insisted that there should be an immediate dissolution, and that the General Election should be fought by the Government on the full Conservative policy. The head of the Conservative central organisation a few days later put the decision of the "1922 Club" into plain words. Sir Douglas Hacking said (on September 26): "The appeal to the country would be made by a 'National' Government which had adopted the Conservative policy." But the Conservative policy was protectionist, and one of the Liberal factions in the Coalition, to say nothing of Philip

Snowden, was ardently free trade. The Liberal faction, led by Sir Herbert (later Lord) Samuel was opposed to an election, and equally strongly opposed to the Conservative policy of tariffs. So was Philip Snowden. They held that the Government's task—and after all it had been in Office only a month—had not been accomplished. The financial dangers which the Government was formed to meet had not been lessened by the abandonment of the Gold Standard. Unemployment had not been reduced. All the arguments that justified the action of the Parties which had combined to overthrow the Labour Government held the foreground still, with undiminished force: if political unity was necessary in August the need for it had not disappeared in September. But all these considerations were powerless to check the Conservative Party's drive towards a General Election in which the "National" Government would be its instrument for changing the century-old national policy of free trade and the weapon by which the Labour Party would be wiped out of British politics. Unless the Conservative Ministers were allowed to have their way it was clear that the Coalition would fall apart. The Samuelite Liberals would not face the odium of breaking up the Coalition by their withdrawal. The resignation of Philip Snowden, although inevitable, would not have deterred the Conservative leaders from their course at this time; and he postponed his resignation, with unhappy consequences as far as his own reputation was in question, by the aid he gave in speech and writing to the "National" Government in the General Election. The Conservative Ministers gave way on one point only: they agreed that the Leaders of each of the Coalition Parties should issue their own election manifesto, and that MacDonald as Prime Minister should make, over his own signature alone, a general pronouncement on the issues of the election, embodied in the formula that the Government sought from the electors "a doctor's mandate."

The three weeks' electoral campaign which ensued was one without precedent in British political history. It generated an atmosphere of panic and hysteria in which the Conservative and Liberal party machinery was set in motion deliberately to defeat every candidate who did not support the "National" Government. Every expedient of electoral propaganda on the platform, in the Press, by wireless broadcasting, on the hoardings, and in door-to-door canvassing was adopted to work up the fears of the people and to turn them against the Labour Party. Although this Coalition of Parties which had been formed to "save the £" had itself thrown over the Gold Standard, it was the Labour Ministers who were pilloried as having "run away from their job." In the same breath that Leaders of the Coalition Parties used to claim that British industry would benefit from abandonment of the Gold Standard, they also set going a wild and fantastic clamour about the effects of the adverse balance of trade. On the platform MacDonald and others waved bundles of depreciated German marks and declared that unless the "National" Government was returned to Office British currency would go the same way: the pound sterling would sink to the value of ten shillings, to a shilling, to a penny, and presently a barrow-load would not buy a halfpenny postage stamp. The climax in this whirlwind campaign of panic-mongering, misrepresentation and false witness was reached on the eve of the poll. Statements were broadcast far and wide alleging that the Labour Government had planned, or were planning, to seize the small savings of millions of people deposited in the Post Office Savings Bank. Nothing that the Labour Party could do to counteract the effects of such outrageous calumnies availed to stop them: there was even a run on the Post Office Savings Bank, and the votes of millions of poor and ill-informed citizens, men and women, were recorded against the Labour candidates. "By exploiting patriotic sentiment, by panic-mongering, by calumny and misrepresentation" as the Party's national executive said in reporting upon the results of the General Election, the so-called "National" Government secured a further lease of power.

The Labour Party put 491 candidates into the field, of whom almost exactly half were Members of Parliament at the dissolution. Only forty-six Labour seats were retained in the new House of Commons. The Conservatives numbered 471; the "National" Liberals, Liberals *sans* prefix, and "National" Labour added another eighty-four to the Conservative voting strength; and there were less than a dozen independent Members in a House of 615.

Yet the smashing effect of the Coalition Parties' victory over Labour was after all more apparent than real. These Parties polled over twice as many votes as the Labour Party. Nevertheless, although the aggregate Labour vote dropped by two million from the high total of 8,362,883 reached in the 1929 General Election, the Party's solid foundations remained unshaken: a total of 6,362,561 votes was secured by the Labour candidates out of the 21,650,000 (nearly) cast in the General Election of 1931, and there were a million unpolled votes to be accounted for when the 1931 total is compared with that of 1929. It is not fanciful to suggest that the raging, tearing propaganda of the "National" Government Parties failed to convince several million citizens—the total poll was 72·28 of the electorate in 1931 as against 79·21 in 1929—that the Labour Party was not as black as it was painted by its political foes.

Changes in the leadership of the Labour Party were inevitable in the circumstances in which the Party was placed. Under the strain of his work as Foreign Secretary in the Labour Government and his distress at the turn of events leading up to the 1931 General Election, Arthur Henderson's health broke down. He had been made Leader of the Party after Ramsay MacDonald's defection, and he decided, moreover, to carry out at Geneva the task he had undertaken as President of the International Disarmament Conference. When the much-attenuated Parliamentary Labour Party assembled in the new House of Commons, Henderson was confirmed in the leadership by a resolution expressing the Party's unabated confidence in him: but the effective leadership of the Party, in his absence at Geneva, devolved upon George Lansbury, who had been made chairman of the Parliamentary Party with Clement Attlee as vice-chairman. The position of the Party in the House was made as unpleasant as it possibly could be. Nothing that the ingenuity of the Coalition Parties could suggest to humiliate and discredit the devoted and loyal band of forty-six Labour Members, was omitted: they were mocked at and derided in the Chamber, and even the ordinary courtesies of the lobbies, dining-rooms and smoke-rooms were denied them. But it could justly be claimed, as the National Executive stated in its report to the 1933 Annual Conference that the Parliamentary Labour Party conducted a gallant fight: "reduced in numbers to less than it possessed over twenty years ago" (said the annual report of that year) "the Group—front benchers and back benchers alike—have been a hard-working 'band of brothers' close-knit in comradeship, diligent in their work, pertinacious in their attack, and versatile in their day-to-day efforts. So much so that the Government and its supporters are constantly aware of the solid unshakable Labour vote in the constituencies. The seven million Labour voters may well be proud of the fifty fighters who have sought to drive the Government to some sense of responsibility to the people in their present plight."

Indeed, the seeds of dissolution sown within the "National" Government from its earliest days were beginning to germinate within a few months of the General Election. Two by-elections in which the Party's candidates (one of them Arthur Greenwood) were successful, and others in which the Labour vote was seen to be rising steadily above the level of 1931, marked the turning of the tide. The protectionist policy which the Conservative faction inside the Government insisted upon enacting, despite the pained protests of their Liberal associates, and the vehement opposition of Philip Snowden, did nothing to relieve the great economic depression. Beginning with a measure, forced through Parliament in two days under the guillotine, imposing duties up to 100 per cent. on commodities which were being "dumped" from foreign countries in abnormal quantities, the Government proceeded to establish a full-blown system of tariffs, in the form of an *ad valorem* duty of 10 per cent. on all imports, with the exception of wheat in grain, and meat. An Import Duties Advisory Committee was set up with the responsibility of recommending additional duties on "non-essential" goods. Retaliation against countries that discriminated against British products, and preference to imports from the Dominions, were features of this protective system. The small Labour Group fought this legislation with skill and determination, but were, of course, unable to arrest its passage through Parliament. One of its political consequences, however, was the withdrawal of the Samuelite Liberals from the "National" Government and the resignation of Snowden in a final flare of vitriolic criticism poured out in a letter to MacDonald. Inside the Cabinet, in the earlier stages of this tariff-versus-free trade controversy, an attempt to keep the uneasy partnership in being was made by an "agreement to differ" which broke the long-recognised tradition of collective Cabinet responsibility and left the dissenting Ministers free to oppose the majority's policy, even to the point of speaking and voting against the Bills. The development of the Conservative protectionist policy at the Ottawa Conference, which brought into existence a system of preferential duties, unalterable for a term of years without the consent of the Dominion Governments, and incidentally necessitated the termination of Britain's trade agreement with Soviet Russia, involved such a fundamental departure from Liberal principles that the dozen Samuelite Liberals in the Government could not connive at it. Consequently, they resigned their Ministerial offices.

The protectionist system was applied by the Conservatives with the most robust assurance to both industry and agriculture. But it did not solve the country's economic difficulties any more than its financial policy could extricate the country from its plight. The Budget had been "balanced" by the expedient of reducing interest on £2,000 million of War Loan from 5 per cent. to 3½ per cent.; by refusing to pay the war debts which Mr. Stanley Baldwin had promised America in 1923 that Britain would pay in full—to the total of £2,200 million in all; by the collection of revenue from the new import duties; and by drastic changes in the finances of the Unemployment Insurance system. Putting into effect the "economies" proposed by the May Committee, insured workers' contributions were raised from 7*d.* to 10*d.* a week, and benefits were reduced from 17*s.* to 15*s.* 3*d.* for men, with corresponding adjustments for women and dependents; the duration of benefit was reduced, the age of entry into insurance lowered to the school-leaving age—and at a later stage the whole business of unemployment insurance was put on to a strict "actuarial basis." This was achieved by setting up an Unemployment Insurance Statutory Committee to maintain the solvency of the Fund by recommending changes in contributions and benefits and the conditions attaching to them. At the same time, the unemployed were divided into three classes who were to be treated respectively as eligible for insurance benefit, unemployment assistance and public assistance. The Means Test governed all.

But unemployment itself remained, chronic and incurable. It reached very nearly the 3,000,000 mark in 1932, when the economic hurricane struck the United States and the election of President Franklin D. Roosevelt gave him the opportunity to inaugurate the bold and resolute measures of control, reconstruction and recovery that made his successive Administrations so notable in the social and political history of the United States and even of such enormous importance to the world at large. From 1932 the trend of unemployment in British industry turned downwards: it stood at over 22 per cent. in that year and fell gradually to about 20 per cent. in 1933, to 16·8 per cent. in 1934, and 15·5 per cent. in 1935. But there were aspects of the unemployment problem which remained profoundly disquieting notwithstanding this tendency towards improvement. There was a "hard core" of workless men and women and "black areas" of the country where industry was stagnant and the population rotted. Although employment was increasing, the expansion of industry and trade failed to keep pace with the numbers seeking work from one year to another. The economic malaise was universal, but no country was more severely affected than Britain and the memory of those dreadful days was not obliterated when the crisis, never truly liquidated, was eased somewhat in the period of rearmament, and "full employment" was literally attained during the second World War.

Overshadowing every question of domestic policy from 1932 up to the outbreak of war in 1939 were the problems caused by the rise of Hitlerism in Germany and the forging of the Axis with Fascist Italy. These were the years which saw Japanese militarism and imperialism beginning the attempt to conquer China by its successful aggression in Manchuria. It was the period in which the League of Nations, reacting feebly to the sternest of tests, progressively revealed its inherent weakness. In these years, the sincere and able leadership of men like Arthur Henderson towards universal disarmament failed to accomplish the aim for which the World Disarmament Conference sat for so many months at Geneva. Instead, as the aggressive and vengeful spirit of Germany became more and more apparent after Hitler's seizure of power in 1933, rearmament became a dominant issue in British politics. It was the inevitable answer to German rearmament, and to the growing insolence and aggression of the Fascist-Nazi dictators.

In many European countries democratic regimes ceased to exist in these troubled years. Dictatorship replaced parliamentary and representative Government not only in Italy and Germany, but in Poland, Hungary, Austria and elsewhere. In the last-named country a terrible social convulsion culminated in bloodshed when the Dollfuss dictatorship succeeded in crushing every democratic organisation, beginning with the free trade unions and the Social Democratic Party. The destruction of the organised Labour Movement in Vienna in 1934 opened the eyes of British Labour to the true portent of Hitler's rise to power in Germany and to the inner meaning of Mussolini's attack upon Abyssinia. Almost simultaneously, counter-revolutionary forces in Spain engineered an armed conflict which deepened and widened into the bloodiest of civil wars. An inexorable pressure seemed to be driving the nations steadily towards war.

Yet peace was the earnest desire of the British people and the Labour Movement shared this desire to the full. A significant event was the Peace Ballot organised by the League of Nations Union with the active co-operation, through the National Council of Labour, of the T.U.C. General Council, and the Executive body of the Labour Party. In this ballot a grand total of over 11,600,000 votes were recorded, giving unequivocal answers to such questions as these: (1) Should Great Britain remain a member of the League of Nations? (2) Are you in favour of an all-round reduction of armaments by international agreement, and of the all-round abolition of national military and naval aircraft, and prohibition of manufacture and sale of armaments for private profit? To these questions a majority of votes were registered ranging from 11,157,000 to 9,592,000, against minorities that were as low as 113,265 and never more than 368,250. Tremendous majorities, too, were in favour of economic and military measures being taken to stop an aggressive nation attacking others. Even to the question whether in such circumstances military measures should be employed, nearly 7,000,000 votes were recorded in favour of such measures against less than 2,500,000 votes in opposition. Nevertheless, the trend towards war went irresistibly on, and with increasing momentum after the General Election of 1935, when the conduct of foreign policy passed into the hands of the Conservative leaders, and in later stages into the inexperienced hands of Mr. Neville Chamberlain.

The Labour Party, before this General Election, was recovering its political influence. But it had not got over the effects on its membership of the protracted economic depression. Trade Union membership had been considerably weakened in consequence of the widespread and apparently incurable unemployment, and the continuing deterioration in the workers' standards of life. The number of trade unionists affiliated to the Labour Party was substantially reduced in these circumstances, especially after the enactment of the Trade Disputes and Trade Unions Act of 1927. From a peak membership of nearly 4,400,000 in 1921, membership of the Unions affiliated to the Party declined, and after 1927 went down sharply; so that by the time of the 1935 General Election it was very much less than half of the total at its peak in 1921. Changes inside the "National" Government also took place which strengthened the hands of the Conservative leaders, whilst reducing to a derisory level the Government's claim to represent a union of Parties: not only were the Samuelite Liberals no longer represented, because of the resignation of their ten Ministers inside the Government, on the protectionist and imperial preference issues, but there were changes of an even more momentous character in the dropping of Ramsay MacDonald from the premiership and the dismissal of Lord Sankey from the office of Lord Chancellor. Ramsay MacDonald remained in the Cabinet as Lord President of the Council, but he was a spent force, and under the renewed premiership of Mr. Stanley (later Earl) Baldwin, the Conservative Party not unreasonably expected to keep the country in its grip, and to prevent a revival of the Labour Party.

These calculations were falsified at the 1935 General Election. Although the Labour Party did not regain altogether the position it occupied at the General Election of 1929 it did, nevertheless, achieve an astonishing recovery. It got back a great many of the seats it held in Parliament before the debacle of 1931. It had less than sixty seats after that iniquitous betrayal; but it returned to Parliament after the 1935 General Election with 154 seats. The Government Parties retained their ascendancy with a popular poll of about 11,800,000 votes against just over 8,325,000 Labour votes. This gave them a clear majority of 3,500,000 over Labour in the country, and a majority of more than 1,750,000 over the combined Opposition Parties. But the strength of the Conservative Party was illusory. Destructive forces had been unloosed in Europe which a Conservative Government in Britain could not cope with; whilst the leadership of the political Labour Movement became steadily firmer and more confident in facing up to the problems and perplexities of those years. It suffered a grievous loss in the autumn of 1935 in the death of Arthur Henderson, and in the same month its Parliamentary Leader, George Lansbury, felt obliged to resign this position because of his disagreement with the Party's decision on the question of rearmament. Clement Attlee was elected to succeed Lansbury as Leader, with Arthur Greenwood as Deputy Leader, and under their guidance the Party both in Parliament and in the country undertook a well-organised campaign to inform the country on the main issues of policy, both national and international, upon which the Conservative leadership was, in the Party's view, at fault. The militant and confident spirit of the Party after the 1935 General Election, found emphasis in declarations made at Annual Conferences, particularly in the address from the Chair by Dr. Hugh Dalton, at the Bournemouth Conference in 1937.

Membership of the Party, Dr. Dalton said, was then rising and had already passed the 2,000,000 mark. The Party's purpose he defined as "to win power and then to use power; to win it by the weapons of democracy, by effective political organisation and by propaganda that stirs, attracts and persuades; to use it to bring Socialism, social improvement and greater social equality, to maintain and extend our democratic liberties, and to restore and consolidate world peace."

The indictment against the Baldwin Government was remorselessly pressed home. At the height of a so-called trade boom at home, Dr. Dalton said, a million and a half workers were still unemployed, hundreds of thousands of them for years on end. Millions were underfed, ill-housed and living in poverty. Millions were over-worked and under-paid, with never even a week's holiday with pay. The cost of living was rising. No preparation was being made by the Government against a further slump. And tremendous dangers overshadowed the nation: "Nothing is to be gained by playing ostrich," Dalton said. "It is foolish to deceive ourselves, and it is wrong to deceive those we represent and those who trust us. The peace of the world today is not merely imperilled—it is being brutally broken without declaration of war, both in China and in Spain, as yesterday in Abyssinia. The abominable massacre of civil populations by air bombardment and the systematic destruction of whole cities, teeming with human life, may, unless Britain speedily reasserts her moral and material influence in the world, soon be repeated on an even greater scale in other European countries."

This prophetic utterance gave urgency to the Party's campaign to secure a change of Government, and a change in the spirit and direction of the country's foreign policy. Significant in Dalton's address as Chairman of the Party in 1937, was his declaration that in the grim international situation, not of the Labour Party's making, the country must be powerfully armed. But arms must be linked with an international policy which would impart new life to the League of Nations and recreate respect for international law. "These last six years the world has rattled back to barbarism at breakneck speed," said the Party's Chairman: "the greatest need today is for a return to honest courage in our foreign policy, and for another Labour Government in Britain to reverse the present helpless slide towards supreme catastrophe."

Two years later the Party Conference, meeting in the same place, decided that it could not give its support, even in the midst of war, to a Government of which Mr. Neville Chamberlain was the head. It was, however, prepared to join with the other Parties in forming a Government under the leadership of Mr. Churchill, for the more vigorous and resolute prosecution of the war until a just and lasting peace could be won by military victory.

CHAPTER XVII

LABOUR AND THE SECOND WORLD WAR

By Herbert Tracey

It lies outside the scope of this chapter to trace in detail the course of events leading, in the period of appeasement, to the second World War. Appeasement was in many respects one of the most squalid and ignoble phases of British foreign policy. It tended in nearly all its manifestations to strengthen the Nazi-Fascist dictatorship. By 1935 the dictatorship had consolidated its resources in Germany and in Italy. From then on to its final act of aggression against Poland in 1939, it acted on the larger stage of world politics with ever-increasing boldness and arrogance. Each new aggression in the appeasement period seemed to lend additional justification to the British Government's policy of non-intervention; but every capitulation to the demands of the dictators strengthened their power to make further demands. Each act of aggression led logically to the next, until in the end the British Prime Minister found himself in Munich to consummate the policy of non-intervention by the surrender of the last citadel of democratic government east of the Rhine. But the decision of the British and French Prime Ministers at Munich in the autumn of 1938 to leave Czechoslovakia in the hands of Hitler was only one of many grievous errors that were committed in the unfolding of the policy of non-intervention.

The road to war led straight from the rape of Manchuria by Japan in 1931 to the invasion of Poland in 1939. On that road every step taken that was intended to prevent war and to reinforce the structure of international order was counteracted by Hitler's planned acts of aggression. The first milestone on the road to war was passed when, at the beginning of 1935, Hitler successfully defied the Western Powers on the question of rearming Germany, secured possession of the Saar territory by a derisory plebiscite in which 90 per cent. of the votes were recorded in Germany's favour, and thence to the reintroduction of universal military service in the Reich. Nazi-Fascist aggression from then onwards went hand in hand with appeasement.

In the very moment when the premiership of Great Britain was transferred from Ramsay MacDonald to Stanley Baldwin (in June 1935), von Ribbentrop signed in London the Naval Treaty which allowed Germany to build up to 35 per cent. of the British naval tonnage. Four months later (in October 1935) Mussolini began the conquest of Abyssinia, and before the end of the year the Hoare-Laval plan carried appeasement a further stage by offering Italy a considerable slice of Abyssinian territory. When in March 1936, Hitler reoccupied the Rhineland with military forces much inferior in strength to the French army which opposed it, France and Britain did not move; though Sir Samuel Hoare (now Viscount Templewood) had given way to Mr. Anthony Eden at the Foreign Office, and Laval's Cabinet had fallen, the appeasement policy was not dropped. It registered another triumph in the Anglo-French joint decision to refer Hitler's violation of the Versailles Treaty to the League of Nations. No stronger action was taken by the British or the French Governments, when, in the autumn of 1936, the rebellion of the Spanish generals against the legitimate Government plunged Spain into civil war. This embittered and bloody class struggle gave the British and French Governments another opportunity to practise appeasement by presenting to the Powers concerned (in August 1936) their joint plan of non-intervention—the plan into which Soviet Russia as well as Germany and Italy found it consistent with its policy forthwith to enter, notwithstanding the ominous reference made by Hitler, in a speech at Nuremberg at that very time, to Germany's neighbours, "swimming in a superfluity of land . . . If I had the Ural mountains with their incalculable store of treasure in raw materials, Siberia with its vast forests, and the Ukraine with its tremendous wheat fields, Germany and the National Socialist leadership would swim in plenty," Hitler said; and he proceeded then to sign the Anti-Comintern Pact with Japan, and to recognise Franco as the active agent of the Nazi-Fascist dictatorship, providing him, with the co-operation of Mussolini, not only with arms and munitions, but with military forces, aircraft and technicians, especially airmen.

Recognition of Franco by both Germany and Italy was co-incident with the joint effort of the British and French Governments (in December 1937) to extend the non-intervention agreement to the so-called "volunteers." The help given by the dictators to Franco was not a more convincing demonstration of their malign purpose than the repeated repudiations they made of the policy of non-intervention. In practice this policy meant that the loyal and legitimate Government of Spain was denied all arms and supplies, except those supplies of food and medical requisites that the international working-class movements were able to provide through their voluntary funds. The rebel forces, on the other hand, under Franco, were able to obtain unlimited supplies of arms and every necessary assistance from the Nazi-Fascist dictators. The inevitable result of this unequal conflict was the defeat of the loyalist forces and the establishment of the Franco dictatorship after two-and-a-half years of bloodshed, at the end of 1938.

Before this stage was reached, however, still another change had taken place in the political leadership of Great Britain. In May 1937, Stanley Baldwin gave way to Neville Chamberlain, and the policy of non-intervention in the hands of the new Prime Minister was pursued with even greater vigour. Positive acts of appeasement took the place of the stricter form of the non-intervention policy which Mr. Anthony Eden tried to follow correctly at the Foreign Office until, in February 1938, he felt obliged to resign on the ground of "fundamental differences" between him and the Prime Minister in matters of foreign policy. Mr. Chamberlain's handling of international affairs was wholly disastrous. In his first speech as Prime Minister he pledged himself to pursue efforts at conciliation. These led him to make a personal effort to come to terms with Mussolini. Following an exchange of letters in the summer of 1937 which seemed to pave the way to a better understanding between Britain, France and Italy, however, came Italy's cynical refusal to join in the Anglo-French agreement of the autumn to guard Mediterranean shipping against mysterious attacks from unidentified submarines. As if to give point to this rebuff, Mussolini a few days later went to Munich and Berlin, a visit which gave Hitler the opportunity (on September 28) to declare that the common trend of ideas revealed in the Fascist and National Socialist revolutions had developed into a similar course of action on the part of the two Leaders. "You who have listened at this very hour, and those who are listening to us in other parts of the world" said Hitler "must acknowledge that two sovereign national regimes have come into contact at a time in which the democratic and Marxist International revels in demonstrations of hatred which must result in dissension. Every attempt to interfere with the understanding between the two nations or to play one up against the other by casting suspicion and by obscuring the real aims in order to dissolve the ideal partnership will be of no avail because of the innermost desire of 150,000,000 people who are united at the manifestation at this very hour, and because of the determination of the two men who are standing here to address you."

Mussolini's signature to the Anti-Comintern Pact followed on November 6, and a month later Italy withdrew from the League of Nations. But these developments of the Nazi-Fascist alliance seemed to exercise no deterrent effect upon the policy of "conciliation" of the Chamberlain Government.

These efforts were obstinately pursued by the British Prime Minister with a new set of advisers on foreign policy, throughout 1938. This was the year which marked the destruction of Austria's independence and its formal annexation by Hitler in March, shortly after he had told the Reichstag that it was Germany's intention to take into her hands the protection of "over 10,000,000 Germans who live in two of the States adjoining our frontiers." The attack upon Czechoslovakia, signalled by this declaration, was consummated in the course of the year by methods of intimidation and violence akin to those practised by the Nazis in the case of Austria. No real attempt was made to save Austria by either the British or the French Governments; but in the case of Czechosolvakia, Anglo-French diplomacy, under the guidance of Chamberlain and Daladier, followed a much more devious course. About their intentions regarding Czechoslovakia the two Governments spoke with contradictory voices.

Although up to the very eve of the crisis assurances were given that France would stand by its Treaty with Czechoslovakia, and that Britain would support France, the effective influence of both the Governments was exercised in the opposite direction. The representations made in Prague by the spokesmen of the two Governments, the Runciman mission, and the visit of the British Prime Minister to Berchtesgaden and Godesberg, all combined to exert pressure upon the Government of Czechoslovakia to yield to Hitler's demands.

So the tragedy of Czechoslovakia unfolded. Over the whole field of diplomacy appeasement went on. The conclusion of the Anglo-Italian Pact (in April 1938) carried with it recognition of Italy's claim to seize Ethiopia, and the abandonment of the British Government's insistence on the withdrawal of Italian troops from Spain by making their withdrawal effective only after the victory of Franco. Mr. Chamberlain's return from Munich (in the autumn of 1938) bringing with him, as he believed, peace with honour and "peace in our time," followed a day or two later by demobilisation in France, received ironical emphasis in Hitler's entry into Czechoslovakia as conqueror in October. Franco's triumph over the loyalist forces in Spain then gave both Britain and France the opportunity, early in 1939, to afford *de jure* recognition to the Franco regime. There was no change in Hitler's strategy after Munich whilst the quarrel he picked with Poland moved on its predestined course through the spring and summer of 1939. The British Government strove hastily to form a "peace front." Guarantees were given not only to Poland, but to Rumania and Greece. An understanding with Soviet Russia, however, was not achieved. Before our political and military mission reached Moscow to negotiate an agreement with the Soviet Government, Litvinov had given place to Molotov as Foreign Minister, and at the height of the Polish crisis the Soviet-German Pact was made public (in August 1939).

Such was the political background of the second World War which began with the invasion of Poland on September 1, 1939. The day after Germany's armed forces crossed the Polish frontier, two declarations were made by the responsible committees of the Labour Party. These defined the position of the whole British Labour Movement in relation both to the war itself and to the Government then in Office. The National Executive Committee of the Labour Party and the Parliamentary Labour Party's Executive Committee jointly declared on September 2, 1939, their resolve to support the action which the British and French Governments were required to take in fulfilment of their Treaty obligations to Poland. But the two Committees at the same time unanimously agreed that the Party could not accept an invitation to join the Government. Almost exactly nine months later (on May 10, 1940) the Labour Party assumed the responsibility of full partnership in the new War Government formed by Mr. Churchill: two of the Party's representatives, its Leader and Deputy Leader, entered the War Cabinet of five members, and a dozen offices of

major importance for the conduct of the war were assigned to Labour Ministers.

The complete list of these appointments is as follows:

Lord Privy Seal	Rt. Hon. C. R. Attlee
Minister without Portfolio	Rt. Hon. Arthur Greenwood
First Lord of the Admiralty	Rt. Hon. A. V. Alexander
Minister of Labour	Rt. Hon. Ernest Bevin
Minister of Economic Warfare	Rt. Hon. Hugh Dalton
Solicitor-General	Rt. Hon. Sir William Jowitt
Minister of Supply	Rt. Hon. Herbert Morrison
Parliamentary Secretary, Board of Education	Mr. J. Chuter Ede
Parliamentary Secretary, Mines Department	Mr. D. R. Grenfell
Under-Secretary of State for the Colonies	Mr. G. H. Hall
Parliamentary Secretary, Ministry of Transport	Mr. Fred Montague
Under-Secretary of State for Scotland	Mr. Joseph Westwood
Parliamentary Secretary, Ministry of Pensions	Miss Ellen Wilkinson
Parliamentary Secretary, Ministry of Agriculture	Mr. Tom Williams
Joint Parliamentary Secretary to the Treasury	Rt. Hon. Sir Charles Edwards
Lords Commissioner	Mr. Wilfred Paling
Comptroller of His Majesty's Household	Mr. William Whiteley
Captain of the Gentlemen-at-Arms	Lord Snell

The decision of the Labour Party to enter the Coalition formed by Mr. Churchill requires some explanation. Its main justification is to be found in the Party's opposition to the policy of non-intervention and appeasement followed by the Chamberlain Government. The position of the Labour Party at the outbreak of war was in no sense inconsistent with its earlier declarations of policy. There was no inconsistency in the Party's unanimous refusal of an offer of places in Mr. Chamberlain's Government when the war began, and its acceptance of Mr. Churchill's invitation nine months later. With the rise of dictatorship which openly proclaimed a reversion to power politics, and particularly after National Socialism revealed its true character in the destruction of the institutions of free citizenship in Germany, in its defiant avowal of rearmament and its earliest acts of aggression and conquest, as outlined in the preceding chapter, the British Labour Movement foresaw that a general conflict in Europe was probably inescapable. The breakdown of the World Disarmament Conference and the growing impotence of the League of Nations as one after another of its member-states repudiated its obligations, did not indeed destroy Labour's belief in the necessity of collective action to maintain peace. Year after year in its annual assemblies, the Party declared its conviction that war could be prevented, the arms race stopped, and the League of Nations made strong again. But it was equally convinced that a change of Government was required to bring these things about.

A clear statement of the policy which controlled the action of Labour's political leaders when war broke out was presented in 1937 to the Trades Union Congress and the Annual Conference of the Party under the title "International Policy and Defence." It summarised fully the sequence of events which marked the worsening of international relations and declared that the situation could be changed only by the advent of a new Government:

> "Such a Government" (said the report) "must be in a position to make a powerful appeal to the Fascist States to agree to the abandonment of the arms race and the acceptance of a general disarmament treaty.
> "Such a Government in the present state of the world must also be strongly equipped to defend this country, to play its full part in collective security, and to resist any intimidation by the Fascist Powers designed to frustrate the fulfilment of our obligations.
> "Such a Government, therefore, until the change in the international situation caused by its assent has had its effect would be unable to reverse the present programme of rearmament.
> "Such a Government, however, would immediately re-examine the whole provision made for defence in the light of the international situation, and the new foreign policy which it would inaugurate.
> "The British Labour Movement, fully conscious of the dangers which today threaten our civilisation, refuses to accept the doctrine of the inevitability of war and will continue to exert all its influence in promoting a durable peace based upon friendship and justice between nations and respect for international law."

This declaration possessed both a practical and historical significance. It emphasised the Movement's fidelity to the principles of a foreign policy which sought to organise peace through international association; but it also recognised the impossibility of escaping war by unilateral disarmament, and accepted the obligation of rearmament for the double purpose of national defence and the reinforcement of Britain's power to assist in securing the observance of international law. Every fresh violation of the rights of free nations by the Fascist Powers fortified the British Labour Movement in its resolve to pursue its two-fold aim.

It involved the Party in Parliament in apparent paradox. The Party's policy, increasingly insistent on the effective organisation of the nation for war, but withholding all support for the succession of "National" Governments that pledged themselves to a vast programme of rearmament, exposed Labour to criticism and reproach. It never slackened during the period of appeasement. It reached the height of vituperation against Labour as the war Party when Mr. Chamberlain brought back from Munich the documents which were supposed to guarantee peace in our time.

Suspicion of a fundamental contradiction in Labour's policy was not finally dispelled until its entry into the Churchill Government. But long before this event took place the Movement had given ample proof of its determination to accept the logical consequences of its demand that resistance to the aggression of the Fascist Powers should be strong and effective. Its declaration of solidarity with the nation when the armed struggle with Nazi Germany began was emphatic and unequivocal: the Trades Union

Congress, meeting at Bridlington on September 4, the day after Mr. Chamberlain, as Prime Minister, announced that a state of war existed between Britain and Germany, lacked nothing in the force and clarity of its declaration:

> "This Congress believes that the Nazi Government, having chosen for its people the way of war, must be resisted to the utmost. It must be opposed by all the forces that the civilised nations can concentrate for its defeat and overthrow. The defeat of ruthless aggression is essential if liberty and order are to be re-established in the world. Congress, with a united and resolute nation, enters the struggle with a clear conscience and steadfast purpose."

Nor was there anything lacking in the response of the Trade Unions to the call for national service. For many months before war was declared the General Council of the T.U.C. was engaged in developing important activities in connection with the organisation of the Civil Defence services and the mobilisation of the country's industrial resources. Labour's share of responsibility in the conduct of the war, and the influence of its representatives in the Government, were in this way materially strengthened. Foundations were laid for Trade Union co-operation in the husbanding of the nation's manpower by the framing of a schedule of reserved occupations. This was designed to prevent the indiscriminate recruitment of workers who could best serve the nation's needs by carrying on with their work. The Unions co-operated with the Ministry of Labour in framing the schedule and in its modification from time to time. They took an active part, too, in the organisation of the voluntary national service scheme for Civil Defence, including the recruitment of A.R.P. workers, for which a national co-ordinating committee, and a network of local voluntary service committees upon which the Trade Unions were fully represented, came into existence. And the T.U.C. General Council were also deep in conversations upon proposals for dealing with important problems of labour in war-time. These did not, however, find a practical solution until the war had actually begun. Developments then took place in the industrial sphere with a rapidity which contrasted rather sharply with the more leisurely and even languid conduct of operations in other fields.

Let it be said that Labour was far from being satisfied at this stage with the Government's handling of industry's war problems. As early as 1935, in the second of its White Papers on national defence, the Government recognised that its rearmament programme would entail a heavy strain on industry, and that the fullest co-operation of employers and workpeople would be required to give effect to it. But very little was done to inform the Trade Unions of what was expected from them or to engage their active interest in the vast scheme for extending industrial equipment and providing the trained personnel for war production. Not only the apathy of individual Ministers, but also the inertia of Government departments concerned with production and supply had to be overcome.

It was almost exactly a month after the official declaration of war, that the first steps were taken on the initiative of the T.U.C. General Council to associate the Trade Unions and employers' representatives more closely with the nation's war effort. A joint conference of the T.U.C. General Council and the British Employers' Confederation was then held under the chairmanship of the Minister of Labour (Mr. Ernest Brown) at which it was decided to set up a Joint Advisory Council to deal with "matters in which employers and workers have a common interest" and to advise the Minister upon them. Fifteen members from each side were chosen to constitute the Council. Two weeks later its scope and composition were agreed upon. A fortnight later still (on November 1) its first meeting was held. This leisured gait did not please the T.U.C. Impatience was intensified by the apparent reluctance of some of the Government Departments to consult with representatives of the Trade Unions upon the multiplying problems arising out of the emergency legislation and the pressure of war conditions affecting the working people. The T.U.C. General Council felt it to be necessary in fact, to approach the Prime Minister himself at the end of the first month of war and put before him its view of the situation.

It was not only Labour's distrust of the diplomacy of the "National" Government, but its slow and reluctant recognition of Labour's place in the community that made it impossible for the Chamberlain Government to win the support of the Labour Party or of the Trade Unions. The Unions, for their part, were convinced that they were not being consulted, nor their co-operation sought by any of the Government Departments as fully and as freely as their help was offered. Mr. Chamberlain was told that this was particularly true of the Ministry of Supply. A definite request was made that there should be Trade Union representation on every national, regional and local committee set up by that Ministry, as the Department charged with the responsibility of producing the munitions of war. It lies beyond the scope of this chapter to describe the Ministry's remarkable system of "controls" and the activities of its still more remarkable host of controllers, practically all of whom were drawn from the trades they controlled. The system was only partially leavened by Trade Union representatives when, as a consequence of a direct instruction from the Prime Minister, the Ministry of Supply, the Ministry of Food, the Board of Trade, the Ministry of Economic Warfare, and the Service Departments, as well, of course, as the Ministry of Labour, took the Unions into a warmer embrace.

The Prime Minister's instruction to the Departments to the effect that the Government desired them to maintain the closest possible relations with the Trade Unions and to create the necessary machinery for systematic and continuous consultation and co-operation, was an important factor in the shaping of Labour's war policy. It made the Party's decision in May 1940 much easier when the question of entry into the Government was reopened. One fairly immediate result of the Prime Minister's instruction was the setting up of District Advisory Committees by the Ministry of Supply to speed up the production of munitions. It cannot be said that these bodies were functioning at all vigorously before the change of Government brought Mr. Herbert Morrison to the Ministry of Supply, but they were an indispensable adjunct of the Government's planning of war production on a nation-wide basis. Their main task was to survey the industrial resources in their areas, and to ascertain how far these resources were being utilised. When representatives of the Board of Trade were added to them these Area Bodies also took account of the requirements of the export trade. Production engineers were also added to assist on the technical side and steps were taken to associate with them the other Government Departments concerned with the supply of munitions, including the three Service Ministries—that is to say, the Admiralty, the War Office and the Air Ministry. Trade panels and Joint Advisory Committees were also established to advise on the control of raw materials and all other requisites of the war trades.

In the work of other Ministries the principle of Trade Union representation was similarly asserted. Thus in the case of the Ministry of Food a central advisory committee was set up to assist the Minister in carrying out the rationing scheme and to advise on the allocation of food supplies and the regulation of prices. As illustration of the scope of this machinery, it may be mentioned that the Government's plan of control for beef and livestock, involving the concentration of slaughtering in selected centres, brought into operation fifty tribunals operating on a county basis. On all of them Trade Union representatives were appointed to serve. A very large number of local food committees, most of them created before the Food Ministry had been sufficiently impressed by the necessity of securing the co-operation of the Trade Unions, had also to be brought into line. These committees were part of the food control machinery of the local public authorities, and the Trade Unions were at first overlooked. The Minister was obliged, under pressure from the T.U.C. General Council, to issue an amending Order providing that a Trade Union representative must be appointed to a local food committee if the appropriate Union organisation in the locality wished this to be done. On some twenty technical committees set up by the Ministry dealing with specific commodities the same principle was observed. So also with the fuel committees, which the Mines Department set up to advise the local fuel overseers, and so, too, with the Board of Trade's machinery for the regulation of prices and the prevention of profiteering: there were some seventeen regional price regulation committees at work in connection with the central committee and Trade Union representation was secured on all of them.

Co-operation between Unions, Management and Government Departments in operating the machinery of Government control in this way strengthened the political association of the Labour Ministers with the Leaders of the other Parties that had joined to form the Churchill Government. But such developments in the mere mechanism of Government control, though they gave the Labour Movement some measure of responsibility, did not lessen the Movement's anxiety as to the general conduct of the war in its opening phases. Repeated attacks had to be made by the Labour Party in Parliament on individual Ministers, and on the Government as a whole, as the country's state of unpreparedness was progressively disclosed and the feeble character of its leadership spread dismay in wider circles. In April 1940, the Government's handling of the manpower problem was bitterly assailed from the Labour benches. Three weeks later, on May 7 and 8, a debate was forced upon the whole issue of the war leadership, in particular connection with the collapse of the Allied Expedition in Norway. As the debate developed the Labour Party felt it to be its duty to challenge the Government's hold upon the confidence of the House. Although on a division the Government secured the vote of 281 of its supporters against 200 in the Opposition lobby, the Prime Minister rightly interpreted the result as a sentence of dismissal for his Administration, and one that was all the more decisive because some thirty-seven of his own supporters, many of them Service members, voted with the Opposition against him. Nevertheless, Mr. Chamberlain in the next twenty-four hours strove to avert execution of the sentence of dismissal by seeking the Labour Party's co-operation in the formation of a new Government under his leadership. Whilst the delegates of the Annual Conference of the Labour Party were assembling in Bournemouth their leaders, Mr. C. R. Attlee and Mr. Arthur Greenwood, took a decisive stand in the negotiations. With the unanimous approval of the National Executive of the Party they refused point-blank to serve in any Administration formed by Mr. Chamberlain. But they made it clear, on the other hand, that the Labour Movement would support a War Government with Mr. Churchill at its head, and that the Party would accept the responsibilities of Office if the Government were founded upon a small War Cabinet capable of conducting the war with energy, efficiency, and determination. It was, of course, implicit in the decision of the Party to challenge in Parliament a vote upon its accusation that the Chamberlain Government was failing in its task, that the Party must assume a real measure of responsibility in any change of Government that resulted from a vote in the House. The effect of the vote was to convince Mr. Chamberlain that he must make way for Mr. Churchill, whose capacity to form a new Administration the Leaders of the Labour Party so strongly reinforced.

Negotiations were, of necessity, conducted under conditions of haste and urgency. The Leader of the Labour Party told the Annual Conference a few hours later that on the very night when they were faced with the question whether they would support Mr. Chamberlain in a reconstructed

Government, or join Mr. Churchill in a new War Cabinet, Holland and Belgium were invaded by the Nazi armies. The great crisis of the war had come. There was no time to consider, from the standpoint of general policy, the implications of the Party's entry into the Government. They could not even stipulate what the representation of the several Parties should be. They had to accept the fact that some persons would be included in the new Government whom they might have wished to exclude, and others left out whom they would wish to bring in. But the National Executive of the Party, having given its Leader and Deputy Leader a free hand in the negotiations, felt no hesitation whatever in sustaining the position they took. When the Conference of the Party assembled for its first session on Whit Monday, May 13, the new War Cabinet was already in being.

Its mandate, as far as the Labour Movement was concerned, found its confirmation in the following resolution adopted at the Bournemouth Conference:

> "This Conference endorses the unanimous decision of the National Executive that the Labour Party should take its share of responsibility as a full partner in the new Government which, under a new Prime Minister, commands the confidence of the nation. This Conference further pledges its full support to the new Government in its efforts to secure a swift victory and a just peace."

The resolution was adopted by 2,413,000 votes to 170,000. The small minority was by no means homogeneous. It comprised delegates who held that the war was the outcome of imperialist rivalries and should be stopped, delegates who urged that only a Socialist Government could win the war, and an ingredient of pure pacifism—from which the Labour Movement has never been entirely immune.

In the course of the discussions upon the composition of the new Government Labour's plenipotentiaries (Attlee and Greenwood) urged upon Mr. Churchill the vital importance of organised Labour having its direct representatives in the new Government—that is, in other words, the industrial wing of the Labour Movement as well as the political wing, should be directly associated with the Government. Mr. Churchill was fully aware of the part played by the Trade Unions in the national war effort, already described, and much too shrewd and far-seeing to wish to deprive his Administration of Trade Union support. He had already, it appeared, taken steps to invite one of the ablest and most influential Trade Union leaders to accept office: during the meetings of the T.U.C. General Council, the National Council of Labour and the National Executive of the Labour Party, at Bournemouth in that hectic Whitsun weekend, it became known that Mr. Ernest Bevin, general secretary of the Transport and General Workers' Union, and a prominent member of the Trades Union Congress, had been asked by the Prime Minister to serve as Minister of Labour. Mr. Bevin sought the support of the T.U.C. General Council and the Executive Council of his own Union before making up his mind to accept this appointment, which was perceived to be a "key" appointment in more than one sense of the word. The General Council of the Trades Union Congress unanimously declared that Mr. Bevin would have their fullest support as Minister of Labour in the new Government. With equal unanimity his Union Executive gave Mr. Bevin "leave of absence" for the duration of his appointment. Mr. Bevin held no seat in Parliament, but he obtained one for Central Wandsworth in an uncontested election a few weeks after he took over the Ministry of Labour.

Importance attached to the inclusion of a strong and able trade unionist of his standing in the new Administration, primarily because the mobilisation of industrial manpower for war production was clearly a necessity of the moment. One of the principal indictments of the previous Government was that it had failed to make use of all available labour; in the debate of the House of Commons on April 16, Mr. Chamberlain and his colleagues had been severely criticised on the ground that they had no real plan for the organisation of production. When the new Government met the House one of its first measures was an Emergency Powers (Defence) Bill which conferred complete control over all persons and property for the prosecution of the war, and many of these powers of control were vested in the Minister of Labour.

Under the new Emergency Act the Minister of Labour was endowed with the authority to direct any person to perform any service required of him, not necessarily service in munitions or factories, and not only workmen; the Minister was empowered to prescribe the terms of remuneration, the hours of labour and the conditions of service: and it was laid down as a guiding principle by the Minister in charge of the Bill (Mr. Attlee) that the rate of remuneration was to be on the basis of the "rate for the job." The control over property was no less absolute than the control over manpower which was vested in the Minister when this Bill was enacted. Industrial establishments of every description whose plant and equipment were necessary for war production came under Government control immediately, and other establishments passed under control as the scope of war production widened. Factories and workshops in the war trades were set to work, in effect, on Government account. Wages and profits were brought under Government control. Excess profits were taxed at the rate of 100 per cent.

Organisation of labour supply raised problems which directly affected the Trade Unions. The advent of an experienced and far-seeing administrator like Mr. Bevin at the Ministry of Labour was, therefore, a development of exceptional interest to the Trade Unions. Relations between the Minister of Labour and the Trade Union side of the Labour Movement were, because of the nature of his task, necessarily more intimate than those of his Party colleagues who were appointed to other Government Departments. But they, too, exercised increasing influence as the war progressed. Mr. Herbert Morrisonat first as Minister of Supply—later he became Home Secretary—was concerned more with technical problems in industry for intensive production of arms and munitions. Dr. Hugh Dalton, at the Ministry of Economic Warfare, like Mr. A. V. Alexander at the Admiralty, toiled in a field of administration with which the leaders of the organised working-class movement outside the Government had fewer points of contact. No such apparatus of consultation and co-operation as Mr. Bevin and Mr. Morrison developed for the Trade Unions on the lines described above were required by the Minister of Economic Warfare or the First Lord of the Admiralty. The detailed explanation given of the machinery of consultative committees and other advisory bodies which established the connection of organised Labour with the Ministry of Labour, applies also to the Ministry of Supply; but Mr. Morrison's administrative talents for getting things done found their exercise in a peculiarly difficult task. He was assigned, at the height of the crisis in the supply of munitions which caused profound anxiety, to a Ministry whose general layout, as he told the House of Commons later, was not his, and he had to take the Department as he found it. It lies outside the scope of this chapter to deal with the work of these various Ministers, and it must suffice to say that Labour's full partnership in the tasks of the War Administration demonstrated their competence for the work they undertook, and gave them invaluable experience for the responsibilities they assumed after the General Election of 1945 in a Government of their own choosing.

Significant changes in the distribution of functions and in the demarcation of the respective spheres of responsibility as between the various Ministers, were announced soon after the War Cabinet was formed. The work of Ministers concerned with defence was necessarily co-ordinated and controlled by the Prime Minister himself as Minister of Defence. He was assisted by a Defence Committee consisting of the heads of the three Service Departments, namely the First Lord of the Admiralty, Mr. A. V. Alexander, the Secretary of State for War, Mr. Anthony Eden, and the Secretary of State for Air, Sir Archibald Sinclair—with the Chiefs of Staffs as advisers. Questions of foreign policy were in the hands of the Secretary of State for Foreign Affairs, who, as a member of the War Cabinet, communicated directly with his colleagues upon these questions at their daily meetings. It was within the sphere of economic organisation that the Government activities were most drastically overhauled, and in which the influence of the Ministers representing the Labour Movement was most potently exercised. Developments that took place during their tenure of Office in the Coalition Government left their mark upon the relations of the Trade Unions with the Government and with the employers' side of industry.

Notwithstanding the Labour Party's assumption of "full partnership" in the country's Government, its Members in the House of Commons held sternly aloof from the politics of Coalition. Mr. Churchill's Government was not founded upon a coalition of Parties: it was a Government of National Union, and the Parties upon whose support it depended were in a curious way at once its friends and its critics. This at least was true of the Labour Party, which continued to occupy the Opposition benches in the House, though its Opposition functions were much restricted. Normal political activities were, of course, pretty much in abeyance during the war. When the Churchill Government was formed, in May 1940, the Parties had already agreed to observe an Electoral Truce. Each Party undertook to refrain from nominating a candidate in any by-election against the candidate of the Party that held the seat at the time of the vacancy. It was explicitly a pledge to observe a truce in electoral contests, and not necessarily a pledge to abstain from political controversy. Even so, the Electoral Truce imposed a very heavy strain on the loyalty of the Labour Party particularly, since it was obviously under-represented in the House of Commons, and could have materially strengthened its position if it had been free to fight in all the war-time by-elections. In the circumstances the Conservative Party had an unfair advantage, as was proved by the fact that in practically all the contested by-elections the Conservative candidates were defeated and seats were won by candidates calling themselves "independent" or belonging to the new Common Wealth Party which had arisen during the war to challenge the position of the Labour Party. It is not surprising, therefore, that resolutions were hotly debated at the Annual Conferences of the Labour Party in 1942 and 1943 proposing to put an end to the Electoral Truce. But these resolutions were consistently rejected by the Conference, and in fact, the conditions of the Electoral Truce were actually strengthened in the middle of the war, as evidence of the determination of all the Parties to continue the struggle until victory was won and as testimony to the value of the Government of National Union as the instrument of that victory.

Political controversy could not, however, be wholly stilled even during the war. It did not touch the measures which the Government brought forward for the more vigorous and resolute prosecution of the war effort. In all these matters of administration and concentration of the resources of the country to win the war, the Government succeeded in sinking all Party differences, and a real unity of purpose was achieved. But on some questions of domestic policy affecting the lives of the people, the differences in the outlook of the Labour Party from that of the older Parties gave rise to controversy. A single example will suffice to show the difficulty in which the Party was sometimes placed by its association with the other Parties in the Churchill Government. In 1942, Draft Regulations submitted by the Government to increase Old Age Pensions, were felt by many members of the Labour Party to be niggardly in the provisions they made. Their protest was not carried to a division, and their opposition to the Regulation was overcome by an undertaking from the Ministers responsible to reconsider the question.

Only on one occasion did the Labour Party in the House revolt in strength and vote against their own representatives in the Government. The occasion of this vote was the debate that arose upon the Beveridge Report, when the Government announced its intention concerning the implementation of its proposals. It was on the initiative of a Labour Minister, Arthur Greenwood, that Sir William (now Lord) Beveridge, undertook the investigation which resulted in the production of his Report. The Government's attitude towards the Report was considered so unsatisfactory that the Parliamentary Labour Party decided to present a motion expressing their criticism of the Government's policy. Despite appeals from the Labour Ministers the Party pressed its motion to a division, and as many as 119 votes were recorded in opposition to the Government, whose position was sustained by 335 votes. All the Labour M.P.s outside the Government, except two, voted in opposition on this occasion. It proved once again that the "condition of the people" question was still the fundamental dividing issue between the Labour Party and the other Parties.

The Party's deep and abiding faith in its social mission, which caused it finally to break with the Parties with which it was associated in the Churchill Government, safeguarded the Party's identity and independence during the war years. Although its opposition functions were much restricted the Party remained on the Opposition benches; and after its leading members entered the Government, an administrative committee was elected by the Parliamentary Party to occupy the Opposition front bench and to act as an Executive Committee with an elected acting chairman as temporary custodian of the Leader's authority within the Party during Mr. Attlee's temporary vacation of such responsibilities. This administrative committee comprised those members of the old Parliamentary Executive who did not enter the Government, together with other members, likewise not in the Government, who were entitled to sit on the front bench; Ministers who were members of the Parliamentary Executive becoming ex-officio members of this committee.

By these arrangements the Labour Party maintained its separate existence and to some extent its independent voice and freedom of action for Parliamentary purposes during the war years. This was quite consistent with the view, officially emphasised by the National Executive in the spring of 1943, that the co-operation of the Party in the Churchill Government involved more than the achievement of military victory. The work of the Labour Ministers was vital, the National Executive said, if the influence of the Labour, Trade Union and Co-operative Movements was to have any effect on post-war plans. As Acting Leader of the Party, outside the Government, Arthur Greenwood, expressing the general view of the Party, rejected in the autumn of 1943 the "Four Year Plan" of post-war reconstruction and reform put forward by Mr. Churchill in the spring of the year, as a programme for a continuous extension of his Government after the war. Mr. Churchill's Four Year Plan proved not to be the programme upon which finally he fought the General Election of 1945. In the end Mr. Churchill chose to act as the Leader of the Conservative Party and abandon the leadership of a united nation he exercised during the war years. The expectation of his Party organisers, which he may have shared, that in the General Election on the morrow of VE day they would profit by the nation's thanksgiving that the war had been won, with the glamour of the Prime Minister's personality as their principal asset, was proved to be a very bad miscalculation.

CHAPTER XVIII

LABOUR'S ADVENT TO POWER

By Morgan Phillips

There was a twofold significance in the victory which the British Labour Party gained at the General Election in July 1945.

First, it was a demonstration of an energetic democracy in action. The Parliament elected in 1935 would have been dissolved in 1940 had circumstances been normal, but the outbreak of war in 1939 and the fall of the Low Countries in 1940, which placed the Nazi forces on the French Coast, made it impossible to hold a General Election when Britain's very existence was at stake. The course of the war had forced Mr. Chamberlain from Office early in 1940, and a new Government was then created with Mr. Churchill at its head and with Labour Ministers taking their full share of responsibility, and the life of this Parliament was prolonged from year to year.

During the five years' interval, the prestige of Mr. Churchill as a great war leader rose to such a high level that to other nations it seemed that all the future hopes and resolves of the British people could be summed up in a single commanding personality. But that is not the democratic way. The essence of democracy is that it is never to be taken for granted, and once the issues of a free Election are placed before the people, those issues are open to be judged on their true values without relation to emotions or personalities.

The choice before the British people at this Election was, broadly speaking, between the respective policies of the Conservative Party and the Labour Party. It was not (as some opponents of Labour implied) an opportunity for the electorate to give a "vote of thanks" to Mr. Churchill. That would have been the very negation of democracy. Briefly, the issue of the Election was whether Britain was to continue under a Conservative Administration whose aim would be to continue and consolidate the existing system of private ownership for private profit, or whether there should be a complete break with the unhappy past and a Socialist Government elected with a policy of public enterprise for public good. That was the choice; and, indifferent to all side-issues and confusions of the Election, the British people gave an uncompromising answer.

That is the first significance. After a Parliament of ten years' duration and five years of electoral truce between the Parties, democracy in Britain has been shown to be more alive and vital than ever before.

Secondly, there is a deep significance in the actual result of the poll. It lies in the fact that despite all the power of the Press and the attempts to confuse the Election issues by capitalising Mr. Churchill's deservedly great reputation, the people took the Election very seriously and refused to be distracted from its real meaning. They saw it as a chance to break away from the misery and uncertainty of an unplanned and unjust economic system. Civilians and Services alike studied the matter gravely and objectively, and voted overwhelmingly in favour of a new deal for the common people.

How the Election Came About.—In October 1944, the National Executive Committee of the Labour Party issued a statement which said:

> "Nothing must be allowed to conflict in any way with the paramount necessity of bringing the war to a successful conclusion. In the view of the National Executive Committee, Labour's participation in the Government should continue just so long as, in the opinion of the Party Conference, it is necessary in the national interest, and for fulfilling the purposes for which the Government was called into being."

All Parties were at this time agreed that there should not be a snap Election on the morrow of victory. Mr. Churchill himself was quite definite on this point. Despite this, however, a number of Conservative Members in the House of Commons were getting restive during the Debate on the Prolongation of Parliament Bill, so much so that Mr. Churchill took the unprecedented course of introducing the Bill himself in the place of the Home Secretary. In the course of his speech on October 31, 1944, he said:

> "We are told there must on no account be what is called a 'coupon' election. By that I presume is meant an agreement between the official Parties not to oppose each other in most of the seats, and to form a solid front against those who criticise or oppose us. . . . One must admit that many people would think this would hardly be a fair way of testing opinion in the country, and in fact it would be quite impossible to obtain Party agreement to such a course. Many people feel that it would impede the electorate in expressing their free choice. . . . I do not find it easy to escape from the weight and force of these arguments.
>
> ". . . The Conservative Party have a majority of more than 100 above all Parties and independents in the present House, and it would therefore fall to us to make arrangements for the inevitable General Election. I cannot conceive that anyone would wish that Election to be held in a violent hurry or while we were all rejoicing together and rendering thanks to God for our deliverance. There must be an interval. Moreover, we have, above all things, to be careful that practically everybody entitled to vote has a fair chance to do so."

In these circumstances, the Labour Movement took the view that the General Election should not take place before the autumn of 1945.

Mr. Churchill's Proposal.—Victory in Europe was officially announced on May 8, 1945. Ten days later "while we were all rejoicing together," Mr. Churchill wrote to Mr. Attlee, Leader of the Labour Party, rejecting Labour's proposal that an Election be held in the autumn. Instead, he suggested a referendum by which the nation should decide whether the existence of the Coalition Government should be prolonged until the end of the Japanese war. His letter to Mr. Attlee was as follows:

"My dear Attlee,
"From the talks I have had with you and your principal Labour colleagues, I have gathered the impression that the Labour Party, instead of leaving the Government on the defeat of Germany, would be willing to continue the Coalition until the autumn.
"I have given the most careful and anxious thought to this suggestion, and I regret to say that in its present form I cannot feel it would be in the public interest. A union of Parties like that which now exists should come together and work together, not for a particular date without regard to world events, but for the achievement of some great national purpose transcending all Party differences. For the last five or six months our Ministerial and Parliamentary affairs have been increasingly affected by the assumed approach of a General Election at the end of the German war. This has not conduced to the national interest so far as domestic affairs are concerned.
"I therefore make you the following proposal, which I earnestly hope you will not readily reject—namely, that we should fix upon another object for our joint endeavours and adjourn the question of our separation until it is gained. The First Lord of the Admiralty has already expressed in his speech in the City of London his regret that a General Election should be held before the Japanese war was finished. It would give me great relief if you and your friends were found resolved to carry on with us until a decisive victory has been gained over Japan. In the meanwhile we would together do our utmost to implement the proposals for social security and full employment contained in the White Papers which we have laid before Parliament. On this basis we could work together with all the energy and comradeship which has marked our long and honourable association.
"I am conscious, however, in the highest degree of our duty to strengthen ourselves by a direct expression of the nation's will. If you should decide to stand on with us, all united together until the Japanese surrender is compelled, let us discuss means of taking the nation's opinion, for example, a referendum, on the issue whether in these conditions the life of this Parliament should be further prolonged.
"I am sending letters in similar terms to Sir Archibald Sinclair and to Mr. Ernest Brown.

"Yours, etc."

Mr. Attlee's Reply.—It will be seen that the letter was virtually an ultimatum. If Labour did not agree to these proposals (and the Prime Minister knew that they could not) the Election would of necessity be held in the summer. Mr. Attlee submitted the following reply:

"My dear Churchill,
"I thank you for your letter of May 18. I have, with my colleagues, given the most careful consideration to the proposal which you make that we should continue together until the end of the Japanese war and seek a further extension of life for the present Parliament.
"The Labour Party, on entering the Government, set no particular date for the termination of the partnership. It has, however, been recognised that a General Election must necessarily bring the partnership to an end if the electors were to have full and free opportunity of expressing their views on future policy.
"The need for bringing to an end, when conditions allowed, a Parliament, the life of which has been prolonged year after year, has been recognised by all of us, and by no one more emphatically than yourself. You stated that the prolongation of the life of the existing Parliament by another two or three years would be a very serious constitutional lapse.

"It is for that reason that my colleagues and I have always held that there should be an interval between the time when conditions permitted an Election to be held and the Election itself. Recognising the possibility of prejudice to the Party holding power during this interim period, we have been prepared to share the responsibilities of Government up to the time when an Election was declared. An autumn Election would provide a more complete and effective register than that now in force and would give to the Service electors the opportunity of more fully acquainting themselves with the candidates' standing and the issues involved in the Election than would be available in July.

"Service candidates would also have a fair chance of making themselves known to the electorate. My colleagues and I do not share your view that the country's interests would be prejudiced by a continuance of the present Government until the autumn. On the contrary, we think that there would be great advantage in the Government which has successfully brought the nation through the war continuing for a short time in order to deal with the immediate problems in the international field, and especially to help to bring to a successful conclusion the San Francisco Conference. We can rely on our Members in the House to do all they can to maintain this unity.

"The increasing success of our arms warranted you, when personally introducing the last Prolongation of Parliament Bill, to assume the probability of the defeat of Germany. As you said: 'We must look to the termination of the war against Nazism as a pointer which will fix the date of the General Election.' Political Parties and the country generally shared your justifiable faith in victory this year, and have, therefore, accepted from you the end of the present session as the terminal date for a General Election.

"It has been the view of the Labour Party, which I think you share, that a rushed Election like that of 1918, before the electorate, and especially those serving overseas, have had a fair opportunity of considering candidates and policies, would be utterly wrong and would gravely weaken the authority of any Government resulting from such an Election at a time when public confidence would be especially necessary.

"We, therefore, consider that the fair and just solution of the problem is an Election in the autumn. You suggest, as an alternative, that we should continue together until the end of the Japanese war. It is unnecessary for me to assure you that, whether in or out of the Government, the Labour Party will give its fullest support to the war until Japan is defeated. But when this will be is uncertain. We hope it may be soon, but if it were to be prolonged we see arising in a much more acute form all those difficulties which you apprehend at the present time in the domestic sphere and which you give as an objection to continuing to the autumn.

"It is precisely on the problems of the reconstruction of the economic life of the country that Party differences are most acute. What is required is decisive action. This can only be forthcoming from a Government united on principle and policy. A Government so divided that it could take no effective action would be a disaster to the country. My colleagues and I do not believe that it would be possible to lay aside political controversy now that the expectation of an Election has engaged the attention of the country. To give a guarantee of agreement to carry on for an indefinite period is not in my power, nor, I suggest, in yours.

"I do not think that it would be right or possible to obtain from Parliament another prolongation of its life. I could not consent to the introduction into our national life of a device so alien to all our traditions as the referendum, which has only too often been the instrument of Nazism and Fascism. Hitler's practices in the field of referenda and plebiscites can hardly have endeared these expedients to the British heart. For the reasons I have given your present proposal is unacceptable. It has been my desire, publicly expressed, that the long and honourable association of the Parties in the Government which has brought the country through so many perils to victory under your leadership, loyally supported by your Labour colleagues, should be brought to an end by common agreement and without controversy.

"I am sure that this would be your own wish, but I am bound to state that the reasons for rejecting an autumn Election seem to me to be based not on national interests but on considerations of Party expediency. It appears to me that you are departing from the position of a national leader by yielding to the pressure of the Conservative Party which is anxious to exploit your own great service to the nation in its own interests. I would earnestly ask you to reconsider your decision to hold an Election under circumstances which are bound to cause bitter resentment among the men of the fighting Services. Should you, however, decide on an Election in July despite all the disadvantages to the electors set out in this letter, with which you are familiar, the responsibility must and will, of course, be yours.

"Yours, etc."

So Ends the Coalition.—This was a reasoned statement of Labour's position, to which Mr. Churchill replied in the following terms:

"My dear Attlee,

"I am sorry to receive your letter of May 21, in which you reject my proposal that we should work together until the defeat of Japan is achieved and the job is finished.

"In this letter you tell me that our only course is to prolong the present Coalition till a General Election in October. This would mean that from now until October, outside the Government, and even within it, we should be continually preparing for an Election. We have already suffered several months of this electioneering atmosphere which, I am sure, is already affecting administrative efficiency and might soon weaken the country before the world at a time when, above all others, it should be stronger.

"I agree with what you say in your letter, that it is 'on the problems of the reconstruction of the economic life of the country that Party differences are most acute. What is required,' you say, 'is decisive action. This can only be forthcoming from a Government united on principle and policy.' I agree also with your statement, 'My colleagues and I do not believe that it would be possible to lay aside political controversy now that the expectation of an Election has engaged the attention of the country.'

"For my part, I am sure that a continuance of uncertainty and agitation would be harmful to the whole process of the recovery of our trade and change-over in industry. It is not good for any country, and it is impossible for any Coalition to live for so long a time under the spell of an approaching General Election. Least of all is this possible in a world where events are so tumultuous and dangerous as now.

"Opinions are much divided as to how Party advantage may lie between a July and an October Election, and I regret the aspersions with which you have darkened this correspondence. I have concerned myself solely with trying to create tolerable conditions under which we could work together. It is clear from the tone of your letter and the feelings of your Party that these no longer exist, and it is odd that you should accompany so many unjust allegations with an earnest request that we should go on bickering together till the autumn. Such a process would not be a decent way of carrying on a British Government.

"I regret that you should speak of 'rushing' an Election. Foreseeing what might arise at the close of the German war, we discussed, as you will remember, the whole question of procedure in detail in the War Cabinet. The normal period between the dissolution and the poll is seventeen days, and it was you and your colleagues who proposed that there should be at least a three weeks' additional interval in view of the special circumstances prevailing. We gladly accepted this reasonable request, and the unanimous decision of the Cabinet was made known to you on January 17, when you announced in the House of Commons that the King had been graciously willing for this occasion to announce his intention to dissolve Parliament at least three weeks beforehand."

"Yours, etc."

On May 23 Mr. Churchill visited the King to tender his Government's resignation. He then telephoned the Labour Ministers who were in Conference at Blackpool, informing them of his action. An official statement was then issued from No. 10 Downing Street, announcing that Parliament would be dissolved on June 15. So ended the Coalition.

Party Alignments.—It was a rush Election, during which a campaign was organised of stunts and scares designed to confuse the electorate and to blind it to the real issues. Only those who were present in Britain during the Election can appreciate the tremendous effort made by the Conservative Party, and various allies, to present the Election as an occasion for expressing gratitude to Mr. Churchill for his magnificent war leadership. This line was pursued by the Conservatives at the expense of a full exposition of their political policy. Deliberately, the Tory Election policy was based on the assumption that the hopes and aspirations of the British people were all embodied in the personality of one man—Mr. Churchill. Their campaign was an effort to induce people to submit their thoughts and judgment to his. A similar trick had succeeded before.

In support of this campaign there were prodigious newspaper and radio efforts to discredit the leadership of the Labour Party and give a false picture of its policy. All this is perfectly permissible, provided it is within the law, and the Labour Party, while avoiding all "stunt" methods itself, answered every challenge as best it could through the *Daily Herald*, the only British Labour national daily, and over the radio. But the forces in favour of private enterprise were very formidable indeed. With ample funds, and the greater part of the National Press behind it, the Conservative Party was able to cover the nation day after day with its Election propaganda. During the Election, however, there were signs that all was not well, that there were stirrings amongst the people, and that although they were all ready to pay their full meed of tribute to Mr. Churchill for his magnificent war effort, they were not prepared to place all their hopes for the future in Mr. Churchill and the Conservative Party. They could not easily forget the tragedy of the inter-war years, with unemployment, with short time and with low wages and malnutrition, and the constant atmosphere of both internal and international strife. They had seen during the war years that they had had (as in fact was the case during 1914-18) a period of full employment. They had seen the State plan for its survival, with the introduction of bulk purchase, with the concentration of industry, and with the selection of priorities, and it was clear that Labour Party propaganda was having a very great effect; that if it was necessary for the State to plan for State survival in war, it was equally necessary for the State to plan for the organisation of a satisfactory peace.

Charge and Counter-Charge.—The pre-war records of the Conservative Party, and some of the people included in Mr. Churchill's "Caretaker" Government after the break-up of the Coalition, were such that the Conservative Party had no hope of winning the Election on their own programme. For that programme offered no effective solution for any of the vital and urgent problems confronting the nation—housing, unemployment, fuel, exports, etc.—it was in essence a plea for a return to the anarchy, the chaos, the insecurity of pre-1939. The Conservatives themselves knew they stood condemned by their own record, and they attempted to cover this up by using the label of "National." In his first election broadcast, Mr. Churchill sought to justify the new Party label in these words:

> "Why do we claim the right to call this Government 'National'? First of all, because those who have left us have left us on Party grounds alone. Second, because the Conservative Party has been willing to abandon Party feeling to such an extent that more than one-third of the members of Cabinet rank in this new Government are not members of the Conservative Party."

The comments on this statement by *The Times* and the *Manchester Guardian* are very instructive:

> "... The motives of those who conscientiously believe that the time to break up the Coalition has come will bear inspection. Convinced Party men are not necessarily putting Party above their country when they persuade themselves that the good of their country requires the adoption of the Party principles in which they believe, or when they argue that the electorate has now a right to be consulted. . . ." (*The Times*, June 5, 1945).
>
> "... Mr. Churchill says this (Government) is 'National' because those who have left it have left 'on Party grounds' and because the Conservative Party has allowed some non-Party and other Party members in. . . . This does not prove that the Conservatives are, as Mr. Churchill pretends, above Party. It only shows that they are experts at camouflage." (*Manchester Guardian*, June 5, 1945).

The Tory machine and the Tory Press between them then tried to lay the responsibility for the rush Election upon the Labour Party, and followed it up with all kinds of fantastic stunts, like "totalitarianism," "Belsen" scares, supposed revolutionary declarations by the chairman of the Party's National Executive: to this they added the "Savings" scare . . . which had served them in good stead in 1931. Commenting on this, the *Manchester Guardian*, June 5, 1945, stated:

> "... (this scare) almost takes the breath away. If there is one political episode in our lifetime which decent politicians should be ashamed of, it is the election of 1931, when a Government was elected in a panic to save the pound and then immediately ate its words and went off the Gold Standard. . . ."

The failure of this scare did not, however, exhaust the resourcefulness of the Tory Party machine. A new one was brought out. Mr. Churchill suddenly discovered that the former Deputy Prime Minister, Mr. Attlee; the Minister of Labour, Mr. Ernest Bevin; and the Minister of Home Security, Mr. Morrison, and other people who had borne their full share of responsibility and worked loyally with him in the Cabinet for a period of four years, were not responsible to Parliament but to some unknown body, the National Executive Committee of the Labour Party. The climax of this was reached when Mr. Churchill in a broadcast insinuated that Labour Ministers would be obliged to divulge State and military secrets to the Party Executive. This led to the following correspondence between Mr. Churchill and Mr. Attlee.

Mr. Churchill wrote, on July 2, 1945:

"Dear Attlee,

"In the violent remarks you have made in your Sunday speech about my Saturday broadcast, you do not seem to realise the new position with which we are confronted.

"I had no idea, during the late Coalition, that the National Executive Committee of the Labour Party possessed the powers which have now become obvious. I have never suggested that you or your Socialist colleagues have in any way made any improper revelations to them.

"I was never aware of any case that had arisen in which the National Executive Committee had demanded secret information from Ministers serving in the Coalition Government, and I have no doubt that you would not have disclosed any such information without previous consultation with me. It seems, therefore, that during these five years of your active co-operation in the Coalition Government, the powers of the Socialist National Executive Committee have remained in suspense, and I am not aware of any complaint which could be made against you or their conduct during this period.

"Now, however, an altogether new situation has arisen. These powers, hitherto latent, have been asserted in a surprising manner. When I invited you to form part of the British delegation to the tripartite conference shortly to assemble in Berlin, I did so because I believed that you were effectively the Leader of your Party, and would have the discretion accorded you which has been customary up to the present time in British politics. It then appeared that the chairman of the National Executive Committee had the right to state that you would go as an observer only, and that no continuity in foreign policy could be guaranteed. I was very glad that you felt yourself able to contradict him on the point of your not going as a mere observer, and we exchanged letters on this subject at the time when I saw you last.

"However, far from withdrawing his original declaration, Mr. Laski has made a series of speeches emphasising his authority and that of the committee over which he presides.

"For instance, at SCUNTHORPE on June 17:

> 'When we win this Election, we want to be free in Socialist terms to make our policy for our own Socialist purpose. . . .'

"At CROYDON on June 18:

> 'I wanted to be crystal clear that, important as it was for Mr. Attlee to be at the Three-Power talks in Berlin, it was not less important that there should be a clear understanding among the electorate of Britain, and clear understanding in the minds of the Russians and Americans, that we Socialists are only committed to decisions which result in coherence with Socialism. I have no apologies for holding that view.'

"At WATFORD on June 24:

'It is now clear that whatever decisions are taken in Berlin are the responsibility of His Majesty's Government, and the Labour Government which will be elected will not be bound by the decisions which Mr. Churchill and Mr. Eden choose to accept. I have no apologies of any kind to make for any of my interventions during this Election. I want to emphasise that the Labour Party is at no point committed to the doctrine of continuity in foreign policy.'

"At WELWYN GARDEN CITY on June 24:

'I have nothing to apologise for, having to deny with emphasis that there is any continuity between the Tory foreign policy and the Socialist foreign policy.'

"Again on June 24, at ENFIELD:

'We do not propose to accept the Tory doctrine of the continuity of foreign policy, because we have no interest in the continuity of Conservative policy.'

"I certainly expected as the days passed by with repeated effronteries that you would make some effort to establish your position against Mr. Laski, and that he would be in some way disavowed by his committee or by the Labour Party as a whole. Nothing like this has, however, occurred, and we are left in the position that he has given you instructions which you have personally rejected but which, nevertheless, remain the official authoritative and reiterated instructions of the Executive Committee of the Labour Party.

"This manifestation of where the real power rests raised far-reaching considerations. We have learnt a good deal more than we knew before about the powers vested in the National Executive Committee, of which Mr. Laski is the undisputed chairman. It certainly appears that they are very wide in their terms and, from your silence, very real. It would appear that a Labour or Socialist Government would be subject to the directions of this committee, and that matters of foreign affairs and also, I presume, if they desire it, military affairs, would have to be submitted to them. So far as I am now informed, they have a right to be consulted and to express opinions which are binding on the Ministers of a Socialist Government or on the Cabinet itself.

"If the Committee is to be consulted and to take supreme decisions of approval or disapproval in regard to Government policy, how can they be debarred from reasonable knowledge of the facts? It might not be possible for Ministers to convince the Committee of the unwisdom of any course without revealing confidential Government matter. Indeed, it might well be argued that, where the power lies there also should be the knowledge.

"When we consider the members of this Committee of twenty-seven, and how very few are responsible in any way to the public or bound by any formal obligation to the State, I feel that the situation is extremely disquieting, and that it ought to be fully explained by you to the nation. The new fact is the demonstration of the power of the Committee and of its chairman, and that apparently you and the Labour Parliamentary Party are not able to challenge Mr. Laski's statement on behalf of the Committee, although it is evident that your public position greatly requires such action.

"The discussion of grave constitutional issues cannot be prevented by anger or strong language.

"Yours sincerely,

WINSTON S. CHURCHILL."

To this Mr. Attlee replied in the following terms:

"Dear Prime Minister,

"I thank you for your letter. I am glad to know that you make no suggestions against your late colleagues.

"The new position with which you state we are confronted exists only in your own imagination.

"The constitutional relationship between the National Executive Committee of the Labour Party and the Parliamentary Party has existed unchanged for years, and is set out in an appendix to the reports of the annual conference published every year. Neither by decision of the annual Party conference nor by any provision in the Party constitution is the Parliamentary Labour Party answerable to, or under the direction of, the National Executive Committee.

"Within the programme adopted by the annual Party conference, the Parliamentary Labour Party has complete discretion in its conduct of Parliamentary business, and in the attitude it should adopt to legislation tabled by other Parties. The standing orders which govern its activities are drawn up and determined by the Parliamentary Labour Party itself.

"I accepted the invitation to go to Berlin as the responsible Leader of the Parliamentary Labour Party.

"Naturally, there are consultations between the Parliamentary Labour Party and the National Executive Committee. No elector will be in the least surprised to hear that this is the case. These consultations are, indeed, arranged for in the Labour Party's own constitution, the clause reading as follows:

> 'To confer with the Parliamentary Labour Party at the opening of each Parliamentary Session, and at any other time when it or the Parliamentary Party may desire a conference on any matters relating to the work and progress of the Party.'

"For instance, when I decided to advise the Labour Party to support you in forming an all-party Government in 1940, I consulted the Executive Committee before bringing it before the Annual Conference of the Party, then in session. You raised no constitutional objection then; indeed, you were glad to have the backing of this democratically-elected conference.

"At no time, and in no circumstances, has the National Executive Committee ever sought to give or given instructions to the Parliamentary Labour Party arising out of the consultations. Indeed, as will be seen from the clause, it has no power to do so.

"The chairman has not the power to give me instructions, nor do his remarks to a Press correspondent constitute the official authoritative and reiterated instruction of the Executive Committee of the Labour Party.

"With regard to continuity in foreign policy, it is obvious that a Labour Government will follow a policy in accordance with the principles in which it believes and on which its Members in the House of Commons have been elected. This is sound constitutional doctrine. Presumably a Conservative Government would do the same.

"The fact that in the late Government Members of all Parties were in accord on the main lines of our foreign policy does not alter the fact that the complexion of the new House of Commons will decide the course of future policy as it did before the war, when you and I both disagreed with the policy of the Conservative Party.

"I am sorry that you should have been so distressed owing to your lack of acquaintance with the procedure of democratic Parties in general, and of the Labour Party in particular.

"Yours sincerely,

C. R. Attlee."

"Dear Attlee,

"Thank you for your letter. While I welcome the assurances contained in it, I regret that I cannot accept your explanation as satisfactory, because it leaves a number of very important points unanswered.

"Under your Party's constitution it is provided that 'The work of the Party shall be under the direction and control of the Party conference . . .' and the Executive Committee shall, 'subject to the control and directions of the Party conference, be the administrative authority of the Party.'

"It is further laid down, as you say in your letter, that the executive may call a conference of the Parliamentary Labour Party at any time on any matters relating to the work of the Party. What is the real interpretation of these provisions?

"It is clear that the conference, working through its Executive Committee, is the controlling body so far as the work and policy of the Labour Party is concerned, whether in Office or not. Moreover, the Executive Committee has the power at any time to call a conference to challenge the actions and conduct of the Parliamentary Leaders. If the Labour Party is in Office the Committee has the power to summon Ministers to 'ad hoc' conferences in order to try and force them to reverse policies which have been presented to the House of Commons by the Government of the day, after full consideration of all the facts and circumstances which only a Government can possess. I am informed that this has actually happened in the past.

"By way of illustration, the constitution would apparently enable the Executive Committee to call upon a Labour Prime Minister to appear before them and criticise his conduct of the peace negotiations. How he could defend his actions without the disclosure of confidential information I fail to see.

"Personally I do not believe that the controversy on these very important issues can be satisfactorily cleared up until the public has a statement signed jointly by yourself and the chairman of the Executive Committee regarding the use of these powers in the future.

"Yours etc.

WINSTON S. CHURCHILL."

Mr. Attlee replied immediately as follows:

"Dear Prime Minister,

"Your messenger with your letter only arrived at my house shortly before 11.30 p.m. when it had already been sent to the Press. I must therefore apologise to you for sending my reply to the Press before my letter will have actually reached you. I am surprised that you, who are apparently becoming acquainted with the constitution of the Labour Party for the first time, should on the authority of an unnamed informant, seek to attach to its provisions meanings other than those accepted by myself and others who have spent years in the service of the Labour Party.

"Much of your trouble is due to your not understanding the distinction between the Labour Party and the Parliamentary Labour Party. This leads you to confuse the organisational work of the Party with the actions of the Parliamentary Labour Party. Despite my very clear statement you proceed to exercise your imagination by importing into a right to be consulted a power to challenge actions and conduct.

"With regard to your final paragraph, I think that you underestimate the intelligence of the public, and I do not share your belief.

"Yours sincerely,

C. R. ATTLEE."

This correspondence is of great historical importance. The terms of Mr. Churchill's letters reveal his anxiety to set up such a barrage of irrelevancy that he hoped would deflect the attention of the electorate from the vital issues of peace, and to blind it to the essential bankruptcy of the Tory Party policy. It is now history how both these aims failed. Local Labour Party organisations, Regional organisations, the headquarters staff at Transport House, together with thousands of voluntary workers, were busy fighting the Election with energy and enthusiasm. Volunteers addressed meetings throughout the country, thousands of people canvassed the door-steps, urging people to exercise their rights of self-expression.

The Labour Party concentrated all these resources in the most effective way by adhering rigidly to the real issues of the Election and by a continual reiteration of its positive policy. Loudspeaker vans were manned in every constituency, and all the essential work of running an election, addressing envelopes and circulars, delivery of literature, etc., was undertaken by many thousands of loyal members of the Movement. These combined efforts made a powerful total, defeated the campaign of misrepresentation, pressed forward the statement of the Labour Party programme; following which there was an overwhelming majority of Labour men and women returned to the House of Commons. The total number of Labour candidates endorsed was 603, of which 33 were promoted by the Co-operative Party and five by the Northern Ireland Labour Party.

Alignment of the Parties.—The total number of candidates of all Parties was 1,683, divided as follows:

Labour	603
Conservative	556
National Liberal	51
National	17
Liberal	308
Communist	21
Common Wealth	23
I.L.P.	5
Others	24
Independents	75

The total poll reached 24,973,298, or 76·1% of the electorate, compared with 22,001,837, or 74·49% in 1935. The votes recorded for each Party were:

Labour	11,992,292
Conservative	9,058,020
National Liberal	759,883
National	142,906
Liberal	2,239,668
Communist	102,780
Common Wealth	110,634
I.L.P.	46,679
Others	195,233
Independents	325,203

PARLIAMENT OLD AND NEW

After the General Election, 1935, the House of Commons was composed as follows:

Labour	154
Conservative	387
National Liberal	33
National Labour	8
National	3
Liberals	17
Independent Liberals	4
Others	9

After the General Election of 1945 the comparable figures were:

Labour	393
Conservative	198
National Liberal	13
National	2
Liberal	12
Independents	14
Others	8

Despite the loss of two seats at Mile End and West Carmarthen, the Labour Party had *a net gain of* 239 *seats* over 1935, or 227 over the number held at the dissolution.

LABOUR'S COMPARATIVE POLL

The following total gives the number of Labour Candidates engaged in contests, their total poll, and the average vote per constituency for the last four General Elections (there were, in addition, two unopposed returns).

	Candidates	*Total Poll*	*Average Poll*	*Comparison with* 1929
1929	569	8,364,883	14,694	—
1931*	508	6,648,171	13,086	— 1,608
1935	539	8,325,260	15,445	+ 751
1945	601	11,992,292	19,953	+ 5,259

*(The 1931 figures include 22 non-endorsed candidates for the purpose of comparison.)

GENERAL ELECTIONS, 1900-45

The complete record of the Party's poll from and including the General Election of 1900 is as follows:

General Election	*Seats Contested*	*Members Returned*	*Labour Vote*
1900	15	2	62,698
1906	50	29	323,195
1910 (Jan.)	78	40	505,690
1910 (Dec.)	56	42	370,802
1918	361	57	2,244,945
1922	414	142	4,236,733
1923	427	191	4,348,379
1924	514	151	5,487,620
1929	569	287	8,364,883
1931	491	46	6,362,561
1935	539	154	8,325,260
1945	601	393	11,992,292

The Election results led inevitably to a change of Government. On July 26 Mr. Churchill tendered his resignation to His Majesty, and Mr. Attlee accepted the King's invitation to form a Government. On July 27 he announced the names and offices of the chief Members of the Government, which were as follows:

Prime Minister, First Lord of the Treasury, and Minister of Defence	MR. CLEMENT ATTLEE
Lord President of the Council	MR. HERBERT MORRISON
Secretary of State for Foreign Affairs	MR. ERNEST BEVIN
Lord Privy Seal	MR. ARTHUR GREENWOOD
Chancellor of the Exchequer	MR. HUGH DALTON
President of the Board of Trade	SIR STAFFORD CRIPPS, K.C.
Lord Chancellor	SIR WILLIAM JOWITT, K.C.

On Saturday morning, July 28, the first meeting of the new Parliamentary Labour Party was held in the Beaver Hall, London. The first part of the proceedings was presided over by Mr. Attlee, and during the course of the morning both he and the new Foreign Secretary, Mr. Ernest Bevin, left to attend the Potsdam Conference. After his return, Mr. Attlee completed his Government, and announced the names as follows:

Secretary of State for the Home Department	THE RT. HON. JAMES CHUTER EDE, M.P.
Secretary of State for Dominion Affairs	THE RT. HON. VISCOUNT ADDISON
Secretary of State for India and Burma	THE RT. HON. FREDERICK WILLIAM PETHICK-LAWRENCE, M.P.
Secretary of State for the Colonies	THE RT. HON. GEORGE HENRY HALL, M.P.
First Lord of the Admiralty	THE RT. HON. ALBERT VICTOR ALEXANDER, C.H., M.P.
Secretary of State for War	THE RT. HON. JOHN JAMES LAWSON, M.P.
Secretary of State for Air	THE RT. HON. VISCOUNT STANSGATE, D.S.O., D.F.C.
Secretary of State for Scotland	THE RT. HON. JOSEPH WESTWOOD, M.P.
Minister of Labour and National Service	GEORGE ALFRED ISAACS, ESQ., M.P.
Minister of Education	THE RT. HON. ELLEN WILKINSON, M.P.
Minister of Health	THE RT. HON. ANEURIN BEVAN, M.P.
Minister of Agriculture and Fisheries	THE RT. HON. TOM WILLIAMS, M.P.
Minister of Supply and of Aircraft Production	JOHN WILMOT, Esq., M.P.
Minister of War Transport	ALFRED BARNES, Esq., M.P.
Minister of Food	THE RT. HON. SIR BEN SMITH, K.B.E., M.P.
Minister of Fuel and Power	EMANUEL SHINWELL, Esq., M.P.
Minister of State	PHILIP JOHN NOEL-BAKER, Esq., M.P.
Minister of Pensions	THE RT. HON. WILFRED PALING, M.P.
Parliamentary Secretary to the Treasury	THE RT. HON. WILLIAM WHITELEY, M.P.
Leader of the House of Lords	LORD ADDISON

Labour's Legislative Programme.—With Mr. Morrison as Leader of the House of Commons everyone waited with eagerness to see how Labour's first Government with a majority would implement the programme approved by the electorate, in which, briefly, they were committed to:

Full employment of national resources, in land, material and labour.
Control of the prices of the necessities of life, including rents.
Planned investment in essential industries and on houses, schools, hospitals and civic centres.
Nationalisation of the Bank of England, and banking generally to be harmonised with industrial needs.

In industry, the Labour Party's first programme was for the public ownership of the fuel and power industries, followed by inland transport, iron and steel; the supervision of monopolies and cartels, a firm and clear-cut programme for the export trade, economic and price controls to ensure the smooth transition from war to peace, and better organisation of Government departments.

In agriculture, County War Executive Committees were to be modified but retained to organise production at the maximum level, and production was to be planned to ensure a stable market. Bulk purchase of food abroad was to continue, together with a well-organised system of distribution at home, and the free and cheap milk schemes which had been begun during the war.

The Party promised that housing and the building programme would be planned in accordance with the principle of controlled prices, and that good town planning and transport facilities would be considered in conjunction with the building programme. Also in the interests of agriculture, housing and town and country planning there would be radical revision of the procedure for the acquisition of land for public purposes.

They were also pledged to implement the Education Act of 1944, raising the school-leaving age to fifteen, and to further the provision of concert halls, libraries, etc., for adult recreation; to place upon the Statute Book a Bill for the creation of a new and comprehensive National Health Service; a new and comprehensive National Insurance Bill to provide security against poverty due to sickness, unemployment or any of the multifarious accidents which beset the worker and his dependents.

With all this, the Party stressed that any of the points in its programme could only be carried out if full employment, the provisions for which were embodied in the first part of the programme, could be ensured, and pledged itself to do all possible to secure this, and to maintain peace in the world to enable this progressive policy to be carried out.

This policy was clearly stated in a pamphlet "Let us Face the Future," of which more than a million copies were printed and distributed during the Election, and on this document alone it was possible for the electorate to make a decision for or against the Labour Government. Now the millions who had voted for that Government were eagerly waiting to see how the policy was to be implemented.

Nor had they long to wait to see how the Government meant to carry on its onerous task. On August 15, 1945, the King officially opened Parliament, and in the gracious address outlined the Government's immediate programme. The King's Speech is a document of historic importance as the first ever made to a Parliament controlled by a Labour majority. In its opening paragraphs it paid tribute to the steady courage and endurance of the armed forces of the Commonwealth, and to all others who had borne their share in bringing about a great Allied victory, and went on to proclaim the firm purpose of the Government to work in the closest co-operation with the Governments of the Dominions and in concert with all peace-loving peoples "to attain a world of freedom, peace and social justice so that the sacrifices of the war shall not have been in vain." The Government were determined, in pursuit of this end, to promote throughout the world conditions under which all countries could face with confidence the urgent tasks of reconstruction, and to carry out in this country those policies which had received the approval of the people. The Government's acceptance of the responsibilities laid down in the Charter of the United Nations, and of the duties entailed in the occupation of enemy countries, was clearly affirmed. Its determination to grapple energetically and boldly with the problems of demobilisation and resettlement of the men and women in the armed forces of the nation was asserted in connection with its resolve to see that the national resources and labour and material are employed with the fullest efficiency in the interests of all, and that the standard of living is progressively improved.

In the speech from the Throne, His Majesty's Ministers went on to declare that they would take up with energy the tasks of reconverting industry from the purposes of war to those of peace, of expanding our export trade, and of securing "by suitable control or by an extension of public ownership" that our industries and services should make their maximum contribution to the national well-being. Specific measures were then outlined in the following terms:

> "In order to promote employment and national development, machinery will be set up to provide for the effective planning of investment and a measure will be laid before you to bring the Bank of England under public ownership. A Bill will also be laid before you to nationalise the coal mining industry as part of a concerted plan for the co-ordination of the fuel and power industries.
>
> "Legislation will be submitted to you to ensure that during the period of transition from war to peace there are available such powers as are necessary to secure the right use of our commerical and industrial resources and the distribution at fair prices of essential supplies and services.
>
> "An urgent and vital task of my Ministers will be to increase by all practicable means the number of homes available both in town and country. Accordingly they will organise the resources of the building and manufacturing industries in the most effective way to meet the housing and other essential building requirements of the nation. They will also lay before you proposals to deal with the problems of compensation and betterment in relation to town and country planning, to improve the procedure for the acquisition of land for public purposes, and otherwise to promote the best use of land in the national interest.

"You will be asked to approve measures to provide a comprehensive scheme of insurance against industrial injuries, to extend and improve the existing scheme of social insurance and to establish a National Health Service. Legislation will be introduced to repeal the Trade Disputes and Trade Unions Act.

"My Ministers will develop to the fullest possible extent the home production of good food. To this end they will continue, with suitable adaptations, those war-time policies under which food production has been organised and the efficiency of agriculture improved, and will take all necessary steps to promote a healthy fishing industry. The ravages of war have made world food supplies insufficient to meet demands, but my Ministers will do all in their power to provide and distribute food to my peoples at prices which they can afford to pay; and they will keep in being and extend the new food services for the workers and for mothers and children which have been established during the war.

"A measure will be laid before you for the reorganisation of air transport.

"It will be the aim of my Ministers to bring into practical effect at the earliest possible date the educational reforms which have already been approved.

"My Government will continue to work in close consultation with the other Members of my Commonwealth on all matters of mutual concern.

"In accordance with the promises already made to my Indian Peoples, my Government will do their utmost to promote in conjunction with the leaders of Indian opinion the early realisation of full self-government in India.

"They will also press on with the development of my Colonial Empire and the welfare of its peoples."

The King's speech at the opening of Parliament is still a programme of unfinished business, half-way through its natural term. But a great deal has been done. Much that was promised in the way of legislation is still in process of enactment. The record of the first thirty months of Labour rule is, however, fairly complete.

Labour's Legislative Output.—Up to the end of 1947, Parliament had sat on more days and worked harder than most of its predecessors. Under the able guidance of Mr. Herbert Morrison as Leader of the House of Commons, the volume of legislation has approximated to 140 measures, many of them of epochal importance. In the words of *The Times*, when Parliament adjourned for its first summer recess (August 1946) "no Government has ever before attempted so much social and economic change in one session." This, indeed, can be said of later sessions too.

From a list of the principal measures passed within this period by the Labour Government, the average reader may not gather a very clear impression of the quality and range of the Labour Government's work. What lies behind the Housing Acts for instance, is a tremendous impetus in building new homes for the people, and in repairing, converting and reconstructing war-damaged dwellings. The mere title of Acts of Parliament are not descriptive of their social and political importance. The legislation enacted for the nationalisation of the coal industry, the electricity industry, the transport system, and other services must ultimately be judged by its results, and the tests cannot be exclusively those of financial profits and losses. Nationalisation of the coal industry has brought great gains to the mine workers, such as the five-day week and higher wages; but it has also brought a higher total production, and more output per mine worker at the coal-face. Nothing in a list of Acts can tell the reader anything about the social benefits accruing from the continuation of rent control and the setting up of rent tribunals for furnished dwellings; or about the succession of Budgets by which taxation has been reduced, and several million in the lower income groups relieved of the payment of income tax, whilst means have been found to increase Old Age Pensions, to start the payment of Family Allowances, to improve Service pay and pensions, to double the consumption of milk in schools, to raise the school-leaving age, to increase State grants to universities, and to double the number of State scholarships. Reference to the Finance Acts in a list of Labour Government's measures will reveal nothing about the financing of the Government's policy to keep food prices stable, to provide priorities for mothers and children in the rationing of milk, and to give guaranteed prices and assured markets for farm products. Nor will a mere list of Acts of Parliament tell the story of the Government's policy for developing the resources of the British Colonies, and to confer freedom and independence upon India, Ceylon, Burma and Egypt.

In the longer view the legislation which embodies the Government's social policy is assuredly of equal importance with the Acts for nationalising basic industries and essential services. Five major measures are linked together in a single pattern to give the fullest protection which the State can devise for the British people against sickness, accident, unemployment, poverty and old age. They include the Family Allowances Act (framed by the Coalition Government), which came into operation in August 1946, to provide an allowance of 5*s.* a week for each child (after the first) up to the age of leaving school. At the other end of the scale is the provision for old age, under the National Insurance Act; and in between is the Industrial Injuries Act, which covers everybody employed in insurable employment, and comprises full compensation for personal injuries arising out of and in the course of a worker's employment, as well as against scheduled diseases, with no contribution test for the payment of benefits. But by far the most far-reaching of these social measures are the National Health Service Act and the National Assistance Bill which will be an Act before these pages are printed.

Under the National Health Act a complete health service is provided embracing every kind of general and special hospital care, provision for maternity, specialist clinics and the advice and service of specialists both at health centres and in the patients' homes, as well as general practitioner services, provided by doctors and dentists of the patients' own choice, either in publicly-equipped health centres or from the practitioners' surgeries and consulting rooms. Supplementary services under the Act include midwifery, maternity and child welfare, health visiting, home nursing, domestic help in the homes when needed on grounds of health, and the provision of spectacles, dentures, surgical appliances, and drugs and medicines. The Act, moreover, revolutionises the administration of hospitals and specialist services. And provision is made for patients who are prepared to pay for additional privacy, and private medical services; though the Act prohibits the buying and selling of medical practices, and provides compensation —to a global sum of £66 million—for practitioners who wish to give up their practice.

The National Assistance Bill, shortly to be an Act, aims at the complete abolition of what remains of the old Poor Law, and the setting up of new and extended public assistance and welfare services for the destitute poor, the aged, and the disabled. Care of the people who do not qualify for pension or insurance benefits under the National Insurance legislation, or who need to have their pension or benefit supplemented because of special circumstances, will be henceforth the responsibility of a National Assistance Board. Local authorities, however, will still have responsibility in providing for the welfare of the aged or disabled part of the population. To encourage them in providing comfortable homes there is to be an Exchequer subsidy, calculated to pay for adequate accommodation for both single residents and married couples. The only qualification for national assistance is the need of the applicant. There will be no household means test, no account will be taken of the earnings of sons and daughters, and even the small savings of the applicant, up to a limit of £375, will not be taken into account in determining needs.

Thus, on the massive foundations of the National Insurance Act, which covers everybody, rich and poor, from school-leaving age to the age of 65 (60 for women), the Government has raised this superstructure of social protection and welfare.

Hardly less revolutionary in its total calculated ends is another measure which Parliament has been called upon to enact, as these pages go to press —the Local Government Bill, which aims at equalising the burden of rates between rich and poor areas, provides payment to members of local authorities for loss of earnings, and transfers to the central authority the financial responsibility for many of the services hitherto carried on by these authorities.

To mention, at the end of 1947, Bills that have yet to become Acts serves to show that the work of the Government in the present Parliament has by no means come to an end. On the record, as unfolded in these pages, it is historically proven that Labour derives its strength, as it does its inspiration, from deep sources in the life of the nation. Its strength lies, as always, in the confidence of the country. By-elections are the best tests, between the General Elections, of any Government's standing in the country. Between the General Election in mid-1945 and the end of 1947, the Labour Government lost no seat in a by-election that it secured in the General Election. It is the only Government during the last fifty years of which this can be said.

CHAPTER XIX

RETROSPECT AND PROSPECT

By Herbert Tracey

The Third Labour Government had not been long in Office when this new book about the British Labour Party was planned. The Party attained power in mid-1945 with a majority in Parliament adequate for all its purposes within the limitations imposed by the interplay of political and economic forces in the world at large over which it could exercise only a limited measure of control. To set in their right perspective the contributions of the many authoritative writers who have co-operated in the restatement of the aims and principles of the Labour Party in this book, it is necessary to trace the course of events in these years, bearing upon the legacy that the Third Labour Government inherited. It was even more an inheritance from history than from its predecessor, the War Government of Mr. Winston Churchill. With the coming of peace, the problems of resettlement and reconstruction arising out of the war itself have been found to be inextricably entangled with historical conflicts extending far back into the past, and conditioned by deep-seated changes in the national economy not only of our own country, but of every country in the world: the statesmen who have been grappling in the immediate post-war years with the gigantic task of re-establishing a semblance of order and law, and respect for human rights everywhere in the world, cannot separate even the short-term problems of an emergency character from the general settlement of political and economic questions that have assumed their present form over a long period of time.

We may take as one example the economic crisis which upset so many of the reasonable calculations of the Labour Government in the first two-and-a-half years of its existence. Although the war hastened the impact of the world's economic difficulties upon Great Britain and added immeasurably to the burden this country has been called upon to bear, the crisis did not originate during the war years: it is the outcome of general tendencies that were in rapid motion in the years between the two World Wars. Its real origins lie, in fact, in the development of the United States and other countries in the western hemisphere as great producing, manufacturing and trading nations. The rise of the United States to the leading place among the nations formerly held by Great Britain as "the workshop of the world" is the capital factor in the economic history of the last hundred years; it is the basic factor in the post-war plight of Great Britain and other European countries.

In the middle of the nineteenth century the United States was third on the list in the order of world production, with Great Britain leading, and with France in the second place. Within a generation America reached the top of the list and placed these two other countries in the second and third place. By the end of the first decade of the twentieth century American production was one-third of the entire production of the world. Between the two World Wars it rose to nearly one-half of the total world production, exceeding the production of the whole of Europe; and during the second World War the American productive system was immensely strengthened and extended whilst that of Great Britain and the countries of the European continent declined heavily. The productivity of American industry expanded by at least one-third during the second World War; output per man-hour increased by at least 20 per cent. As a consequence of the renovation of plants, the improvement of the productive processes, and the development of mass production methods in great new factories created during the war, the American industrial apparatus is now certainly 50 per cent. larger than when the war began: a federal expenditure of many thousands of millions of dollars was authorised for the purpose of building new plants and extending existing factories, and it has been estimated that the value of the new factories built during the war by the American Government amounted to $16,000 million, which was equal to one-fourth of the value of all American factories before the war.

To this gigantic increase in the productivity of the American industrial economy, and allowing for the fact that before the war American industry worked often at no more than 50-60 per cent. of capacity, must be attributed the more or less persistent disequilibrium in world trade which is the ultimate cause of the current crisis, as it is the explanation of preceding crises including the great depression which nearly wrecked the massive economic structure of the United States between 1929 and 1932. This disequilibrium is the cause of the extreme difficulty, if not the impossibility, of countries with an adverse balance of trade—an excess of imports over exports—securing enough dollars to buy what they need from the United States or other countries which claim payment in dollars. The "dollar shortage" is a chronic condition which assumed a positively menacing aspect after the war ended in 1945, and the termination of the lend-lease arrangement—which had temporarily disposed of the dollar problem—combined with the precipitate winding up of UNRRA, confronted Great Britain and other countries in Europe with the problem of establishing a new balance of trade with the countries in the dollar area.

To meet the situation and afford a breathing space to this country, the United States, in July 1946, extended "a line of credit" amounting to $3,750,000 million, and a credit of $1,250,000 million was provided from Canada, in the expectation that these credits would be spent at a lessening rate in the first three years, leaving a surplus which could be used in the next two years to build up a balance of payments before interest and loan repayments began. Contrary to all intentions, all but $400 million of the U.S. loan, and $500 million of the Canadian credits were expended by August 1, 1947. The purchasing power of the American loan, moreover, was reduced by perhaps about $1,000 million by the rise of the American price level in the immediate post-war years. For this country the exhaustion of the American and Canadian credits had necessarily painful consequences: among them a drastic reduction of imports which required to be paid for in dollars, the reimposition of control over labour, withdrawal of many of the Treasury subsidies, a much stricter rationing of food for the people and raw materials for industry, a reversal of the decision to make sterling freely convertible into other currencies, and a concentration of the nation's productive resources in the effort to close the gap between imports and exports by the setting of export targets which had to be achieved at the expense of domestic consumers.

In this manner a world-wide change in the trend of economic forces, and in the commercial and financial relations of Great Britain with other countries, assumed an aspect of urgency in the immediate post-war years. The War of 1939-45 not only bequeathed to the Labour Government a whole host of economic and political troubles: it accelerated tendencies towards an unbalancing of trading and industrial relations which would have presented an increasingly difficult set of problems for this country, and the world at large, if the war had not taken place. For decades before the war this maturing crisis, extending over the whole world, but affecting most deeply the great industrialised countries, was signalled for our own working people by a heavy downward movement in wages, mass unemployment, and the spreading desolation of the distressed areas where the population was dependent on one or two basic industries. Nor were these related phenomena of chronic unemployment, of hunger and privation in the midst of plenty, and of intractable industrial and financial troubles, apparent only in this country. They appeared in an almost identical form during the inter-war years in every other country—not excepting the United States, a highly favoured country that might have seemed to be immune from such economic and social disorders. In the United States there was not only mass unemployment on a colossal scale, but a financial convulsion which at one stage brought about the complete collapse of the American banking system.

In its historical setting the nature of the crisis was such that only a temporary alleviation, in the United States as in Britain and on the continent of Europe, particularly Germany and France, was found in the demand for labour, capital and materials for rearmament and the full employment of industrial equipment to prepare for the second World War. Whether a recurrence of the terrible tragedy of the inter-war years can be prevented is a question that can only be answered when the current discussions on measures to be taken with America's aid to promote political stability and the economic rehabilitation of Europe, to say nothing of Asia, reach some practical conclusion.

A wider view has thus to be taken of the Third Labour Government's task. Complete success in closing the gap between British imports and exports and obtaining a more plentiful supply of dollars to keep up an adequate flow of food and raw materials to meet our national needs will not dispose of the whole complex array of problems that have come into the forefront of discussion whilst this book has been in preparation. Foremost in these discussions are the problems connected with the making of the peace: the breaking of the deadlock with Soviet Russia in the Council of Foreign Ministers and in the United Nations; the settlement of Germany's future relations with its neighbours; a solution of the racial and religious conflicts that convulse Palestine and India, and of the political and economic troubles that distract China and cause unrest and disorder throughout the East; the control of economic warfare and the promotion of general disarmament; the development, through the projected International Trade Organisation, of a more rational policy of international trade than the world pursued in the era of autarchy and protective tariffs, the manipulation of foreign exchanges and currency control—and many other intricate and stubbornly contested issues of policy. On all of them the Labour Government has been required to take action consistent with the aims and principles set forth in this book. It is necessary therefore to take account of such specific post-war developments as the Truman doctrine and the Marshall Plan, the controversy about the veto inside the United Nations, the Bretton Woods Agreement, the suspension of the Articles dealing with the convertibility of sterling and non-discriminatory trade in the Anglo-American Loan Agreement, and a great many other questions which have become a subject of controversy and targets of policy whilst some chapters of this book passed the stage at which additional material could be brought in.

It is indeed very necessary to keep clearly in view the fact that a great deal has taken place in world affairs during the existence of the Third Labour Government. Many high hopes and exalted sentiments have been frustrated by the course of events since the war came to an end; many noble aspirations and statesmanlike efforts have still to produce the desired results.

Let us look more closely, therefore, into the work of the peace makers first, in the light of actual events.

The Leaders of the Labour Movement were not blind to the difficulties that would attend upon the effort to work out the principles of a just and lasting peace. They recognised that these principles would be exposed to a searching test in the treatment of Germany and the other States that had been defeated on the field of battle. In particular they were conscious of their responsibility in applying these principles in the settlement of Germany's future under conditions that would help to bring into being a genuinely democratic regime and help to found and fortify the institutions of free citizenship among the German people.

In the actual course of events since Germany's military defeat it has been found impossible to keep out, even in the early stages of the occupation of Germany, political and social questions of far-reaching import. Experience proved this to be the case even with the comparatively simple and uncomplicated armistice terms upon which the first World War was brought to an end. Those terms, drawn up by Field-Marshal Foch and signed by the German plenipotentiaries in 1918, raised such difficult problems as the Eastern frontier line of France, along with the question of bridgeheads over the Rhine and the occupation of the Rhineland. It was primarily as a soldier that Foch incorporated in the armistice claims concerning the Rhineland, with the aim of making the Rhine France's Eastern frontier. "Whoever holds its bridges," he said, "is master of the situation: he can easily repulse invasion, and if attacked can carry the war into the enemy country." A political solution of the problem of France's Eastern defences has not yet been reached. Foch's political solution was to convert the Rhineland into a buffer State separated from Germany and unarmed, while under the military control of France. In Downing Street, in December 1918, he developed his proposals in talks with the military and political leaders of the Allied and Associated Powers, to combine all the French, Belgian, Luxemburg, and Rhenish Provinces into one Confederation, which would have had then a population of 54,000,000: but his scheme was opposed at the time—particularly by Lloyd George and Bonar Law as creating "another Alsace-Lorraine."

To recall these discussions of 1918 is merely to emphasise the fact that the same problem has re-emerged now in a far more concrete form. It is complicated by the nature of the military-political occupation of Germany, and its division into zones, in which the original plan of co-ordinated control has not been implemented. Out of the failure to pursue a common policy in their zones, the occupying Powers have been faced with a very difficult situation affecting their relationships one with another in the preparation of the final Treaty of Peace with Germany. Certainly the original plan for the occupation and control of Germany, before the final Treaty has been signed, has been to all intents abandoned.

In February 1945 at the Conference in the Crimea (commonly known as the Yalta Conference) the British Prime Minister, the President of the United States, and the Chairman of the Council of Peoples' Commissars of the U.S.S.R.—otherwise Winston Churchill, Franklin D. Roosevelt and Joseph Stalin—agreed on common policies and plans by which the military forces of the three Powers would each occupy a separate zone of Germany: co-ordinated administration and control being provided for, under the plan, through a Central Control Commission. This was to consist of the Supreme Commanders of the three Powers with headquarters in Berlin. It was also agreed that France should be invited to take over a zone of occupation, and to participate as a fourth member of the Control Commission, if she so desired: and at a later date, following the restoration of more stable political conditions in France, the limitations of the French zone were agreed upon by the four Governments concerned acting through their representatives on the European Advisory Commission.

In the Yalta Conference at the same time the broad general principles were laid down in respect of reparations by Germany. It was agreed that Germany should be obliged to make compensation in kind to the greatest extent possible for the ruin and devastation she had caused: a Commission for the Compensation for Damage was to be set up with instructions to consider methods of compensation. Agreement was also reached by the three Heads of Government on their attitude towards Poland after her liberation by the Red Army. Reaffirmation of the common desire—as the Crimea Conference report put it—to see established a strong, free, independent and democratic Poland was reflected in their support of a Polish Provisional Government of National Unity, and the establishment with it of diplomatic relations by the Government of the United Kingdom and the United States Government—the Union of Soviet Russia being already in diplomatic relations with Poland. On the question of liberated Poland's Eastern frontier the three Heads of Government laid it down that the frontier should follow the line of the western Neisse, but the Polish boundary was not definitely fixed. It was agreed that Poland must receive substantial accessions of territory in the North and West, but that the final delimitation of the Western frontier of Poland should await the Peace Conference. There was some agreement, too, among the three Heads of Government on their attitude towards Yugoslavia; and other Balkan questions came under review without any clear or comprehensive statement of the problems that had to be surmounted there or how they were to be dealt with. But the Crimea Conference did agree upon permanent machinery to facilitate regular consultation between the Ministers responsible for Foreign Affairs, and a Council of Foreign Secretaries came into being, with the intention of meeting every three or four months, in rotation in the three or four capitals, to enable them and their advisers to consult together in laying the foundations for permanent peace, and the completion of formal Peace Treaties.

Six months later, in July-August 1945, at the Berlin (Potsdam) Conferences, the decisions of the Yalta Conference came under review. Political conditions had changed in the meantime. The military struggle was at an end. Germany and Japan, as well as Italy and the smaller allies of the Nazi-Fascist States, were soundly defeated, and military occupation of Germany and other vanquished countries had become an accomplished fact. Two of the three great war leaders who had met together in the Crimea were no longer in the picture. Franklin D. Roosevelt had died on the very eve of victory, and his place as President of the United States had fallen to Harry S. Truman, until then U.S. Vice-President, a man of character and of high standing in the Democratic Party in the United States, but still without the wide experience and strong judgment that his predecessor possessed. Winston Churchill, too, had gone, swept from his position as Prime Minister by the tidal wave of the Election which had placed the Labour Party in power even while the Berlin Conference was in progress. Joseph Stalin was the only one of the three who had laid down the basic principles of a common peace policy in the Yalta Conference, who was present throughout the proceedings in Berlin. Winston Churchill went to Berlin at the beginning of the Conference (on July 17), but he took with him Mr. Attlee, who was Deputy Prime Minister; and with them went Mr. Anthony Eden as Foreign Secretary, to meet Mr. Truman and Generalissimo Stalin who were accompanied by the Foreign Secretaries in their Governments, James F. Byrnes and V. M. Molotov. The Conference in Berlin was interrupted for two days when Mr. Attlee was recalled to his own country to take over from Winston Churchill in consequence of the Labour Party's victory in the General Election: when he returned to the Conference as Prime Minister he was accompanied by Britain's new Secretary of State for Foreign Affairs, Ernest Bevin.

The Berlin Conference can therefore be said to mark the true peace-making activities of the Third Labour Government. The most important decision of the Berlin Conference involved the setting up of a Council of Foreign Ministers representing the five principal Governments among the United Nations, namely, Britain, the U.S.S.R., the United States, France and China. Their task was to go on with the necessary preparatory work for the peace settlements, taking up other matters which might be referred to them by agreement of the participating Governments. It was decided that the Council should meet normally in London where the permanent seat of the joint secretariat to be formed by the Council would be located. Provision was made for each of the Foreign Ministers to be accompanied by a high-ranking deputy who would be authorised to carry on the work of the Council in the absence of his Foreign Minister. A small staff of technical advisers was attached to it. And it proceeded, as its first commission, to frame the Treaties of Peace on behalf of the United Nations with Italy, Rumania, Bulgaria, Hungary and Finland.

Broadly, in fact, the responsibility of the Council of Foreign Ministers was to formulate proposals for the settlement of the territorial questions outstanding at the conclusion of the war in Europe, and to prepare a Peace Settlement for Germany which would be presented finally to whatever Government emerges from the chaos of Germany in the course of time. Political principles and economic considerations were agreed upon in the Berlin Conference to govern the treatment of Germany in the preliminary period of occupation and control. Foremost amongst these considerations was the necessity of bringing about the complete disarmament and demilitarisation of Germany and putting an end, once for all, to the possibility that German industry could be used for military production. Another consideration was the necessity of convincing the German people that they had suffered a total military defeat, and that responsibility rested upon them for the consequences that they brought upon themselves by yielding to the leadership of Hitler and his criminal associates.

That Germany must be completely convinced of its defeat in arms was felt to be an absolute condition of the situation. There was no question of Germany's surrender under conditions, such as confused the settlement with her after the first World War. No pretext was to be left for anybody to say that Germany laid down arms under terms such as the German militarists manufactured out of the acceptance of President Wilson's Fourteen Points at the end of the first World War. The myth of Germany's invincibility cannot be allowed to survive. Future generations of German youth are not to be allowed to grow up in the midst of war memorials with street-names, tablets, and statues proclaiming German military victories and glorifying her military leaders. Destruction of the National-Socialist Party and all its allied organisations and institutions was another of the Berlin Conference's directives. And along with it went a directive to prepare Germany for the eventual reconstruction of its political life on a democratic basis affording a foundation for Germany's peaceful co-operation in international life.

Among the economic principles which were accepted as almost axiomatic by the leaders of the United Nations in the Berlin Conference was the elimination of Germany's war potential. It involved the prohibition and prevention of any means of producing arms, ammunition, and implements of war, as well as all types of aircraft and sea-going ships; with rigid control over the production of metals, chemicals, machinery and other prerequisites of a war economy—these having to be rigidly controlled and restricted to Germany's approved post-war peace-time needs. Germany's productive capacity, beyond the limits of permitted production, was to be dealt with in accordance with the reparations plan. The German economy was to be decentralised with the object of removing the excessive concentration of economic power as exemplified in particular by cartels, syndicates, trusts, and other monopolistic arrangements. In the reorganisation of the German economy, the primary emphasis was to be placed on the development of agriculture and peaceful domestic industries.

The most significant decision of the Berlin Conference was the stipulation that during the period of occupation Germany was to be treated as a single economic unit. This meant that common policies were to be worked out in their application to mining and industrial production, to agriculture, to wages, prices and rationing, and to the financial system, to import and export programmes, and to the obligation to provide reparations. This decision has failed to find fulfilment in the earlier period of occupation and control. The economic unity of Germany asserted in the Berlin Conference and emphasised in the agreement reached at Potsdam (in August 1945) was not, in fact, achieved, and the British and American Governments found it necessary, before 1946 reached its end, to take an independent decision to fuse the British and American Zones of occupation, a decision which took effect on the first day of January 1947. The arrangements set forth in the Anglo-American Agreement were to be taken as the first step towards the achievement of the economic unity of Germany as a whole. The two

Governments declared their readiness at any time to enter into discussions with either of the other occupying powers on the extension of the Anglo-American arrangements to their zones of occupation.

The declared aim of the two Governments in consenting to the economic fusion of their zones of occupation was to achieve a self-sustaining economy for the area by the end of 1949. With this end in view the indigenous resources of the area and all imports into it, including food, were to be pooled in order to provide a common standard of living. Joint control by the U.S. and U.K. Commanders-in-Chief over the German administrative agencies necessary to the economic unification of the two zones was provided for in the agreement. It was agreed, too, that the two Governments would share equally the financial responsibility for the necessary importations of food and raw materials, the cost of which was not met by export proceeds; with the stipulation that the costs incurred by the two Governments for their two zones before the date of the agreement, and thereafter for the fused area, should be recovered from future German exports in the shortest practicable time consistent with the rebuilding of the German economy.

In one sense this agreement revealed the failure of the Occupying Powers to reach a common understanding upon their policy in dealing with Germany. But it was also a testimony to the good intentions of the British and American Governments. Such measures, however, constituted only a short-term programme: the long-term problems involved in the settlement with Germany remained, up to the end of 1947, a matter of controversy. These problems are manifestly bound up with the question of national security and the struggle for power. Organised labour, with its strong sense of international solidarity, and its faith in the principles of international co-operation which determined its attitude, first to the League of Nations and then to the United Nations Organisation, is slow to believe that security for any nation and for all nations is, in the final analysis, a problem of geopolitics—that is to say, a problem of a nation's geographical position and its relations with the centres and the sources of military power.

The basic facts of the power structure of continental Europe, after the first World War were obscured, from the Labour standpoint, by the creation of the League of Nations. Beyond and beneath the hopeful experiment in international co-operation represented by the League of Nations, there were fundamental factors which jeopardised its success. The power structure of continental Europe before the second World War rested upon (1) the disarmament of Germany, (2) the demilitarisation of the Rhineland, and (3) the system of Alliances which the great continental powers entered into—particularly the alliances of France with the successor States of the Austro-Hungarian Empire as political make-weights in the power balance against Germany. It was a system that could be effective only in so far as there was no fortified barrier in the West—such as the Siegfried Line—to prevent France, with or without any Western Ally, going to the help of any smaller Ally in Central and South-Eastern Europe.

The course of power politics in the inter-war years demonstrated the weakness of this system. The post-war power situation after the 1914-18 War was determined by the following sequence of events. France gave up very reluctantly, in the peace discussions after the first World War, her claim to the Rhine frontier: she was dissuaded from it by the offer of a military alliance with Britain and the United States. For reasons of internal politics which it is here unnecessary to recount, the United States failed to confirm and implement President Wilson's offer: America neither ratified the Versailles Treaty, nor the proposed Treaty of Alliance and, moreover, did not enter the League of Nations; and as a consequence, Britain, too, did not implement its pledge as a third party to the proposed military agreement. The inter-war period, therefore, began for France with the unhappy feeling that the two most powerful States in the world were not parties to a military alliance with her. Thus the question of her territorial security became for France her most anxious preoccupation. It produced the Maginot Line as a first barrier against the danger of another German invasion: and the Maginot Line was the very symbol of the sense of insecurity felt by the continental nations. To that sense of insecurity, intensified by the fact of German rearmament and a renewal of Germany's policy of aggression under Hitler's leadership, can be traced the tortuous course of European politics in the inter-war years. It was the fear of the eventual rearmament of Germany which led the European countries to seek assurance through pacts and treaties. It was the cause of the unilateral plans for the post-war expansion of Soviet Russia; it was the reason for the partition of Poland; it gave birth to the Anglo-Soviet, the Czecho-Soviet, and the Franco-Soviet Treaties—all of them measures against a rebirth of German aggression—which proved to be of a very flimsy character.

In their approach to the final settlement of Germany's place in the Commonwealth of Nations, therefore, the question has arisen whether treaties, even of the most solemn and binding character, and with specific obligations as to combined military action, are a sufficient guarantee that Germany, which has been for generations an aggressor power, will make war no more if she is left with the means to make war. Treaties and pacts, in an age of power politics, may have their uses: but we have learned by bitter experience that their uses now are not what they once were. It was one of the greatest of Britain's Prime Ministers, Sir Robert Walpole, who said two centuries ago, that the use of alliances

> "has in the last age been too much experienced to be contested; it is by leagues well concerted and strictly observed, that the weak are defended against the strong, that the bounds are set to turbulent ambition, that the torrent of power is restrained, and Empires preserved from those inundations of war that in former times laid the world in ruins."

By alliances, Walpole said, "the equipoise of power is maintained, and those alarms and apprehensions avoided which must arise from the vicissitudes of Empire and the fluctuations of perpetual contests." But this was said two centuries ago, at the time when the sanctity of treaties was an article of faith, even among statesmen: and the echo of these eloquent words had scarcely died away before the turbulence of ambition and the torrents of power which the treaties of that age were to restrain, raged with unparalleled violence in the French revolutionary wars and the rise of Napoleon's Empire. And we have only to remind ourselves of the melancholy record of the world between the two World Wars, between the framing of the Covenant of the League of Nations and the writing of the Versailles Peace Treaty, to the Kellogg Pact and the network of European alliances through which Hitler thrust his jack-boot, to realise that treaties can all too easily become "scraps of paper."

Whether the Allied Nations, and indeed all the nations of the world, will find their security in something more massive and abiding than a flimsy network of paper guarantees, is the great question which still awaits an answer in the assemblies of the United Nations and the Council of the Foreign Ministers. Whether we like it or not, it has to be recognised that a new era of power politics has begun, and integral to the struggle for power is the position of Germany, formerly the centre of military power on the European continent. The present occupation and control of Germany. the disbanding of its armies, the confiscation and destruction of its armaments and its naval power, are only a first step to the demilitarisation of Germany. It is recognised that all these measures will prove of no avail if the structure of German militarism and imperialism can be rebuilt upon strong economic foundations. British policy aims at a solution of these problems in a way that will draw the free nations of Western Europe more closely together. The British, American, and French Governments have sought on these lines to break the deadlock with Soviet Russia.

It could indeed be said that a unilateral solution of many of these problems affecting Germany has been taken by Soviet Russia. Transfers on a large scale of Germany's industrial equipment have been made, and it is contended that these are in accordance with the decision of the Yalta Conference that Germany must be compelled to compensate to the greatest possible extent for the loss and suffering caused to the United Nations, and that the reparation claims of Soviet Russia in particular should be met by removals from the Soviet Zone of Germany, and by the appropriation of certain German external assets. It was agreed at the Berlin Conference, in conformity with the view taken at the Yalta Conference, that in addition to the reparations that Soviet Russia should take from its own zone of occupation, industrial capital equipment and other assets should be transferred to Russia from the Western Zones: the agreement covering 15 per cent. of such usable and complete industrial equipment in the first place from the metallurgical, chemical, and machine manufacturing industries, in exchange for an equivalent value of food, coal, potash, zinc, timber, petroleum products and the like. The Soviet Government undertook, in the Berlin agreement, to settle the reparation claims of Poland from its own share of reparations, and renounced all claims to shares of German enterprises located in the Western Zones of occupation, as well as German foreign assets, with specified exceptions apart from those transfers of property already mentioned.

One of the difficulties that the Council of Foreign Ministers had to face in dealing with the final Treaty with Germany, arose from the dynamic policy that the Soviet Government has pursued with no regard to the views or the interests of its war-time Allies. Apart from the transfer to Soviet Russia of physical assets on reparations account, there have been political and territorial settlements enforced by the Soviet Union which have had the effect of extending its Western frontiers and bringing many of its Western neighbours under its direct control.

Among the political changes involving the redrawing of the boundaries of the U.S.S.R. must be recorded the transfer, in January 1945, of territory from Esthonia and Latvia, Lithuania and Finland. Moreover, at the Berlin Conference the Soviet Union was provisionally awarded a section of East Prussia, and in September of the same year the Czechoslovak Government ceded Ruthenia (Carpatho-Ukraine). About the same time under the Soviet-Polish Agreement of August 1945, a new Soviet-Polish boundary was drawn on the basis of the Curzon Line. The conclusion of Treaties of Peace with Italy, Rumania, Bulgaria, Hungary and Finland must also be recognised as having strengthened the political and economic influence of the Soviet Union over these countries.

The Treaty with Italy, for example, ceded territory to Yugoslavia and fixed a new frontier between the two countries. It also constituted Trieste as a free territory under the guarantee of the Security Council of the United Nations, and embodied Italy's renunciation of its African possessions, namely Libya, Eritrea, and Italian Somaliland: the final disposal of these possessions being left for joint determination by the Governments of the Soviet Union, the United Kingdom, the United States and France. As regards reparations the Treaty provided for the payment within seven years of $100 million to the Soviet Union out of current industrial production after the first two years. It is stipulated that the reparations must include a share of the Italian factory and tool equipment designed for the manufacture of war materials, and the quantities and types of goods to be delivered were to be the subject of agreements between the Soviet Union and Italy.

Under the Treaty with Rumania, likewise, the Soviet-Rumanian frontier was redrawn in accordance with the agreement between the two countries in June 1940, and the Soviet-Czechoslovak agreement of June 1945. The Treaty also laid down that the Soviet Union's claim for reparations should be liquidated within a period of eight years by the transfer of such commodities as oil products, grain, timber, sea-going and river craft, machinery and the like, to the amount of $300 million. No territorial changes were made by the Treaty with Bulgaria. But the Treaty prohibited permanent fortifications on the Greco-Bulgarian frontier, and stipulated the payment of reparations to Yugoslavia and Greece to the amount of $25 million and $45 million respectively. Restoration of a frontier between Hungary and Rumania as it existed in 1938 was stipulated in the Treaty of Peace with Hungary, and a new frontier between Hungary and the U.S.S.R. was fixed along the former frontier between Hungary and Czechoslovakia. Reparations in the case of Hungary were fixed at $300 million payable over eight years in such commodities as machine equipment, river craft, grain and the like; two-thirds of the amount to be paid to the Soviet Union and the remainder to Czechoslovakia and Yugoslavia. In the Treaty with Finland the territorial changes made under the Armistice agreement ceding to the Soviet Union the Province of Petsamo were confirmed. The Soviet Union confirmed its renunciation of the lease it held on the Hango Peninsula; Finland for its part confirming the lease of a Soviet naval base, and the use of railways, waterways, roads and air routes for fifty years at an annual rent of 5 million Finnish marks to be paid by the Soviet Union. The Treaty provided that reparations to the amount of $300 million should be paid by Finland over a period of eight years in such commodities as timber products, paper, cellulose, sea-going and river craft, machinery, and similar goods.

It proved to be no easy task to negotiate the Peace Settlements with Italy, Rumania, Bulgaria, Hungary and Finland. It was not made less difficult by the revelation of Soviet Russia's determination to exercise a dominating influence beyond its Western frontiers, in the Balkans, and in Central Europe. The Soviet policy of expansion brought forth a counteracting policy embodied in what came to be called the Truman doctrine and the complementary programme known as the Marshall Plan. The essence of the American policy which the Truman doctrine and the Marshall Plan were designed to reinforce, was resistance to the spread of Communism in Western Europe. It was bound up with the offer of material, financial, and economic assistance to the governments of those countries, beginning with Greece and Turkey, that were prepared to oppose the spread of Communist doctrines, and to withstand the expansion of Soviet Russia. As the year 1947 reached its close it became more than ever apparent that the peace-making governments represented in the Council of Foreign Ministers had not accepted the principle of equal treatment for all, either in the matter of reparations or in the settlement of standing political controversies, upon which the Labour Government in Britain conducted its foreign policy.

Much of this became clear when the British Foreign Secretary explained in the House of Commons in the autumn of 1946 how the claims to preferential treatment insisted upon by Soviet Russia had complicated the settlement of the problem of the Danube. The Anglo-American policy, supported by France, was that the Danube should be free for all States to navigate on equal terms. It was proposed that the four major Allies and the Danubian States should join in a conference, within six months of the Peace Treaty coming into force, to consider the establishment of a new international regime for the Danube, which would take into account present-day conditions. The Soviet view, however, was that it was not necessary to include in the Peace Treaty any reference to a future regime along the Danube. In effect, the Soviet Government denied the right of any country other than the Danubian States—most of them entirely under Soviet domination—to have any say in the control of navigation on the river. It was found to be impossible to include in the Treaties with the Balkan States any Article stipulating for freedom of navigation on the Danube. Soviet policy has so far successfully obstructed the re-establishment of any form of international control on the river.

Against this background of political conflict must be set the proposals which divided the Council of Foreign Ministers in their approach to a settlement of Germany's future. At the meeting of the Foreign Ministers in Moscow in the spring of 1947, Ernest Bevin put forward a plan for a central administration in Germany which envisaged the ultimate formation of a Federal German Republic. This plan is in conformity with the policy of decentralising the political structure of Germany and developing local responsibility which the British Government laid down as guiding principles in the Berlin Conference. Mr. Bevin proposed that the Central Government in Germany should be based upon a bicameral legislative assembly and a Supreme Court, with a President as constitutional head of State without an independent executive authority. Of the two Chambers one was to represent the nation as a whole by popular election, and should alone be responsible for the initiation of national legislation. The other Chamber was to be representative of the German Provinces (Länder) to be elected on the basis of equal representation for each Länd. A suspensory veto on legislation from the popular chamber was to be vested in the Chamber representing the Länder, and the Supreme Court would be the guardian of the constitution. The main function of the Länder would be to see that legislation enacted by the Central Government was carried out in the Provinces.

A three-point plan of procedure moving in the same direction was put forward at the Moscow Conference by the United States' Foreign Secretary. It emphasised the principle of Federal decentralisation, imposing upon the provincial (or State) governments all powers not specifically assigned to the Central Government.

French policy, as explained at the Moscow Conference by France's Foreign Minister, conformed generally to the foregoing outline of Anglo-American policy, but with many reservations. French proposals relating to the future structure of Germany were conditioned by the demand of the French nation for security against any possibility of Germany aggression and the revival of German militarism. The French Foreign Minister did not go beyond a proposal that popularly elected assemblies should be established for the different Länder to develop the organisation of separate States on a democratic basis, together with central technical administrations. Soviet policy, on the other hand, definitely challenged the conception of a Federal Germany. The Soviet Foreign Minister indicated a preference for a German political structure on the lines of the Weimar Constitution, enacted after the first World War. The decisions of the Hitler regime which abolished the State or Provincial Diets in Germany should be reversed, according to the Soviet Foreign Minister, and the decentralised pre-Hitler system should be restored: essentially Soviet policy favoured, at the Moscow Conference at least, the re-establishment of Germany as a single unitary State with an all-German bicameral Parliament and under a President elected by Parliament and not directly by the people.

Into the vast historical background of this question, it is impossible to enter. It is hardly possible indeed to summarise even briefly the history of Germany as a Confederation of States during the whole period, extending over eight centuries, in which the so-called Holy Roman (Teutonic) Empire had the hegemony of Europe, through the much smaller German Confederation which Napoleon I created when his conquests broke up the Holy Roman Empire, to the still smaller German Confederation which was Bismarck's handiwork in the later decades of the nineteenth century. The German Confederation which once consisted literally of more than 1,000 principalities, duchies, archbishoprics, and smaller lordships, was reduced by the Napoleonic conquests, and by the Council of Vienna (in 1815) to a few hundred, by Bismarck to a few score, and by Hitler to a single unitary State. But in all this long historical process by which Germany was transformed into a centre of power, the lead was always taken by Prussia. Historically, the power structure of Germany grew and was fortified by Prussian annexations: beginning with the historic crime of Frederick the Great (the third King of Prussia) in seizing Silesia, in repudiation of the Treaty by which Prussia and all the other States of the Empire, and most of the States of Europe, had bound themselves to defend under the terms of the Pragmatic Sanction by which the female succession of the crown of Austria was guaranteed.

Prussia is the source of German militarism, and Prussia derived its military strength and its warlike resources from the possession of Westphalia, the richest Province of Germany from the industrial standpoint, with immense mineral wealth, especially coal and iron, and with extensive manufacturing industries. For more than three centuries Westphalia, originally a part of Saxony, has been a Prussian Province. Its material resources, combined with those of Upper Silesia, were the foundation of Prussia's war industries. Germany's sea power, too, rested upon the fact that Prussia was the only German State with a seaboard. The conditions for Germany's growth as a naval power were created when Prussia obtained control over the Jutland Peninsula by the incorporation of the Danish

Provinces of Schleswig-Holstein and control of the Baltic, carrying with it control over the whole of Scandinavia. Not only the control of the Baltic and the inland waterway system of the Gotha Canal, and the land routes connecting the North Sea with the Baltic, but its possession of the Jutland Peninsula, across which the Kiel Canal was cut, strengthened Prussia's strategic position in the North Sea. As the only German State with a North Sea coast, in possession of her own ports and the cities of the old Hansa League, Prussia held practically the entire foreign trade of Germany in its grip. From the standpoint of geopolitics the control of Prussia over Germany's sea power based on the Baltic and the great naval bases of the Kiel Canal, combined with the industrial resources concentrated in the Rhine Provinces of Westphalia and Silesia, established the conditions under which German heavy industry developed, with a high war potential. It stabilised Prussia's hegemony over Germany and gave Prussia political leadership of the German States.

Seen in the perspective of history, the permanent demilitarisation of Germany and the abrogation of its war potential, must necessarily, therefore, involve drastic treatment of Prussia. The case for a Federal German Republic, on the plan envisaged by Anglo-American policy at the present time, finds its justification in history. But conflicting viewpoints have to be reconciled in the Council of Foreign Ministers before a final settlement of the German problem can be reached. Bound up with it is the question of what to do with Germany's industrial regions—Westphalia, the Ruhr, the Rhineland—which constituted the foundation of Germany's power structure. Control of the Rhine, flowing through the most populous parts of the Continent, in which so many countries are interested, is a related problem of great complexity and importance.

Relevant to the discussion of the interrelated problems briefly summarised in the foregoing paragraphs, is the fact that the constitution of the United Nations adopted in the San Francisco Conference in June 1945, a month before the change of government in Britain, provides for regional arrangements within the framework of the general international security organisation. In the preliminary consideration of the draft scheme for a World Organisation, at the Dumbarton Oaks Conference in the autumn of 1944, attention was directed to the regional system already operating in the Western Hemisphere. One of the principal spokesmen of the United States foreign policy at that time (Mr. Sumner Welles) urged a study of the inter-American system as a possible form of international organisation constructed upon a federation of regional authorities, subordinated to and co-ordinated with a supreme international body representative of all nations and all regions. This conception of a regional grouping within the framework of the general security scheme was not advocated for balance of power purposes, or for strategical reasons, but to promote the interdevelopment of economic, cultural, and political relations, and not the setting up of a super State. Labour's international policy has favoured large experiments in international economic organisation and, in the current discussions, the principle of regional groupings has been considered in application to the great river systems in which the interests of many nations are inextricably woven: the Rhine and the Danube, for example, which have been theatres of war and a source of much political conflict in the past.

Whether in the final stages of the peace-making labours of the Council of Foreign Ministers a solution of the power conflict which has so far delayed the peace settlement will be sought, remains to be seen. On this basic question of the relationships of power in the post-war world, Field-Marshal Smuts has perhaps come nearest to the Labour view of the desired solution. The argument presented by Field-Marshal Smuts, in the remarkable address entitled "Thoughts on the New World," delivered in November 1943, derived from a penetrating analysis of the power situation arising out of the war. Such an analysis found its confirmation when the Foreign Ministers of the victorious powers came to grips in the making of the peace. The war left Britain and Russia as the two great centres of power in Europe, as Field-Marshal Smuts predicted, with Russia as the new colossus in Europe, bestriding the continent and the others down and out. Russia's power position was immeasurably strengthened because the Japanese Empire went down, too, leaving no check or balance in the East, save that of the United States, looming up outside Europe as the other great World Power. The combination of Britain and America might constitute a political Axis, Field-Marshal Smuts suggested, but it offers but a one-sided and unstable alliance as a guarantee of international peace. The deadlock that arose inside the United Nations as between the Soviet Government representatives and the British and American statesmen on many questions of policy, and especially the question of the veto, serves to emphasise the reality of the power conflict. In a statement on Britain's foreign policy made by the Prime Minister in Parliament in the autumn of 1946 the question of the veto in the Security Council of the United Nations organisation was singled out as a matter of vital importance. Russia's use of the veto created an impression of disunity and ineffectiveness, and had raised doubts (Mr. Attlee said) about the value of the Security Council as an instrument for the preservation of international peace and security.

At the San Francisco Conference, which Mr. Attlee attended as Deputy Prime Minister, the creation of the veto was agreed to, he explained, as something to be used only in the last resort in extreme cases where the five Great Powers might find themselves in disagreement. It was not conceived to be a device to be used constantly whenever a particular Power was not in full agreement with the others, Mr. Attlee said. Yet that was what had happened: the veto was used for every trifling thing, and he pointed out that it was reducing to a nullity the Security Council's usefulness, and losing it the confidence of the nations.

"It is the desire of His Majesty's Government that this Body should return to and fulfil its original intention so that the world may feel that there exists an instrument which, when matters cannot be settled by negotiation between countries, stands ready to intervene and bring impartial minds to bear upon the issues involved. Nothing will be so disastrous to the peace of the world as to allow the respect, dignity and power of the Security Council to be brought to nought. While His Majesty's Government are not at the present time prepared to move that there should be any change in the Charter, we certainly are of the opinion that there should be a review of the use of the veto with a view to restraining it to its original intent."

It cannot, unhappily, be said that discussion of the veto question and other important issues of policy in the United Nations' Assembly, affords convincing evidence that the power conflict will be resolved, and a return made to the policy of collaboration between the three Great Powers. At the end of 1947, indeed, it seemed that the three Great Powers were hopelessly deadlocked. The Council of Foreign Ministers broke up at that time with nothing settled, leaving the British Government quite convinced that the Soviet Government was intent upon the pursuit of a policy to gain control, not only over the Eastern European States on her borders, but to extend Communist control to the West. To counteract the dangers of this Soviet policy, the British Foreign Minister set himself to develop the principles of the Anglo-French Treaty of Dunkirk with the object of achieving a union of the Western European countries. In close accord with France, negotiations were set on foot with the Benelux countries—Belgium, Holland, and Luxemburg—on the basis of the Dunkirk Treaty, for the organisation of a Western Union with which "other historic members of European civilisation" (in Mr. Bevin's phrase) including the new Italy, could associate themselves. Thus, the network of Eastern European pacts which Soviet Russia has been busily engaged in knitting together has forced upon the Western Governments an alternative pattern of political and economic co-operation. The Western Union is not in form a Customs Union, but this too, fits into the conception of a closer association of the European countries called for by their acceptance of the Marshall programme.

From the purely political standpoint the most salient feature of the period under review has been the stability of the Third Labour Government as tested by parliamentary by-elections. It is possible to make too much of the fact that no by-election fought to hold seats for the Government up to the end of 1947 has been lost: but this state of affairs, without precedent in modern times, is significant in view of the adverse criticism to which the Government has inevitably been exposed because of the "austerity" measures it was compelled to adopt to meet the conditions of economic crisis. Up to December 1947 there had been some thirty contests for parliamentary vacancies. In three of them—namely, the City of London, Kensington South and the Combined Universities—Labour candidates were not nominated; and in one case, the Ogmore Division, the Conservative Opposition did not contest the seat. In all other contests in which the Labour Party defended seats held by the Government supporters, they were held, though with reduced majorities. On the other hand the vote of Opposition Parties in these by-elections fell in some instances below their General Election level, too.

More significance, perhaps, as an indication of the "swing of the pendulum," attaches to the local government elections. Following the General Election in mid-1945, Labour made a tremendous stride forward in the November 1945 municipal elections. For nearly 9,000 vacant seats in these municipal contests there were nearly 8,000 Labour candidates, of whom about 5,000 were standing for the first time; and no more than 2,500 of these vacant seats were formerly held by Labour. The net gain of seats in these municipal elections of 1945 was 1,348, a result never remotely approached by the Labour Party in previous years. Out of 83 County Boroughs Labour gained control of 46, whereas previously there were Labour majorities on no more than 15; and the non-County Boroughs under Labour control increased 23 to 73; whilst of the 28 metropolitan Boroughs only five were left with anti-Labour majorities, and in all but one of these there was an increase in the Labour representation. Labour gained control also over 24 Scottish Burghs and held its control over 14 more.

In the November 1946 municipal elections, contrary to the general impression created by newspaper headlines, Labour again achieved a net gain of nearly 200 seats in England and Wales, and 57 seats in Scotland. In the District Council elections in March 1947 a net gain of 68 seats was secured. But this tale of success in local government elections assumed a somewhat darker colour in November 1947. A net loss of about 644 seats, despite an increased Labour vote of over 900,000, against considerable gains for the Conservative Party—which fought these municipal contests more openly on party lines than ever before—gave ground for some misgivings about the ability of the Labour Party to keep its hold on the electorate and ensure a majority for the Labour Government in the next General Election.

If the Government could rest upon its legislative achievements its position could be regarded as fairly well assured. In the first half of its term of Office it enacted the principal measures of socialisation to which it was pledged in its General Election manifesto: "Let Us Face the Future." In addition to nationalisation of the Bank of England, the mining industry, the transport services, the electricity supply services, the gas industry, the Government carried through its far-reaching social security programme, and made indubitable progress in its housing programme and town and country planning. Under the New Towns Act preparations have been made for the development of at least half a dozen new town areas; and large-scale works of public importance like the Tyne Tunnel, Scottish hydro-electric projects, and the Severn Suspension Bridge have been put in hand.

In conformity with the principles laid down by the United Nations Assembly for the control of atomic energy, the Government has instituted arrangements for research and development in this new field under public control. In the Industrial Organisation and Development Councils Act steps have been taken to establish a more rational order in industry, by the setting up of machinery which gives the workers a share in the responsibilities of management. This Act is based upon investigations carried out by Working Parties appointed by the President of the Board of Trade (then Sir Stafford Cripps) with the object of examining the present-day equipment of nearly a score of important industries and to make recommendations for their development. A striking feature of the reports of the Working Parties so far published—about a dozen—has been their practical unanimity in recommending that each industry shall have set up a central body to co-ordinate and stimulate its activities in the public interest. From the industrial standpoint, too, there are great potentialities in the operation of the Wages Councils Act, which authorises the establishment of joint bodies representing both the employers and the workers along with the consumers' interests, and transforms the old Trade Boards into Wages Councils: a betterment of industrial relations will certainly follow the extension of this joint machinery.

In the field of social policy, more particularly, the Government has pursued the task of safeguarding the people's welfare by putting into operation the system of Family Allowances by which over 4,000,000 children are benefiting; by increasing the Old Age Pension rates for over 3,250,000 old people; by revolutionising the system of Workmen's Compensation, through the enactment of the National Insurance and the Industrial Injuries Acts; and by the passing of the National Health Service Act, and the Act abolishing the last traces of the old Poor Law. The legislation establishing a National Insurance system gives protection to the whole population from the cradle to the grave, whilst the measure dealing with National Health provides a comprehensive scheme, including all forms of general and special hospitals, health centres, and a general practitioner service, with supplementary services for maternity and child welfare, ambulance, midwifery and clinics for special treatment, along with better medical inspection of children in schools and special provision for those disabled by deafness.

During the Third Labour Government's tenure of Office four Budgets have been introduced into Parliament. The first of them was an interim Budget in which the standard rate of income tax was reduced, with the effect, amongst others, of lightening the burden of income tax on the smaller taxpayer, and increasing the allowances for families and for earned incomes; and taking steps also to lower the purchase tax over a wide range of household requisites. In his second and third Budgets the Chancellor of the Exchequer provided for the increased State expenditure arising out of the extension of the social services under the Education, Family Allowances,

Old Age, and Widows' Pensions, and other Acts; carrying farther the reduction of the purchase tax, and the relief from income tax of the lower-paid wage earners.

The fourth of Labour's Budgets rather reversed the Government's policy in view of the necessity of bridging the "inflationary gap" and reducing the volume of spending power in the hands of the people generally. To lessen the dangers of inflation the purchase tax was increased on a wide range of commodities in general use, and the subsidies payable from the Treasury in respect of raw materials, such as cotton, wool and leather, were removed. Food subsidies, however, were left untouched, with the proviso that they would not be allowed to rise above the level at which they stood in the main Budget of 1947. The tax on profits was doubled, and new imposts were laid upon spirits, wine and beer, along with an innovation in taxation upon stakes laid in dog racing, and football pools. This supplementary Budget was called for by the deepening gravity of the economic crisis, and by the requirements of the Government's export programme which involved the utmost possible concentration of the country's resources in manpower and materials upon essential trades and industries, and a contraction of both production and expenditure in less essential spheres while the crisis remains to be overcome.

In the sphere of international affairs the event of major importance has been the adoption of the Labour Government's policy for India and Burma. India has ceased to be a Dependency or possession of the Empire in the historical meaning of the term, and has become independent and self-governing, though divided politically and in a territorial aspect by the setting up of two States—India and Pakistan. Under the settlement, however, India and Pakistan remain within the British Commonwealth as self-governing nations, unlike Burma, which has decided to sever its connection with Britain upon its achievement of full self-government. Anglo-Egyptian relations remain unsettled, but British naval, military and air forces have been withdrawn from the country, and negotiations for a revision of the Anglo-Egyptian Treaty of Alliance of 1936 were set on foot. A solution of the problem of the Jewish settlement in Palestine has become the responsibility of the United Nations under the decision to partition the country between Jews and Arabs. A virtual state of war has prevailed as between the British authorities and the Jews on the one hand, and on the other between the Jews and Arabs: a federal scheme was formulated and became the subject of discussion; but when the British Government decided that it could no longer accept responsibility for the situation in Palestine, the problem passed to the United Nations.

Agreement has been reached by delegates of twenty-three nations assembled in the International Trade Conference at Geneva embodying a general understanding on tariffs and trade, which is interpreted as the opening of a new chapter in international economic relations. At this conference, in Geneva, a determined effort was made to lower tariff barriers, and to deal with the problem of preferential trade relations and currency restrictions affecting the movement of trade. The aim has been to promote an expanding multilateral trading system as the objective of national policy by all the participating countries. The agreement embodied in what has come to be known as the I.T.O. Charter, derives from the declarations in the Atlantic Charter and the Lend-Lease arrangements between the United States and the countries allied in the struggle against the Nazi-Fascist dictatorship. At the beginning of 1948 it is expected that the I.T.O. Charter will be confirmed at the Havana Conference on Trade and Employment summoned by the United Nations to assemble there in November 1947. Seventy-five States and territories are represented at Havana, and their acceptance of the Charter will not only facilitate national and international action in maintaining a balanced and expanding world economy, but will lead eventually to the elimination of tariffs and trade barriers, and of discriminatory international taxes and regulations, import quota systems and exchange controls, and bring about a general application of the principle of most-favoured-nation treatment in international trade.

Parallel with its efforts to promote greater freedom in international trade are the far-sighted plans of the Labour Government to promote the economic development of the colonial empire. Legislative effect will be given to these plans by a measure under discussion in the House of Commons for the setting up of a Colonial Development Corporation which would be financed by loans or advances from the national Exchequer up to £100 million at risk at any one moment. It is the purpose of this Colonial Development Corporation to undertake every kind of activity, designed to promote agricultural production and food production, and of such raw materials as these colonial territories possess, such as Malayan tin and rubber, and Rhodesian copper. The Government's policy is avowedly an alternative method to the old system of colonial exploitation. It applies the same technique of the Public Corporation invested with statutory powers which is a feature of the Government's nationalisation policy for domestic industries and services.

As the Minister of Food (Mr. John Strachey) said in opening the second reading of the Overseas Resources Development Bill, in November 1947, the public corporation is a characteristically British institution, and the instrument of the future in furtherance of Government policy. He described the public corporation, in its structure, as very like any large private organisation and public company, but with an essential difference in that its capital is publicly owned, and in the last analysis it works, therefore, for public purposes. Hitherto, the public corporation was an instrument of public enterprise which has not been used to promote productive activity in hitherto undeveloped areas of the world. It is perhaps fitting that this Epilogue, closing the wide survey of Labour history, organisation, policy and programme—to say nothing of Labour's leading personalities, pioneers and founders—should bring into sight this most significant development of British political institutions. For more than a generation the public board or commission has been the chosen instrument for the carrying on of vital public utilities and great national industries. The history of these public bodies can be carried back to the period in which the management of ports and harbours was entrusted to such bodies as the Mersey Docks and Harbour Board, and the Port of London Authority. The principle found further application in the setting up of the Forestry Commission, under an Act of 1919, to carry out an ambitious programme of reafforestation, and to promote schemes of land settlement in connection with forestry, to foster marketing schemes and similar activities. Diverse characteristics of the public corporation are revealed in the British Broadcasting Corporation, created under Royal Charter in 1927, in the Central Electricity Board, set up about the same time under the Electricity Supply Act, 1926, the London Passenger Transport Board, projected in a Bill drafted by the Second Labour Government and enacted in 1932-33 by its successor, and the Agricultural Marketing Boards, which came into existence under the Act of 1931. A more mature form of public control is represented by the National Coal Board, the Transport Commission, the Electricity Commission, and kindred authorities established under the nationalisation legislation of the Third Labour Government.

Although this new type of administrative authority serving public enterprise represents an empirical application of a new principle, it is one that meets most of the objections urged against Socialism as a theory of economic organisation. Parliament, in setting up such public bodies as the National Coal Board and its earlier prototypes, divests itself to some extent of its authority over the sectors of economic enterprise these Boards take under their control; but the ultimate sovereignty of Parliament is not impaired, but reinforced, and the interests of the commonwealth are safeguarded. Bureaucratic administration of public enterprise is being replaced by a more flexible system which guarantees a high standard of technical competence. The spirit of public service is being steadily strengthened by new instruments of public administration. In the words of the revised constitution of the Labour Party the objective of organised Labour in seeking to secure for the workers by hand and brain the full fruits of their industry and the most equitable distribution thereof, is based upon common ownership of the means of production, distribution and exchange; and is being achieved step by step in the development of the best obtainable system of popular administration and control of each industry or service. This book bears witness page by page to the progress that has been made towards the realisation of these aims and purposes of organised labour.